PRISCILLA SHIRER

UNSEEN

THE PRINCE WARRIORS

365 DEVOTIONAL

B&H
PUBLISHING GROUP
Nashville, Tennessee

978-1-4336-9018-1

Published by B&H Publishing Group
Nashville, Tennessee

Dewey Decimal Classification: J242.2
Subject Heading: DEVOTIONAL LITERATURE / SPIRITUAL WARFARE /
CHRISTIAN LIFE

2 3 4 5 6 7 8 9 • 21 20 19 18 17

For . . .

Micah
Cameron
Chloe

Introduction

Hey there, Warrior.

The devotional you are holding in your hands is much more than just a book. It's a manual for victory, filled with strategies designed to help you defeat a very real enemy—an enemy who wants you to believe that because he is invisible, he is also fictional. But that isn't true. He is real.

And so are your God-given armor and weapons that can shut him down!

Here's what you need to know about every day's strategy session. Each one is divided into two sections: Reconnaissance (or *Recon*) and Actionable Intelligence (or *Actionable Intel*).

Here's what they mean:

Reconnaissance (ree-CON-eh-sence) is the process of locating and watching an enemy. Usually in secret. Undercover. Think camouflage. Think high-powered binoculars. Think sensitive listening equipment, gathering real-time, fact-based information so that you can be prepared to use your God-given resources to counteract the enemy's plans, movements, and whereabouts.

Each lesson will start here, with *Recon*. Together we will observe some insights and truths that will help us be prepared to stand firm and claim victory. Solid recon will lay the groundwork for a lifetime of victory.

After you've gathered your intelligence, then you must plan a strategy to put into action. After all, what good is acquired information if it's never transferred into a plan for launching a preemptive strike or preparing a counterstrategy? *Actionable intel* (INN-tell) is your opportunity to implement a strategy against your opponent so you can always be on guard.

Each day, remember: your all-powerful God is FOR YOU! You are His Warrior, armed with His armor. Did you hear that? Armor! You can wear the armor of God every day, anywhere, any time, any place. In fact, you *must* wear it if you want any chance of defeating the devil. Listen: "Put on the full armor of God so that you can stand against the tactics of the Devil" (Ephesians 6:12).

He has given you:

 A belt to fortify you

 A breastplate to protect you

 A pair of boots to stabilize you

 A shield to cover you

 A helmet to guard you

 A sword to fight for you

 Prayer to constantly connect you to His divine power and strength

Most days you'll notice one or more of these symbols at the top of your day's reading. This is to show you how that lesson connects to a specific piece of armor and helps you to know how to put it on. As you read and pray, God Himself will help your *reconnaissance* brim with important insights and revelation. Then He will help you to organize your *actionable intel* into a package that will enable you to be victorious. He hates your enemy as much (or more) than you do, so He'll do anything it takes to help you WIN.

You ready, soldier? Let's go!

Really and Truly

I will always remind you about these things, even though you know them and are established in the truth.
—2 Peter 1:12

Recon

Hey, you made it. *Day One.* Fun. I'm so glad you're here. But I'm not going to sugarcoat it for you, because I think you're brave enough to know. We're here to do some battle. We're here to learn how to fight. And win.

I mean, if everybody else wants to goof around all the time, spending every waking minute just watching TV or playing video games, that's fine for them. But not for you. There's nothing wrong with enjoying any of those things. But I've got a feeling you want to be different. I believe you want the truth, and I believe you want to hear it straight up.

So that's what we're going to be doing. Talking truth. And the truth is this: *you're a warrior.* You can do big things because you serve a big God. You can have victory in every area of your life, even the most difficult ones. And we've got a whole year together now to see what some of that means. So let's go—this is going to be great!

Actionable Intel

Try to pick a time and place—same time, same place—where you're going to be reading your devotional book and praying. Every day. See you back here tomorrow.

Wonder Why

I do not understand what I am doing, because I do not practice what I want to do, but I do what I hate.
—Romans 7:15

Recon

Yesterday I suggested that you figure out a specific time and place to set aside for spending a few minutes with God and with this book every day. Think of it like an appointment. Like your 10:00 class, let's say, in room 215 or something. It's important, so you go there. At that time. At that place.

But here's what I want you to notice. It won't be long (if it hasn't happened already—maybe right here on Day Two!) before you think, *Ugh, I really don't want to read my devotional today.*

Wonder why? Because you're such a terrible person? *No.* You just feel like doing something else. And like Romans 7:15 says, sometimes it's really hard to carry through with the things you really want and intend to do.

But have you ever considered *why* you may feel this way? Is it possible that someone is fighting your desire to do the right thing? An enemy who wants to keep you from getting power and planning a strategy to defeat him?

Cannot. Let. Him. Win.

So make your plan, and then commit to follow through.

Actionable Intel

The next time you sense yourself struggling to do something you know you should do, pray for God to help you overcome the temptation. And when you feel a tug to rebel, let that be your tug to pray instead.

Armored Up

Put on the full armor of God so that you can stand against the tactics of the Devil. —Ephesians 6:11

Recon

If you've been paying attention in English class, you already know how every story is built around a conflict. Some kind of problem or difficulty exists, often brought on or made worse by someone called an antagonist. The one who's working to overcome the problem is called the protagonist. The hero.

And God, my friend, is your protagonist. Your hero. But here's something special I want you to know about Him: He's not satisfied flexing His spiritual muscle all by Himself. He's decided to hand out some weapons and body armor so that through Him, you can be victorious.

Ever heard about this armor? Ever heard what it can do for you when you put it on and trust God to show you how to use it? It's how you become a warrior. And every single piece of it is vitally important. It's like Kryptonite to the enemy.

Actionable Intel

Read Ephesians 6:10–18, paying special attention to six specific pieces of armor that are listed there, starting with verse 14. See if you can spot them all, and underline them when you do.

Wrestling Match

We do not wrestle against flesh and blood.
—Ephesians 6:12 ESV

Recon

I have three boys, probably near the same age as you. They are now getting bigger and stronger than I am. And one of their favorite things (for some reason) is wrestling with me. Sometimes one of them will spring from around the corner, toss me up on his shoulder, and pin me down onto the sofa, while his brothers all stand around laughing. Thanks.

Wrestling. You know how it feels. Somebody grabs you. You push back. But if they're bigger and stronger, you sometimes can't get away. Can't turn the tables on them.

See that word at the top of this page? In the verse there? *Wrestle.* That's what you and I are dealing with in life. A fight. A struggle. A contest with a real opponent, waged up close, in hand-to-hand combat. His goal is to pin us down so that we have no hope of enjoying life and fulfilling our God-given purpose. But you don't have to take it lying down. Not anymore.

Actionable Intel

Write down some words that describe how you'd feel if you were pinned down in a wrestling match (you can use the blank pages at the back of the book). Then write some that describe how you'd feel if you were the one on top—the one doing the pinning. Circle the words that you'd prefer to describe your life on a daily basis.

Strength in Your Corner

*The One who is in you is greater than the
one who is in the world.* —*1 John 4:4*

Recon

Yesterday I mentioned my boys liking to wrestle me. But I forgot to mention one part. The best part. Right in the middle of our matches—when I feel like I'll never be able to get myself unpinned—the boy's huge, six-foot-three, burly father will round the corner and come to my rescue. And at the sight of him, all my sons will hop off me and scatter in all directions like they're being shot out of a cannon.

They know when they've met their match.

I realize that if I had to fend for myself, I'd likely never have much luck against any of my big sons. I'm just not as strong as they're becoming. But I'm in a relationship with someone who's stronger: their father. And thanks to him, I can get out from under my three wrestlers and back on my feet. *He* is my rescuer and my strength.

Because of your relationship with Jesus Christ, you are stronger than any enemy you'll ever face in life. He can rescue you from any situation and then give you strength to stay on your feet.

Actionable Intel

If you don't know what it means to be in a "relationship" with Jesus Christ, talk to someone today who you *know* to be a Christian. He or she will love telling you about it and about how to set up your first line of defense against the enemy. If you'll turn to page 371 in the back of this book, I'll tell you a little more about it too.

Eye-Opening

I pray that the eyes of your heart may be enlightened.
—Ephesians 1:18 NIV

Recon

Paul was a first-century missionary whom God worked through to make disciples all over the known world, from the Middle East throughout Greece and all the way to Rome. He wrote the book of Ephesians as a letter to the church in the Greek city of Ephesus.

When he listed the armor of God, his main goal in writing was to help them recognize the many blessings they'd received and the power that God Himself had given them access to use. He wanted their spiritual eyes to be open so they could see all the amazing resources available to them for experiencing victory.

Part of the reason why we sometimes lose ground in our battle against the enemy is because we, like the Ephesians, are walking around unaware, uninformed about who we are and Who we belong to. We're sure nobody cares about us. We think we're losers. We don't see the point. We just think we're supposed to take whatever comes at us without putting up a fight.

Open your eyes! Paul prayed. God's power is greater than you can even imagine, and he chooses to work through you.

Actionable Intel

In the journal pages at the back of this book, write down three words that describe positive traits about who you are in Christ, or who you are becoming. Ask your parents if you can tape them up on your bathroom mirror, on the wall beside your bed, or someplace where you can see them every day to remind yourself of your importance.

Writing on the Wall

When you pray, go into your room, close the door and pray to your Father, who is unseen. —Matthew 6:6 NIV

Recon

I've got this closet, see. Just a little one. It's no more than a few feet wide. I keep some shirts and pants in there. Various scarves, belts, purses. You know . . . stuff. But if you were to look inside, among all that chaos, you'd see something else as well. Taped to the walls. Up one side and down the other.

They're prayers.

Written-out prayers.

I used to think praying was supposed to be completely spontaneous, just words off the top of my head. Which it *can* and *should* be. God wants you to pray to Him at any point during the day, no matter where you are. But prayer can also be a lot more strategic than that. It can be carefully written and repeatedly delivered. Very specific and very intentional—like the prayers I've written during my devotions and then taped to the wall of my closet. These pages are regular reminders of what I want to say to God.

Prayers that are focused and purposeful are sometimes the most direct hits.

Actionable Intel

If you were to write out a prayer on paper, what would you write? Think about taping it inside your closet somewhere where you can see it, and say it again and again.

Winnable War

*Rouse the warriors; let all the men of war
draw advance and attack!—Joel 3:9*

Recon

In the movie *The Two Towers,* the middle film of the Lord of the Rings theatrical trilogy, Théoden, king of Rohan, refuses to accept the advice of Aragorn, who is urging the king to make some trusted alliances or else be doomed to destruction. "I will not risk open war," Théoden proclaims to him defiantly. But then Aragorn replies with a line I want you to remember:

"Open war is upon you . . . whether you would risk it or not."

Because sin is part of our world, escaping hard things and being immune to attack is not possible. Sure, we'll enjoy this kind of freedom *one day,* in heaven, safe forever from all evil and danger. But for now we fight—though not without an arsenal of weapons capable of helping us win.

Remember that you face an enemy who wants you filled with fear and discouragement so that you won't enjoy life as it was meant to be lived. Then use your armor, forged through your alliance with Christ, to push the enemy back and put him in his place. These weapons give you spiritual brawn for battle.

Actionable Intel

Do you remember the pieces of spiritual armor you underlined in your Bible a few days ago? Write down as many of them as you can remember in the journaling pages in the back of this book.

The Belt of Truth

Stand, therefore, with truth like a belt
around your waist. —Ephesians 6:14

Recon

The apostle Paul's letters make up a huge chunk of our New Testament, and he most likely wrote many of them while in prison. Colossians. Philemon. Philippians. Also Ephesians, where the Lord inspired him to speak about spiritual warfare and our spiritual armor.

So perhaps, using your imagination, you might see him sitting there, locked up, thinking about what to write while a real-live soldier of the Roman Empire might have been somewhere within view, dressed in traditional uniform. (I don't know for sure, but it's possible.)

The belt was a foundational piece of the soldier's uniform. It served an important, practical purpose. And for believers, it serves a critical, practical purpose as well.

That's why I can't wait to see you put on this belt yourself. Because it's yours, you know. God has given it to you. And having this belt—His truth—wrapped completely around your heart and life could make a lot of the things you struggle with a whole lot easier.

Actionable Intel

In the journaling pages at the back of the book, list the one or two most important benefits that a belt provides.

Supporting Role

The LORD surrounds His people, both now and forever.
—Psalm 125:2

Recon

The belt worn by a Roman soldier was actually more like a . . . uh—*ahem*—like a . . .

Well, it was like a *girdle*, all right? Do you know what a girdle is? Women who are trying to fit into a nice formal outfit that might hug them a little too close around their hips and middle often wear a girdle underneath their dress to make their stomach lie a little flatter.

But trust me, this ancient kind of girdle in a Roman soldier's uniform was a manly sort of thing. Sturdy. Leathery. And very important. Because it gave him support at his core. With this extra support, he could carry the weight of all his other armor and endure long marches against the enemy.

This is exactly what truth does when we commit ourselves to it. It gives us support. It keeps us steady and strong when the enemy is coming against us. Without it, we'll be unprotected and spineless, and the enemy will take advantage. Nothing else in our lives will fit together right. Because we're not solid at the core.

Truth provides the essential kind of backing we need for spiritual war.

Actionable Intel

Look at the drawing of the Roman soldier in full gear on page 373 in the back of this book. Notice where the girdle is located on his body. Why do you think this piece of standard equipment was so necessary?

Heavy Lifting

With You I can attack a barrier, and with my God
I can leap over a wall. —2 Samuel 22:30

Recon

I want to give you another, more modern picture of the kind of support that the belt on a Roman soldier's uniform provided. (I'm still afraid I may have worried you a little bit by calling it a girdle.)

Have you ever seen the guys who drive around in the big trucks delivering packages to people's houses? Or have you ever seen the workers at a hardware or home improvement store who haul heavy things to your car for you? They often wear a thick, elastic brace that gives support to their waist, keeping them from throwing their backs out of joint from all that bulky stuff they carry around.

That's the power of truth. It strengthens you. It supports you. It keeps you going. It helps you sleep better at night. You wake up the next day not hurting or tired, not sorry you did what you did. You've worked hard, but you could still do more because you were protected and built up. That's what truth is for.

Actionable Intel

The next time you see someone wearing one of those back braces I described, try asking him how the brace helps him. See if any of his answers somehow relate to how the belt of truth is designed to support you.

The Heart

*Guard your heart above all else, for it is
the source of life. —Proverbs 4:23*

Recon

Right this moment—without any deliberate action on
your part—your heart is beating away inside your chest,
pumping blood throughout an intricate network of veins
and arteries. Along the way, this blood is providing oxygen
and other nutrients to various parts of your body, while also
removing harmful materials that need to be eliminated
from your system. Your heart is your life source.

Without the work that this vital organ is quietly doing,
largely without our notice, you and I wouldn't be here
minutes from now. Its job is so important, so necessary,
that we literally can't survive without it.

Today's verse is trying to tell us is that our *spiritual*
heart (our soul) is equally as crucial to our survival as our
physical heart. It is our "source of life." That's why we're
commanded to guard it with all our might . . . because our
enemy knows this too. And he's sure to be targeting it.

Actionable Intel

Hold your hand to your chest, and sit quietly for a couple
of minutes. Feel your heart working at its steady, nonstop
pace. Thank God for this incredible gift of life-giving power
to you.

The Breastplate

*Stand firm therefore . . . having put on the breastplate
of righteousness.* —*Ephesians 6:14* NASB

Recon

Once a Roman soldier had secured his belt around
his waist, the next piece of armor he put on was his
breastplate. This was a metal shield, usually made
of bronze, that covered his body from the neck to the
thighs. The Romans called it a *thoraka*. (The *thorax*, you
probably know from science class, is still what we call the
area between the neck and abdomen, where the heart
and lungs are; it's also what we call the center section of
an insect's body, like on an ant or a honeybee.)

This breastplate often fit over an undergarment made
of leather. And if the soldier was wealthy enough, he also
stretched a "coat of mail" over the *thoraka*, which is the
chain-link, metal material that might remind you of a
knight's armor. It was almost like a dragon's scales.

Three intense layers of protection. Back to back.
Because, honestly, it didn't matter how tough a soldier
was or how good a fighter; just one dagger to his heart
and he was most likely done, maybe for life.

The breastplate is what protects a warrior's heart
against a full-frontal attack by the enemy. Good thing
you've got one to wear then, huh?

Actionable Intel

Looking again at the picture of the Roman soldier on
page 373, locate the piece of armor that served as his
breastplate. How do you think a soldier going into battle
without this vital piece of equipment would feel about his
chances for survival?

Righteousness

Offer yourselves to God, and all the parts of yourselves to God as weapons for righteousness. —Romans 6:13

Recon

Wearing the breastplate, Paul told us, has something to do with "righteousness," which basically means "right living." So *obedience* to God and His Word is what puts the breastplate on. Doing the right things as you are enabled by God's Spirit. Fulfilling the expectations that come with being not only a *child* of God but a *warrior* under His command and leadership.

Now, the belt of truth, as we've seen, is symbolic of how we *affirm* God's standards in our life. We find them in the Bible. We agree with them. We fly them like a banner, like a flag that declares our allegiance. They set the unchanging benchmark for what we believe.

Righteousness takes it one step further. It is how this truth becomes practical and translates into behavior. It's how the truths we *know* become the truths we *live*. And the truths we *live* become "weapons." (Did you notice that term in today's verse?) Righteousness is like a weapon. It deflects the enemy's attacks and positions you, God's warrior, for victory.

Actionable Intel

Have you ever thought of your righteous actions—your obedience, your devotion to doing what God's Word says—as being *weapons*? How does this fire up your desire to do them? To use them?

Following in His Tracks

These are the ones who follow the Lamb
wherever He goes. —Revelation 14:4

Recon

Here's an analogy that might help you fully understand the connection between the *belt of truth* and the *breastplate of righteousness*. Because even though they are separate pieces of equipment, they work together.

Think of *truth* like a railroad track. If there's a railroad track anywhere near your house, it was probably marked out and hammered into the ground decades ago. And if you walked or rode your bike over to where it's located, you'd find it in exactly the same place it was when it was laid.

Righteousness is like the train that travels on the track. If not for the rails, the train wouldn't have anything to run on.

The track *and* the train together allow each to serve the purposes for which they are intended.

Since your enemy is so determined to prevent your "train" from following the truth, count on him to be working overtime—either to weaken your trust in the integrity of the track or to derail you from riding on it.

Actionable Intel

Personal evaluation: In what ways has your "train" been running well in alignment with the "tracks" of God's Word lately? Is there any way it hasn't?

Defensive Tactics

The Lord is faithful, and He will strengthen and protect you from the evil one. —2 Thessalonians 3:3 NASB

Recon

In battle, defensive protection is equally as important as offensive weaponry. Perhaps even *more* important. Because without the ability to take a blow or absorb an attack, the opportunity to actually fight and defeat the enemy may never come.

A breastplate is almost entirely a protective device. There would rarely be a scenario where a soldier would use it to hurt somebody. They would use it for protection and defense.

Because your enemy will never tire of launching assaults against you, protection is a constant need. The best *offense*, as they say, is often a good *defense*.

Now, God Himself, of course, is your Protector, who will "protect your coming and going both now and forever" (Psalm 121:8). But part of how He offers protection is through the rugged strength that a righteous life provides you, as pictured in the breastplate of righteousness. Obedience is about much more than doing what God says; it's about creating a tight line of effective defense against the enemy.

Actionable Intel

On a football team, what are the different goals and strategies between the players on the *offense* and the players on the *defense*? What happens to a team if their offense is great, but their defense is terrible?

This Little Piggy

Those parts of the body that we think to be less honorable,
we clothe these with greater honor. —1 Corinthians 12:23

Recon

Feet are really important. You usually don't think of them.
They're down there at the end of your legs. They're kind
of weird shaped. But if you stub a toe, peel back a nail, or
crack a bone—even on the little pinkie one—your whole
body feels it.

During the days of the Roman Empire, footwear for
both men and women consisted of soft leather shoes that
were more like slippers. The shoes of a soldier, however,
combined the flexibility of a sandal with the rugged
toughness of a boot, especially in the thick sole. These
shoes provided lots of benefits, but their basic function
was simply to protect the feet. To guard them. To keep
them safe from cuts, bruises, and other injuries.

Because one sore foot can take the rest of you
completely out of commission.

Worry can do the same thing. That's why God has
given you *shoes* of peace (Ephesians 6:15)—to make sure
your whole body is safe from an enemy who's after your
peace.

Actionable Intel

In the picture of the Roman soldier's gear on page 373, also
notice the look and features of his shoes. These soldiers
didn't take their feet and footwear lightly. Neither should
you. Every piece of spiritual equipment is necessary.

Burglar Alarm

A thief comes only to steal and to kill and to destroy. I have come so that they may have life and have it in abundance. —John 10:10

Recon

Your enemy is a thief. Out to steal from you. And he'll take anything he can get.

It might be a full night of sleep, if he can worry you enough about an upcoming test or a medical result you're nervously awaiting. It might be your confidence, if he can get inside your head and talk you into doubting your abilities. It might be trust in a friendship, causing you to wonder if a friend is being disloyal. It might be the security of the relationships in your home. It might be your appetite, your patience, your self-discipline . . . you name it.

Here's the truth: a hardened thief like him is never going to stop trying. And on your own, you cannot seal up enough windows or lock enough doors to keep him from trying to sneak in. But because Jesus defeated Satan on the cross, His work not only counteracts the Devil's effectiveness, He also destroys it. The result is that you have life so abundant that it is eternal and transforms every part of your existence.

And part of this "abundance" is a pair of burglar-proof, God-sized shoes He puts in your spiritual closet. These shoes are marked with peace—a deep, internal comfort that not even a persistent prowler can take away from you.

Actionable Intel

Look up Ephesians 6:15 in two or three different Bible translations. Pick out the key words in the verse. Then spend a few minutes asking God to help you understand how these ideas tie together.

Boots on the Ground

*Now to Him who is able to protect you from stumbling
and to make you stand in the presence of His glory . . .
the only God our Savior . . .—Jude vv. 24–25*

Recon

One of the most unforgettable features of a Roman soldier's
shoes were the spikes that protruded downward from
the thick leather soles. These spikes, or *hobnails*, turned
sandaled boots into something more like football cleats,
only much grittier, much sharper. Industrial strength.

The hobnails were an essential element. They were
potentially the difference between victory and defeat,
because these soldiers didn't get to choose the ground they
were called to take or defend. It might be uphill or straight
downhill or slick with rain or dew from the night before.
And unless those shoes could dig into the earth, securing a
foothold, the army could not advance or hold the line.

When you think of the *shoes of peace* as part of your
spiritual arsenal, your mental image may be sort of soft
and marshmallowy. Sissy shoes. But trust me, peace is a
rugged, battle-tested piece of protection that's equal to the
toughest situation.

Actionable Intel

Do you own a pair of sports shoes that have cleats on the
bottom? Or even something that has a tough sole with a
good grip? Run your fingers along some of those ridges
and protrusions. Write down some of the benefits they
provide. And think of yourself standing strong, thanks to
the shoes of peace that can hold their ground—and thanks
to God, who keeps you from falling.

All Together Now

From Him the whole body, fitted and knit
together by every supporting ligament, promotes
the growth of the body. —Ephesians 4:16

Recon

Hobnails on the bottom of the Roman soldier's shoes helped the army perform one of its standard, successful formations. Here's how it worked. A line of warriors would stand shoulder to shoulder and dig their cleats into the ground. Together, their firm stances formed a nearly impenetrable wall of defense.

Satan doesn't like that. *Unity*. He's much more likely to come after you if you consider yourself more of a gladiator than a soldier. An army of one. That's one of the reasons why God has given you an entire community of faith—the church—to help defend against and attack the enemy.

Any of us, of course, can lose our footing from time to time. But if we're connected with our brothers and sisters, arm in arm along this advancing line of God-given power and might, we can help lift each other up and restore fallen soldiers to battle readiness.

One believer united with dozens, hundreds, thousands of others. There's peace of mind in that.

Actionable Intel

Pray today for other Christians you know, especially those who are part of the same church as you. Ask God to show you how to support each other in ways that cut off more and more of the enemy's attack lanes—against all of you.

Faith

You stand by faith. —Romans 11:20

Recon

The uniform of the spiritual warrior is the belt of truth, the breastplate of righteousness, and the shoes of peace. These represent the all-the-time, all-weather, protective fighting gear that no soldier can do without. Ever.

But "in addition to all this," Paul said in Ephesians 6:16 (NIV), the well-prepared warrior has been given a number of other pieces of essential equipment, ready to be put into practice at a moment's notice.

The first one mentioned is the "shield of faith" (v. 16).

Faith is what God activated in you so you could receive His gift of salvation in the first place. This was a *saving faith*. But faith is much more than the one-time access code that welcomes you into God's family. *Active faith* is a vibrant, ongoing requirement for doing battle in the unseen realms where only spiritual weapons will work. It is the spiritual virtue that will help you stand firm and stand tall against the schemes of the Devil.

Actionable Intel

There's so much we'll discover about the shield of faith. But for now, write down your working definition of *faith*. What do you think faith is? How do you think it works? Leave some room so you can add to your definition as you go along.

Shield of Faith

Take up the shield of faith, with which you
can extinguish all the flaming arrows of the evil one.
—Ephesians 6:16 NIV

Recon

Two kinds of shields were used in the ancient world during the time when Paul was writing. One was more the Captain America type—about the size of a trash can lid. But the type of shield Paul was describing in Ephesians 6 was called a *scutum*—pronounced SCOOT-em. (That's a fun word to say.)

The scutum was sort of shaped like a small door. (The drawing of the Roman soldier on page 373 will help you visualize it.) About two-feet wide, four-feet high. It was made from planks of wood and was covered by canvas. Then by leather. Then it was typically reinforced with iron, making it able to withstand the hard-hitting strokes of an enemy's broadsword in battle. The shield was so large, in fact, that an average-size soldier could basically crouch behind it and hide his entire body.

Our faith is that kind of shield—massive, protective, and able to cover us when we're under enemy fire. And because our God Himself is a shield, we'll never have reason to be afraid.

Actionable Intel

Read Proverbs 30:5, focusing on just the second half of the verse. God is truly "a shield to those who take refuge in Him." Consider memorizing this short piece of a verse, and repeat it to yourself often as a reminder of God's protection over your life.

Weapons of Mass Distraction

He shatters the bow's flaming arrows, the shield,
the sword, and the weapons of war. —Psalm 76:3

Recon

Flaming arrows were one of the more common assault weapons during the days of ancient Rome. Soldiers would slather tar on the pointy tips of these long spears (sort of like the javelins you see in the Olympics), then set them on fire before shooting them across to the opposing side.

The objective of these fiery arrows was less to kill someone and more to *distract* them. When launched into the enemy's camp, they would set the other side's tents and supplies on fire. Then the soldiers would have to stop advancing and defending themselves, needing to put out fires instead.

The Devil employs this strategy as well. *Distraction.* He wants you so busy trying to put out fires like temptation, turmoil, or relationship difficulties that you'll be too worn out to fend him off and claim your victory.

What you need is the same thing that ancient soldiers in battle needed: a shield that can extinguish fiery darts.

Thank God you have a shield that can do just that.

Actionable Intel

In the journal pages at the back of the book, write down some of the main things you're trying to achieve or stay focused on in life today. Now write the top two or three issues that are distracting you from being zoned in on your most important things. Ask the Lord to show you how faith can help keep you protected from them.

Meant What I Said

"If I tell you the truth, why don't you believe Me?"
—John 8:46

Recon

Here's a simple definition of what faith really is: *Faith is acting like God is telling the truth.*

When you read the Bible and discover the amazing things God did through ordinary people, your first reaction might be to dismiss it, to downplay it. Abraham. Noah. Ruth. Rahab. Paul. The stories seem to have happened so long ago. God's power in you doesn't really feel that powerful.

But maybe instead of thinking up all the ways He must be exaggerating, instead of discounting His Word as something that's too old to really apply to you, what about just . . . believing it? Trusting in what He is telling you and showing you about the amazing things He's able to accomplish in you?

Have faith!

What if the Bible is the actual, absolute truth? How would that change what your faith looks like? How would it change what your lifestyle looks like?

Actionable Intel

Read the verse that follows Jesus' words from today—John 8:47. How does He say a child of God responds to God's Word? What does He say about a person who's *not* a child of God?

And . . . Action!

We must not love with word or speech,
but with truth and action. —1 John 3:18

Recon

I didn't know a lot about how movies were made until God gave me the opportunity to actually *be* in one. But I know this: if all the actors ever did was sit around reading the script and rehearsing their lines—if all the filmmakers ever did was build screen sets and select wardrobe and raise money to pay for the cost, cast, and crew—there would never be any movies made.

There's no movie until actors get hired and sets get built, until the director yells, "Action!" and the actors act.

Our enemy really doesn't mind if we put on our dress clothes, go to Sunday school, read our Bible, and plop a few dollars in the collection plate at offering time. He doesn't care . . . as long as all this faith we're building up never leads to any action. As long as when God says, "Action!" we stand still and do nothing about it.

It's the *action* of faith—the living out of our faith—that becomes the *shield* of faith, able to guard us against enemy attack.

Actionable Intel

The next time you're at church or Bible study, don't just follow the script and try to get through the hour. Concentrate on how what you're hearing and learning and experiencing can be turned into everyday *action*!

Top-Level Protection

Take the helmet of salvation. —Ephesians 6:17

Recon

When military planners develop war strategies, they build them around primary objectives. They know what they want to accomplish—whether it's taking a bridge, seizing a compound, or destroying an oil field—and they strategize accordingly.

Well, we've been tipped off in Scripture to our enemy's primary objective: he seeks to influence your *heart* as well as your *mind*. That's why each piece of spiritual armor God has given you is designed to guard these key areas against all the various strategies your enemy has devised for meeting his goals.

But one piece of armor—the helmet of salvation—is specifically intended to protect your *mind*. Because believe it or not, a huge part of the battlefield is located right there, right behind your eyeballs, in a portion of your body that never shuts off and requires twenty-four-hour surveillance.

You want to win this battle for your mind? Never leave home without your helmet on.

Actionable Intel

Why do you think Satan would be so interested in infecting your thinking patterns and habits?

Head Protection

Our God is a God of salvation, and escape from death belongs to the Lord God. —Psalm 68:20

Recon

The helmet worn by those in the Roman army was made of iron and was typically covered with bronze. Its primary function was to protect the soldier's skull and brain from the swing of the massive broadsword. Picture any swordfight from ancient or medieval times, and you know what I'm talking about—a huge, heavy, three- to four-foot-long weapon of sharp, sudden death. Warriors would usually need to cradle the sword's massive handle with both hands as they swung it. And if it ever landed a direct blow—*Clang! Thud!*—it was immediate lights-out for the loser.

Your enemy is not coming after you with light artillery. He is swinging weapons to strike. And to kill—your joy, your future, your destiny. One of his key targets for taking you down is your mind.

But you're protected by the helmet of salvation. It is your guard against his attacks. You can't keep him from trying, but in Jesus you *can* prevent him from succeeding. Keep your mind covered in the strength of your salvation.

Actionable Intel

Our picture of the Roman soldier on page 373 shows his broadsword—the larger one, the one that's tucked in his belt. Note its weight and bone-crushing capabilities. Now you know how strong you need your helmet to be, and how sure you need to be that you're wearing it today.

Salvation

He was amazed that there was no one interceding;
so His own arm brought salvation. —*Isaiah 59:16*

Recon

We hear the word *salvation*, and our minds immediately want to make it more difficult than it is. We complicate an idea that—while, yes, is the hugest experience in the world—is simply the ultimate example of a concept we already know well.

God has *saved* us.

Now, obviously it's bigger than a basketball player saving the game by hitting a half-court shot at the buzzer. Or a family saving a puppy dog by adopting him from the pound. But it's not completely different from these things either.

The truth is, all of us were completely lost. The future looked tragically bleak. There was nothing we could do to stop it. But God stepped in and saved the day, saved our lives, saved our everything.

And for this, we should worship Him. For this, we should praise Him every day. No one else could do it for us. But He did it.

He *saved* us.

Actionable Intel

Look up *salvation* in a dictionary or thesaurus. List any words from the definition that help give you a better handle on what Christ's salvation means.

The Jackpot

You do not lack any spiritual gift. —1 Corinthians 1:7

Recon

One of the enemy's tactics is to cause you to focus on what you lack instead of what you actually have and who you really are. Then, while you are weakened, discouraged, and vulnerable, he strikes. But when you know how abundant and lavish your spiritual blessings are, you can live like the warrior you were always meant to be.

Ephesians 1 lays out your blessings like a huge, delicious buffet. There's salvation "through His blood"; "forgiveness" of your sins; grace that's been "lavished" upon you; not to mention the promised "Holy Spirit"; a rich "inheritance" from your Father; and of course the "immeasurable greatness of His power" (vv. 7, 8, 13, 14, 19). And that's just a sample from one chapter, in one book. Imagine what else you could find in some of the 1,188 other chapters, scattered among sixty-five other books in the Bible.

And you thought being a Christian was just about going to heaven one day. No, it's a *whole* lot more than that! It's about all the blessings that give you victory while you are right here on earth.

Actionable Intel

Keep a running list somewhere, maybe in a journal or notebook or cell phone, every time you discover a new gift or blessing that God has given you. Leave lots of room. It can get to be a long list.

Full Coverage

He has delivered me from every trouble. —Psalm 54:7

Recon

At one time in history, a Roman soldier's helmet was basically a skullcap. It covered nothing other than the top of his head. But around the time when Paul was working and writing and serving churches, the helmet was redesigned to include some valuable upgrades and features.

For one thing, a flared piece was added that covered the back of the neck. The new helmet also included metal guards that curved around each side to protect the face and cheekbones. With the exception of the soldier's eyes, nose, and mouth, everything else was basically covered.

Your helmet of salvation gives you comprehensive coverage as well. All-around protection. Morning, noon, and night. Past, present, and future. Body and soul.

The salvation that God has given you leaves nothing unprotected.

Actionable Intel

Look at the Roman soldier's helmet in our drawing on page 373. Notice its various levels of protection. What are some of the spiritual analogies you can draw from how the helmet of salvation provides protection?

Somebody New

If anyone is in Christ, the new creation has come: The old has gone, the new is here!—2 Corinthians 5:17 NIV

Recon

I know it still *looks* like you. Same eyes, same hair, same nose, same hat size. But the helmet of salvation you've been given to wear on that head, after receiving Christ as your Savior, is for a different person than you used to be.

Salvation has given you a new *identity*. "The old has gone, the new is here!"

Your "old" identity, spiritually speaking, was a person dying a slow death, disguised in a healthy body. It was the death of a heart held captive by sin, mastered by a cruel enemy. This simply wasn't going to end well. It never does. It can't.

Your "new" identity, however, is a person who is adopted by God. You are freed from guilt, filled with the Holy Spirit, changed from hopeless to hopeful. Even your physical death now will only lead to new life.

That's who you are, warrior. Wear that helmet. And wear it well.

Actionable Intel

Consider designing a new birth certificate for yourself to commemorate being "born again" (John 3:3) into a new identity in Christ. Be creative with it. Share it with your parents and family.

Sword of the Spirit

[Take] the sword of the Spirit, which is God's word.
—*Ephesians 6:17*

Recon

There are six pieces of armor listed in Ephesians 6, as we've seen. But one of the qualities that makes the sword unique among them is that it's the only one designed for *offensive* rather than *defensive* warfare.

The belt, the breastplate, the shield, the helmet—each is extremely important and necessary in its role of protection. Protecting your heart, protecting your mind, protecting your whole self from enemy assaults. But the sword is an active weapon. It's designed for attack. Where the others help you stand firm, the sword helps you strike out.

The power you've been given by God's Spirit is not for sitting back and taking the enemy's best shot. It's for taking the fight to the battlefront, moving ahead on your mission of victory.

Actionable Intel

Have you ever heard anybody refer to their Bible as their "sword"? I have. Because that's what it is. From now on, think of the Word as your sword.

Shooting Daggers

The One who has the sharp, double-edged
sword says . . .—Revelation 2:12

Recon

The sword that Paul described as part of your spiritual armor actually refers to a specific type of weapon. Roman soldiers of his day utilized two types of swords, one of them the *broadsword*. It was long and heavy, crushing in power. Even when it wasn't razor sharp, it still packed deadly force.

A second type, however, was what Paul had in mind for the sword of the Spirit. The *dagger* was much shorter, usually eighteen inches or less, easier to cloak, and able to be wielded easily with one hand. It was sharp as a needle at the tip. Double edged along the sides. Quick to draw and use against an opponent.

When you're armed with the Word of God, that's the kind of weapon you're fighting with. Pinpoint. Stealth precision. Striking from out of the blue. Think of your sword as quick and slashing. Think of your enemy as unable to stop it.

Actionable Intel

Notice the difference between the broadsword and the dagger in our drawing of the Roman soldier on page 373. What makes God's Word more similar to the shorter, quick-strike weapon?

Didn't See It Coming

Amasa was not on guard against the sword in Joab's hand. —2 Samuel 20:10

Recon

In a drastic transition among his leadership team, King David replaced Joab as commander of the army with one of David's relatives, Amasa—a move that obviously didn't sit well with Joab. But the old warrior didn't go easily into retirement. He gathered a group of men on his side and stayed in the action.

That's how he found himself bumping into Amasa one day amid the battle preparations. As Joab reached to embrace him in a show of fake respect, his dagger slipped out of its sheath and fell to the ground. As he picked it up—quicker than Amasa could see—he stabbed his rival in the stomach from close range. Face-to-face. Amasa was dead.

There's the power of the dagger. Undetectable. Nearly impossible to defend against.

So use yours well, warrior—your sword of the Spirit, the Word of God—and your enemy, the Devil, will fall before you.

Actionable Intel

Don't just read your Bible today. Realize you're sharpening your dagger for action.

What's in a Name?

*"Be gone, Satan! For it is written, 'You shall worship
the Lord your God and him only shall you serve.'"
Then the devil left him. —Matthew 4:10–11 ESV*

Recon

Just to be clear, your enemy's name is Satan (which means
"foe" or "adversary"). He's known as the Devil (which
means "slanderous").

Oh, and he goes by some other names and labels as
well. Perhaps you've heard him called Lucifer, which
means "day star" or "shining one." He disguises himself as
an "angel of light" (2 Corinthians 11:14). He's a tempter,
an accuser, a liar, and a blasphemer—meaning he treats
God's name and God's truth like they're worthless garbage.

We have no need to fear him, of course, since "if God
is for us, who is against us?" (Romans 8:31). But his anger,
arrogance, deception, and treachery are serious business
and are meant to bring us down. So as problems and
difficulties circle around your life, resist the urge to blame
other people, like your parents or your classmates. Call
it like you see it—like Jesus did. It's not *them*. It's *him*—
the *enemy*! Let him know you're on to him, and that you
won't let him get away with what he's trying to do. Then
put your armor on, pray, and get ready to win.

Actionable Intel

What have you typically thought the Devil was like? How
do some of the descriptions from today's devotion help to
rebuild your thoughts about him?

Big, Bigger, Biggest

"I am the Alpha and the Omega," says the Lord God, "the One who is, who was, and who is coming, the Almighty."—Revelation 1:8

Recon

I don't ever want to mention Satan's names and attributes, as I did yesterday, without making a whole lot bigger deal of Jesus' names and attributes. And even if I wrote all His mind-bending characteristics in the tiniest print size possible, this whole book wouldn't be space enough to tell the half of it.

He is the First and the Last, the Beginning and the End. He's the author of creation and the creator of all. He's the originator of the universe, and He orchestrates all of time and history. He eternally remains unmoved, unchanged, and undefeated.

He soothes pain and offers healing. He bestows grace on the most undeserving. He offers freedom to every captive and resurrection where dead things persist. He awakens hearts, renews minds, and reforms lost souls. He is power, peace, and provision. And He's only getting started. He is everything you'll ever need.

Actionable Intel

In the journaling pages at the back of the book, write a list of who God is to you. How many one- or two-word attributes can you think of? Tape this list somewhere (where your parents won't mind) so that you can see it every day.

Always There

*Who can hide in secret places so that I
cannot see them?—Jeremiah 23:24* NIV

Recon

Hey, I told you yesterday that your God and your enemy
(the Devil) are not on the same level. God is all-powerful
and in control of the universe; Satan has a whole bunch
of limitations. For the next several days, I want to show
you just a few of the many differences that exist between
them . . . and why you can always be victorious because
your commander is Commander in Chief.

God, for example, is everywhere all at once. The Devil
isn't. It's called being *omnipresent* (*omni* comes from
Latin, meaning "all"). Always present.

That's why you can never get in enough trouble, or be
in so much danger, or make such a mess of things, or feel
so far away from Him that He doesn't see you and watch
you and take care of you. You can always have confidence
that He is near no matter where you are.

The enemy wants you to think that you can run but
never hide from him. The truth is: God protects you in
spiritual safe places where no devil can ever find you.

Actionable Intel

Get your Bible and read Psalm 61:3–4. Realize even with
war raging around you, God is your "refuge" and "shelter,"
that you are protected under His wings from the enemy's
prying eyes.

Inside Information

Before a word is on my tongue, You know
all about it, LORD. —Psalm 139:4

Recon

The enemy only wishes he knew what you were thinking. *He doesn't.* He's limited in the amount of intel he can gather on you. He can't hear those silent prayers and strategy sessions of yours where you're talking to God all day in your own mind and heart.

God, however, not only knows your innermost needs and hurts—and will help you with problems and situations you may not even know how to ask Him about yet—but He also knows your *enemy's* mind. He knows exactly where and when the next attack is being mounted against you, and He has given you the perfect gear and guidance to keep you standing in a strong position.

God is *omniscient*. He knows all. With Him on your side, you always have the information advantage in every battle.

Actionable Intel

Some prayers are worth praying out loud, where even the enemy can hear the promises of God's Word! But what prayers might you want to keep locked away in your heart, between you and God alone?

Unlimited Power

Who can this be? He commands even the winds and the waves, and they obey Him!—Luke 8:25

Recon

Let's say you want people to think you can do something—like get backstage passes to a big concert because your dad went to school with one of the guys who does the sound or lighting—but you know you probably can't really get the tickets because your dad doesn't know the guy *that* well and only said he'd give it a shot . . .

Then all you can do is talk a big game. Tap dance and pretend. You weren't truly capable of pulling it off unless a lot of details fell in line. But you sure wanted to act like you were.

The Devil does a lot of that play-acting too. Giving the illusion of unlimited power and invincibility. But don't let him deceive and mislead you. Only God is *omnipotent*, able to do whatever He wants whenever He wants. The One behind *your* power is the only One who has *all* power.

Actionable Intel

Think of a time when you tried to (or were tempted to) give the impression that you could do something you really couldn't. How did someone call your bluff?

For All Time

From eternity to eternity the LORD's faithful love is toward those who fear Him. —Psalm 103:17

Recon

Our God is *omnipresent* (He's everywhere all at once). He is also *omniscient* (He knows everything there is to know), and He is *omnipotent* (He does anything He wants to do).

That's a whole lot of things to be all-everything at.

But you know what's even better? He will be all of these things *forever*, for eternity—just as He is all these things already, from an eternity ago.

Our enemy has been around a long time too. But he will not have power forever. He'll be around a long time still. But he will be crushed. That's because the Bible says he's in line for a date with destruction when he will be "thrown into the lake of fire and sulfur" to be "tormented day and night forever and ever" (Revelation 20:10). That's what *he's* going to be doing for all eternity.

But that's not what's going to happen to God. And not you either, if Jesus is your Lord and Savior.

Actionable Intel

Picture an ocean completely dry, hundreds of miles wide. If a bird dropped a grain of sand from the shore into that enormous, ocean-size ditch, just once a year, there's no telling how many billions of years it would it take to fill it up. And when the bird dropped in the very last grain of sand, eternity would only have just begun.

The Unseen

This grace was given . . . so that the manifold wisdom of God might now be made known through the church to the rulers and the authorities in the heavenly places. —Ephesians 3:8–10 NASB

Recon

"Heavenly places." Sounds so nice, doesn't it? And heaven, of course—oh yeah, that's going to be nice. But when Paul was talking to the Ephesians about "heavenly places," he was talking about the invisible, unseen realm where the real battles of life are actually being waged. Not here on the physical, three-dimensional, five-senses world where war is fought with fighter jets and missile launchers and sniper drones. War in the "heavenly places" calls for *spiritual* weapons, not *physical* ones.

You and I can waste a lot of time getting mad, getting even, getting up in people's faces when they don't do what we want them to do, when we don't like the way they're treating us. But why fight our battles with weapons that don't work, *can't* work, won't *ever* work? When you know where the *real* fight is coming from, you can fight back with weapons that really do the job.

Actionable Intel

What are the most common earthly weapons you use when fighting typical daily battles? Sarcastic words? The silent treatment? A bad attitude? What kinds of spiritual weapons can you use today instead?

Home Court Advantage

[God] raised us up with Him, and seated us with Him in the heavenly places in Christ Jesus. —Ephesians 2:6 NASB

Recon

"Heavenly places." There it is again. It's where the "rulers and authorities" in our enemy's army are scouting their war plans against you, remember? But if all this up-in-the-air talk about fighting spiritual battles seems just a little too "out there," here's what I want you to notice from this verse. *You*, my friend—if you've given your life to Jesus—are actually spiritually present *right this minute* in "heavenly places" too.

Isn't that cool?! And you thought you were just an earthling. Bound by gravity and time and Newton's laws of motion. But . . . nope. You're not. The heavens are actually more *your* home court now than the enemy's, because you're sitting there with the One who created them and owns them and has put you on His team.

Don't ever think you only have limited access to Jesus or limited ways of fighting and winning. You're already in perfect position to do some major-league damage to the enemy and his efforts against you.

Actionable Intel

In your favorite sport, what are some of the factors that give the home team the edge? Pray and ask the Lord to help you remember the home-court advantage you have, now that your home is with Christ in heavenly places, so that you can live like the victor you are.

Prayer Warrior

*Pray at all times in the Spirit with every
prayer and request. —Ephesians 6:18*

Recon

When most people read about our spiritual armor in
Ephesians 6, they see only six pieces listed: (1) the belt of
truth, (2) the breastplate of righteousness, (3) the shoes of
peace, (4) the shield of faith, (5) the helmet of salvation,
and (6) the sword of the Spirit.

You've already made this list yourself if you've been
following along in your devotional.

Turns out, though—there are *seven*. And though it's
mentioned last, it's the one that holds all of the armor
together.

It's prayer. Prayer is what activates all the other pieces
of your spiritual armor. Every battle must be fought with
prayer. Constant prayer. "Pray at all times" praying.

So "stay alert in this," Paul said, "with all perseverance"
(Ephesians 6:18). There's no spiritual warrior who's not
also a prayer warrior.

Actionable Intel

Commit today not just to being a person who knows it's
important to pray but to be someone who's growing up
into a real prayer warrior. There's a difference, you know,
between knowing about prayer and actually praying. YOU
are a prayer WARRIOR!

God's Armor

He put on righteousness like a breastplate, and a
helmet of salvation on His head. —Isaiah 59:17

Recon

Looking at today's verse, you might notice that some of
this armor God is wearing sounds a whole lot like the
spiritual armor listed in Ephesians 6—something else I
asked you to read and report on. (It's been a while, but do
you happen to remember?)

Here's my question: Why do you think they look so
similar? Why would these two sections of the Bible sort
of repeat themselves? Here's the answer: Because the
spiritual armor you've been given for wearing in battle
is not just any old armor. It is *God's* armor! He's not
keeping the good stuff to Himself and making you settle
for leftovers. Only the best will do for God's warrior kids.
That's why He's giving you the battle clothes off His own
back. Each piece is a gift from Him to you. They are full
of His own power to guarantee you success against the
enemy.

How does it feel to be a warrior who wears the armor
of the King?

Actionable Intel

Take some time to compare and contrast Isaiah 59:16–20
with Ephesians 6:13–17. Which pieces of armor are in
each passage?

Warning Signs

God is not a God of disorder but of peace. —*1 Corinthians 14:33*

Recon

Warriors in combat learn to look for anything that might signal the presence of the enemy. The sudden movement of troops. The distant beat of helicopter blades. The chatter of communication picked up through phone and radio traffic.

Being able to spot the advance warning signs of enemy activity is key to defeating them.

The same thing goes for warriors in unseen combat. And one of the telltale signs to watch for is an increase in *chaos*.

Know what I mean by chaos? It's when you're feeling more worried than confident. Confused, not sure what to do. Instead of getting along with people—friends, parents, siblings—you're angry, hurt, or upset.

And the moment you start to sense it—instability, conflict, uncertainty, touchiness—pray and ask God to show you if it's your own sinfulness that is leading to the unrest, or if it's your enemy who is trying to mess with you. Don't get mad at the *seen* sources if that is where the trouble appears to be coming from. Direct your prayer attack against the *unseen* source who's out to steal your peace.

Actionable Intel

Today, if you feel frustration building between you and other people, take it as your cue to pray for them, and say something kind to them instead.

Under Armor

My strength will be refreshed within me, and my bow will be renewed in my hand. —Job 29:20

Recon

Most of the Roman soldier's armor and weaponry connected in some way to the belt he wore. And all the gear he carried around for fighting and protection could weigh, all together, up to seventy pounds. Yeah, *sixty or seventy pounds*. He was packing a load.

So the belt was foundational and critical. Without it, he was like a police officer missing his holster. Nowhere to keep anything.

If he needed his sword, he yanked it from his belt. If he needed his dagger, it came from there too. If he needed his hands free for . . . whatever . . . then the belt was where he stuck everything while he was punching somebody out. The belt, it seemed, was always in play. Always part of the action.

Truth may not be the fanciest and flashiest thing. But it helps keep you protected and prepared where it counts.

Actionable Intel

Have you ever noticed all the things police officers carry on their belts or in their holsters? How much harder do you think their job would be—the kind of danger they could potentially be in—if they didn't have all that stuff at hand? If you know a police officer, why don't you ask him or her the same question?

Truth in Action

*The fruit of the light results in all goodness,
righteousness, and truth. —Ephesians 5:9*

Recon

For the next few days, I want to highlight again all the
pieces of spiritual armor from Ephesians 6, because each
of them represents a spiritual virtue. What I want you
to see in particular right here is how *truth*—the virtue
behind the "belt of truth"—is key to helping us experience
all the others.

Like, for example, the *breastplate of righteousness*
(Ephesians 6:14). *Righteousness* is a pretty big word, I
know, and it sounds all churchy and everything. But it's a
lot simpler than you might think.

Righteousness means living right. But if we don't
know the truth from God's Word that tells us what "living
right" is supposed to look like, how do we know what to
do? It's not enough just to *feel* like doing the right thing.
We need God's Spirit—the "Spirit of truth" (John 14:17)—
to work through our minds and hearts to change the way
we think and live.

Actionable Intel

What happens when you're playing a game where not
everybody knows the rules? How many mistakes get made
before people start playing it right?

Partnered with Peace

*Grace, mercy, and peace will be with us
from God the Father and from Jesus Christ
. . . in truth and love.* —2 John v. 3

Recon

The next pieces of armor are the *shoes of peace* (Ephesians 6:15). Peace is as crucial to your life as a pair of good boots would be to any soldier who hoped to fight well and win. For you, *peace with God* means that nothing can ever crop up in your life—no setback, no circumstance—big enough to separate you from the confidence of God's love for you. You're safe. You're settled. That's the truth, no matter what the enemy says.

What's more, it also gives you *peace with others*. I'm not saying everyone will always be easy to get along with. But for your part, you can always choose the way of peace and harmony in all your relationships.

That's because the truth of God's power—the truth of what God can do in any situation—is greater than any obstacle that ever stands in its way. Walking in truth will help you walk in peace.

Actionable Intel

Where do you wish for peace the most? What parts of life cause you the greatest sense of turmoil and frustration? How much of this chaos or confusion could be resolved if the truth came into play?

Two for One

Faithful love and truth will join together. —Psalm 85:10

Recon

Next comes the *shield of faith* (Ephesians 6:16).

If it weren't for truth, faith would be, well . . . it *wouldn't* be. Because faith doesn't just need something to believe in; it needs the something it believes in to be completely capable of doing everything it claims it can do. Otherwise, faith is wasted. Or misguided. For example, if you believe your bed can hold your weight, but it crumples to the ground as soon as you lie down on it, it was not something worth having faith in after all.

The truth of your God is what makes your faith worth having. Truth is the anchor that brings faith down to earth. Down to Tuesdays. Down to mornings that aren't Sunday morning and to evenings that aren't Christmas Eve.

With truth around your waist—with truth feeding into your mind and heart—what you believe becomes what you live. The two are not so separate anymore. That's how faith hardens into a shield that makes you tough and battle-ready.

Actionable Intel

Think of one thing you believe about God, based on the truth of His Word. Now think of three everyday actions you can do or attitudes you can have now that this one truth has established as your foundation.

Everything Rolled Together

*His divine power has given us everything required
for life and godliness through the knowledge
of Him who called us. —2 Peter 1:3*

Recon

We're looking today at the *salvation* behind the *helmet of
salvation* (Ephesians 6:17).

Let me try it this way: If I were to ask you what a
vacation is, would you say it's a week at one of your
favorite places—the beach, the mountains, a theme park?

The truth is, a vacation isn't just about the destination.
It starts as soon as you leave home. It's the fun you have
while you're getting there. It's the stuff you do when you
arrive. The things you eat. The laughs you enjoy with
people you love. The nights sitting around with your
family or going out to see things. It's *all* of that . . . and
more. *That's* what a vacation is.

So if I were to ask you what salvation is—well, it
works the same way. It's not just this one thing: being
saved. No, it's *everything*: it's real-time relationship with
Jesus, the promise of heaven, the forgiveness of all your
sins, an inheritance of incredible blessing.

Knowing the truth about salvation means you know
it's a whole lot more than just a walk down the church
aisle.

Actionable Intel

I've asked you to create several lists, I know, but here's
another one to start. Get someone to help you think of all
the blessings that come from being saved. You might be
surprised by how many there are.

Fighting Words

The entirety of Your word is truth, and all Your righteous judgments endure forever. —Psalm 119:160

Recon

When we think of the *sword of the Spirit* (Ephesians 6:17), we're talking about the Word of God. When God speaks personally to you through the truth of the Bible, it's like a sword that helps us take stabs and gashes at Satan's lies, ripping them up into slivery smithereens.

Now, I'll tell you, I don't like to fight. I like things a whole lot better when they're just peaceful and calm and settled down. But when it comes to being lied to by this enemy . . . lies about my relationship with Jesus, lies about the nature and character of God, lies about what people said and meant, lies about what he wants to do to my parents, my friends, in my house, on my property . . .

Listen, I'm getting my sword out. I'm swinging and striking. Because I'm not living under the enemy's lies. Neither should you.

We have a sword. And we know how to use it.

And that's the truth.

Actionable Intel

What do you think is the best way to use the sword of the Spirit against the enemy in your everyday life? What does that look like?

Prayer Power

*"If you remain in Me and My words
remain in you, ask whatever you want and
it will be done for you."*—John 15:7

Recon

The last stop on our little mini-tour takes us to *prayer* (Ephesians 6:18).

Truth is vital to prayer . . . because prayer is not only the action of talking with God. It's not merely a communication device. It's not just a "now I lay me down to sleep" kind of thing. Not for a warrior like you.

When you know the truth of what God has done for you in Christ, prayer becomes your point of access to it. Prayer is where you go to receive His promises. Prayer is how you experience His confidence and victory. Prayer is the place where God's power isn't just something you sing about, but something He starts to give to you and infuse through you. Prayer is the doorway to all God's blessings in heavenly places, and it is Kryptonite to the enemy and His plans.

Make sure, more than anything, that you are a prayer warrior. Your enemy can't stand the sight of a young person who knows its power and uses it.

Actionable Intel

I'm going to ask you today to spend a little more time praying than usual. Look back over the last several days, at all the spiritual armor and virtues we've been talking about. Ask God specifically to help you apply and experience them all.

A Tale of Two Strongholds

The LORD is the stronghold of my life—of whom should I be afraid?—Psalm 27:1

Recon

Strongholds are like military forts—built up and secure, keeping people in, keeping people out. And God, the Bible repeatedly says, is like a stronghold for His people. A place of safety and security, of confidence and victory.

Life is a daily decision to see whose stronghold you're going to live in.

Because, you see, the enemy knows how to build strongholds too—not to *protect* you, but to *trap* you. He does it by taking isolated sins, isolated events, and then tempting you into making them habits and cravings, into reasons for staying bitter, angry, and unforgiving. All too soon (and often before you realize it) the choices you've made have allowed him to box you into a competing stronghold. You've let him pin you inside the cage of his chaos, when you *could* be resting within God's peaceful provision.

But you can escape the enemy's strongholds . . . by running back to your one and only Stronghold. The door is always open to you. And always ready to shut behind you and keep your enemy out.

Actionable Intel

Turn to Psalm 62, and read verses 5–8. If you have time today, write these verses word for word in the journaling pages at the back of this book. Underline the words that speak to you the most.

What If?

Moses answered, "What if they won't believe me and will not obey me but say, 'The LORD did not appear to you'?"—Exodus 4:1

Recon

What if? It's one of your enemy's favorite questions.

And here's why he likes it. It's open-ended, so it can't be answered with a simple yes or no. It's an opinion, so he can always argue his side of it.

It's sort of a *gotcha* question. A squishy question. Just the kind of question you'd expect from someone whose goal, if not to defeat you, is at least to frighten you and distract you and get you off your game.

But the next time you hear his "What if?" question, pick up your shield of faith as quickly as you can by moving forward confidently on God's promise. As you do, He'll turn that "what-if" sound into a fizzly sort of *pffft* sound. Let it hit the sweet spot of your faith. Hear it being extinguished. As if held under water. Drained of power. Drowned into silence.

So let him ask all the "What if" questions he wants. You can keep them from hindering you every single time.

Actionable Intel

Write down some of the "What if" questions you most struggle with every day. Then pray and ask the Lord to give you His courage to push past them and extinguish them by faith.

Eight Thousand Promises

*Every one of God's promises is "Yes" in
Him. —2 Corinthians 1:20*

Recon

There's a little series of children's encyclopedias called
8000 Things You Should Know. These big, fat, kid-friendly
books are just chock-full of facts and information—
everything from animals to science to space to world
geography. Tons of stuff. There's always something new to
learn, from the fun to the fascinating.

Now, of course I'm not suggesting that we change
the name of the Bible. But it would ring true if on the
back cover somewhere we called it *8000 Promises You
Should Know.* Because inside the pages of Scripture are
thousands and thousands of promises from God, made to
you as a believer in Jesus Christ.

That's thousands of opportunities for you to trust God
by faith. Thousands of opportunities for you to take up your
shield of faith and see God respond to your trust in Him.
Thousands of opportunities to knock down the arrows of
your enemy.

Actionable Intel

Turn to Ephesians 6:16—the verse that talks about your
shield of faith—and read the promise that applies to you,
every time you raise it up.

Setting the Standard

"Your word is truth."—John 17:17

Recon

Since you've been so faithful to make it this far in your devotional reading, I consider it my distinct privilege to tell you: you're already doing the first thing needed for strapping on the belt of truth. You're learning and living by the Word of God, by the Bible.

That's because *truth* can basically be condensed to this short definition: *truth is God's opinion on any matter.* And God's opinion on everything that matters to you and me has already been hand delivered to us . . . in the Bible.

The Bible is our standard. Immovable. Never changing. Ephesians 4:14 warns us against staying spiritually ignorant and immature, or else we'll be "tossed by the waves and blown around by every wind of teaching." Well, the Bible is everything that the wind and ocean waves are not. God's Word never shifts to another direction. Never comes and goes. Never looks or acts differently in different kinds of weather.

Are you staying in the Bible? Then you're staying in the truth.

Actionable Intel

I'm going to be sharing four—count 'em—*four* ways you can surround yourself with the belt of truth. Start a list of these four strategies, beginning with this one about staying in the Word. Write it in your *own* words. In fact, feel free to decorate the journal page any way you like. We'll look at number two tomorrow.

Testing, Testing

*Examine everything carefully; hold fast to that
which is good. —1 Thessalonians 5:21* NASB

Recon

You may not be in control of all your decisions yet. (News flash: Some decisions will *always* be made for you, by someone else or something else, no matter how old you get.) But like everybody, you make enough of your own decisions—related to what you do, what you're planning, and how you spend your time—that you always need to wear your belt of truth.

I'm going to use the word *systematically*. It means repeatedly and on purpose. Whenever you come up against a decision that needs to be made—whether it calls for immediate action or whether you have a week or more to think about it—get in the habit of *systematically* applying what you know to be true to every question it brings up.

Ask. Get information. From your parents. From your authority figures. From your experience. And certainly from what you're learning in the Bible. Every decision is worth basing on the truth.

Actionable Intel

What decision is weighing on you right now? Maybe it's not just a single decision but one of those choices you make almost every day. How might knowing the truth affect the way you make it? Write down today's reminder, tip number two: "Systematically line up your decisions with truth."

Follow the Leader

Follow my example, as I follow the example
of Christ. —1 Corinthians 11:1 NIV

Recon

Maybe there's someone you know—even if you only know them as a celebrity and only see their public image—who you sort of try to imitate. They inspire you. You look up to them. They interest you. You listen to what they say. You watch how they act. How they dress.

There's nothing wrong with that, if your role models are good ones. But when we are looking for a hero, what we need are people whom King David called the "holy people who are in the land." They were his "delight," he said—"all" his delight—these "noble ones" whose character was truly worth being followed (Psalm 16:3).

If you really want to keep the belt of truth secured tightly around your waist, make sure your greatest goal is to be more like Jesus by reading about Him in the Bible—and to be more like those who strive for the exact same thing.

Actionable Intel

See if someone who knows the Bible well can help you identify some of the greatest character traits of Jesus. What are some situations in your life where you need to stay more true to these qualities? Write down tip number three for wearing the belt of truth: "Learn about the character of God."

I'm Just Not Feeling It

Whatever is true, whatever is honorable,
whatever is just, whatever is pure . . . dwell
on these things. —Philippians 4:8

Recon

Have you been keeping up with some of the ways you can put on the belt of truth? (1) Use the Bible as your standard of truth. (2) Test every decision against the standard of truth. (3) Follow the example of Jesus and those who follow the truth.

And here's one more. (4) Don't confuse your feelings for the truth.

You may have noticed that your moods, your emotions, your feelings—they're a lot more consistent with the "winds and waves" kind of experiences. They can bounce all over the place. You can be happy and feel good one second, then be bummed out and upset the next. You just never know. Feelings aren't driven by logic—by the *truth*—but almost completely by circumstances and situations. Your enemy is hoping you'll follow your feelings instead of the truth because then you'll always be vulnerable.

Truth doesn't run through the belt loops of emotion. Truth runs on established promises and on the timeless wisdom of God's Word.

Actionable Intel

How have your feelings often only succeeded at getting you into more trouble? What usually happens once you've cooled down or taken a deep breath? Which side of the reaction is more in line with what's really true? Tip number four for wearing the belt of truth: "Don't rely only on your feelings."

Buckle Up

"When the Spirit of truth comes, He will guide you into all the truth."—John 16:13

Recon

I've got some prayers written out and taped to the wall of my closet, dealing with specific issues that I need God's help with.

Today I want you to start writing a prayer too—asking God to keep you fitted with the belt of truth.

The prayer doesn't need to be long and involved. Make it very short, if you like. But flip back through this book or whatever kind of journal you might be keeping, and locate a verse or two or three that have been important to you in this devotional.

Combine the truth of those verses with words from your own heart, and compose a prayer—written out, on paper—that you can repeatedly pray. In it, ask God to protect you from enemy lies and deception of every make and model. And thank Him for giving you His Word and His Spirit to "guide you into all the truth" and keep you fortified as the warrior for His kingdom that you are.

Actionable Intel

I've given you your challenge for today. I pray, as you follow it through, that you'll discover the power of praying. Of really, *really* praying.

Invisibility

*"Everyone who practices wicked things hates
the light and avoids it, so that his deeds
may not be exposed."*—John 3:20

Recon

What if you had the superpower of being invisible? Wouldn't that be cool? You could sneak into places without being seen. Nobody would even know you were there. You could cause a lot of havoc that way, keeping people guessing. They wouldn't be able to tell where all this weird stuff happening to them was coming from.

But imagine being suddenly exposed. Your disguise undone, decoded, reversed. *They can see you now.* You're standing there, where you're not supposed to be, where you were depending on your invisibility to cover for your pranks and actions.

That's what your enemy is depending on too. On his invisibility. On your not knowing he's there making things difficult for you. But God's Word is filled with decoding techniques that bust his cover. That's why spending as much time as possible reading the Bible, thinking about what God is saying, is so important. Truth exposes lies. Truth turns on the light. Truth makes the invisible . . . visible.

Actionable Intel

Here are some tactics the enemy uses: division, discouragement, jealousy, worry, fear. If you detect these things happening, you can know he is at work. Once his cover is blown, you can deal with him using the spiritual weapons you're learning about in this devotional.

Truth or Fiction?

We did not follow cleverly devised stories when we told you about the coming of our Lord Jesus Christ in power. —2 Peter 1:16 NIV

Recon

Books in libraries are sorted into different categories—history books, sports books, books on animal life, books on monsters, and books about space battles set in futuristic societies. But there are really just two main categories: *nonfiction* (stories that have actually happened or are still happening) and *fiction* (stories from an author's imagination).

This enemy who's fighting against you, and against me, and against everybody who's seeking to follow Christ would love for you to think he hangs out only in the fiction section, where people make up stuff that's not really true. Just pretend. Like a video-game world. Harmless. Nothing to worry your little head about. Just a myth.

But, no—he's real, all right. And your God is very real as well, although Satan would like for you to think God isn't real either. So you have no reason to ever be afraid. Through God and His power, you can live your own true story of good conquering evil.

Actionable Intel

Make a list of some things happening in our world today—or even just in your life today—that let you know how real the enemy is.

Put It to Good Use

Let the righteous go on in righteousness; and let the holy go on being made holy. —Revelation 22:11

Recon

Having the breastplate of righteousness is good. But it's not just something to *have.* You need to know how to use it.

For instance, if you were given a new video game console for your birthday last year, I'm sure you had it hooked up and were playing with it ten minutes after taking it out of the box. Without even looking now, you've learned how to press just the right buttons at just the right time to make your character jump or drop or dodge things or throw things.

But put that same controller in my hands, and I'm all thumbs. I'm *holding* the thing—I *have* it—but I don't know how to *use* it.

Like the angel said to John the apostle in some of these last words of the Bible, you and I need to "go on in righteousness," meaning we have to live out what we know about God, not just sit around admiring His Words.

Actionable Intel

What's something in your house (maybe some of your dad's tools or your mom's cookware) that you don't know how to use? Ask your parents to teach you how to use it. Knowing how to *use* something gives you a confidence leap in that area. It can happen in your spiritual life as well.

Just Do It

Happy is the person who trusts in You,
LORD of Hosts. —Psalm 84:12

Recon

One of the most amazing people I've ever known lives each day with a secret weapon, and it makes her life a fantastic adventure. She *takes up the shield of faith*. She simply does what God asks her to do. No matter what.

If He gives her the idea to do something special for someone? *She does it*. If He wants her to mend fences with one of her friends who's upset with her? *She does it*. If He leads her to put more money than usual in the offering plate on Sunday? *She does it*. She doesn't waste time questioning or doubting God, nor does she let fear and insecurity talk her out of being obedient to Him. *She just does it*.

She doesn't merely have faith in what God can do. She has faith that He can do it in *her*. She believes that when she responds to Him in faith, He will lead her to the most amazing, most thrilling, most happy and satisfied life that anybody can ever live. And trust me, her life is living proof of it.

So trust God and . . .

Just do it.

Actionable Intel

Ask God to give you an opportunity to trust Him and act in faith during the next twenty-four hours. Then make a commitment to do whatever He tells you to do.

Inside Wiring

I will put my laws into their minds and write them on their hearts. —Hebrews 8:10

Recon

Every single function of your body—whether a tiny movement of your pinkie finger or a mile run in gym class—comes from the signals and impulses your brain sends out. And unless the information flowing through all those nerve endings is correct, a part of your body will end up malfunctioning.

Well, what your brain is to your body, your faith is to your soul. The soul is what makes you who you are. And if you choose to base all your thinking and emotions on something false, then you will not live the way God wants you to. You will malfunction and end up in chaos and fear. But if you base your faith on the truth of God, you will lead a life of peace and confidence.

The helmet of salvation is what God has given you to keep your mind on its proper wavelength. Because when it's on and working properly, everything else will run better too.

Actionable Intel

If you're experiencing any anger, doubts, or insecurities today, try tracing them back to faults in your spiritual wiring—flawed thinking about God or who you are in Him. Do a little electrical repair, and see if it doesn't start clearing up.

Seen and Heard

This is the confidence we have before Him:
Whenever we ask anything according to His
will, He hears us. —1 John 5:14

Recon

Here's one of God's promises: *When we pray, He hears us.* Do you ever doubt that? Do you ever think prayer is probably just a superstitious waste of time, like talking to an invisible friend? Just words in the darkness?

Not according to the Bible. God hears you. Every word. You can be confident of that.

In fact, you *need* to be confident in it. Because built on this truth is an even greater truth: "If we know that He hears whatever we ask, we know that we have what we have asked Him for" (1 John 5:15). When we pray, He not only *hears* us; when He hears us, He *answers* us.

I know why that's hard to believe. He's so big, and we're so small. Why should He care? But wrap your life in the truth that God both hears and answers your prayers, and He will show you, over time, that your confidence is in the right place.

Actionable Intel

As you pray today, take special notice that every word you speak—or even think—is being heard by God. Don't doubt it for a second. Believe the truth.

Pathfinder

I will lead the blind by a way they did not know; I will guide them on paths they have not known. —*Isaiah 42:16*

Recon

Life comes with a lot of question marks. What will you be when you grow up? Where will you go to college? Who will you marry, and how can you know you're choosing the right person? How can you ever really know God's will? About anything?

Here's a promise from God: *He will show you how to follow Him.*

"Whenever you turn to the right or to the left, your ears will hear this command behind you: 'This is the way. Walk in it'" (Isaiah 30:21). Yes, you'll need to be listening. Yes, you'll need to consider His plans more trustworthy than your own feelings. And yes, you'll need to be ready to do whatever He shows you. But the truth is, even for those of us who feel lost and blind sometimes, our God is a faithful leader who knows how to show us the right paths to take.

Actionable Intel

Write down the two or three biggest questions that are on your mind concerning your life, your future, your family—big things. As you pray about them over the next few weeks and months, keep a record of how God begins giving you even small answers to your questions.

Value Statement

A demonstration of the Spirit is given to each person to produce what is beneficial. —1 Corinthians 12:7

Recon

God loves to give gifts. In fact, He is the ultimate gift giver. And the truth is, *He has given you a special gift*. Not only did He knit you together in your mother's womb (Psalm 139:13), not only did His hands form you in His image (Psalm 119:73), and not only has He infused you with physical or musical or academic talents for you to grow and develop, but He has also blessed you as a believer with a certain gift or two (or more) that can help you serve Him and others like no one else can.

Listen to me now. Your enemy will try anything to convince you that you're worthless. He'll piggyback on a cruel word spoken to you, a poor grade on an important test, a dropped pass or missed layup. He'll try anything. But God has already declared you to be a person of immeasurable value. Useful to Him. Gifted by Him. Anything other than that is a lie.

Actionable Intel

Ask someone who loves you and knows you well—a parent, a grandparent, a special teacher at church—to tell you what gifts they can see that God has given you. I promise you're going to like what you hear. And you will probably be surprised by what you haven't recognized in yourself.

Not Enough Ink

*If every one of them were written down, I suppose
that even the whole world would not have room for the
books that would be written.* —*John 21:25* NIV

Recon

There are 365 devotions in this collection. One for each
day of the year. But even with all these readings and
all these words, they're still not enough to cover even a
fraction of God's promises to you. His truth already fills
more than a thousand pages of Scripture. And the way His
Spirit personalizes it to your life as you go along—there's
not a calculator on the earth that can possibly compute
how many strands of truth reach out from His heart to
yours each day.

It's a b-i-i-i-g belt, this belt of truth.

So I hope you'll wrap it snugly around you today . . .
because there's nothing in your life that can't fit inside. No
problem. No worry. No fear or loss or embarrassment or
trouble. No confusion. No misunderstanding. No decision
to make or dilemma to figure out.

When the truth is at your side, and at your front, and
supporting you from behind, you're living with the all-
around protection of God's promises.

Actionable Intel

Do you happen to have a belt you don't wear anymore
but still hangs in your closet? Ask your mom or dad if you
can write "Belt of Truth" on it, and then keep it hanging
nearby as a reminder to put on the belt of truth every
morning.

What Every Sinner Needs

Whoever knows the right thing to do and fails to do it, for him it is sin. —*James 4:17* ESV

Recon

Any salesperson or advertisement trying to get you interested in their product must first convince you of your *need* for it. And when it comes to the breastplate of righteousness—listen, we all desperately need it.

For starters, the Bible tells us "there is no one righteous, not even one . . . no one who understands . . . no one who seeks God" (Romans 3:10–11 NIV). Even those of us who've been saved from our sins, who've been given the Holy Spirit to guide us into truth—yes, even those of us who "know the right thing to do"—keep finding ways to sin.

Again, it's not just you; it's all of us.

So the *need* is established. Sin has proven to be not only our *original* problem but also our *ongoing* problem. And that means our need for righteousness is ongoing as well. Our need for this breastplate is critical. No home or heart should be without one. And God has made sure we can have one.

Actionable Intel

Are you confident that you've received Jesus into your heart? If you're not, today's devotion tells you the place to begin: realizing you're a sinner, realizing your need for Him. If He's made this obvious to you today, talk to a Christian friend or family member about how to receive God's forgiveness for *all* your sin. This is where righteous living begins.

Your Father's Shoes

Stand firm then . . . with your feet fitted
with the readiness that comes from the gospel
of peace. —Ephesians 6:14–15 NIV

Recon

My youngest son likes to wear his daddy's shoes. Granted, they are waaaay too big for him. But still, I often see him (and hear him!) clomping around the house like a Clydesdale or slogging through the yard, trying to stay upright in those oversized shoes.

Before he started doing this, if I ever saw huge, muddy footprints tracking through the house, I would've gone to my husband and asked him to please be more careful where he was walking. But lately, there's just as good a chance that a six-year-old made those muddy prints—because when you're wearing your daddy's shoes, your footprints look a whole lot like his.

As a warrior in God's service, you too have been given your Father's shoes to wear—and your Father's footprints to make. Only instead of being hard to fit into, these shoes actually bring you more comfort and stability in your life than you can ever imagine. And instead of making a mess that you'll have a hard time cleaning up, they'll leave prints of victory . . . and peace.

Actionable Intel

If someone asked you to define *peace*, what would your answer be? Try writing it down, and then keep it in a place where you can find it later. We might come back to it . . . to see if your answer changes a little.

So . . .

So we do not focus on what is seen, but on what is unseen. —2 Corinthians 4:18

Recon

My father is a pastor. He says lots of memorable things. Here's one of his sayings that is one of my favorites: "Faith means acting like it *is* so, even when it's *not* so, so that it *might* be so, just because *God said* so."

Let's break this down a little bit. *Acting like it is so*: this tells me that faith is something you do, not just something you think about. *Even when it's not so*: this means that very often you will not be able to see any visible proof of God's presence or His promises. *So it might be so*: this means if you don't act on faith, you'll miss out on seeing what God wants to do in you and through you. *Because God said so*: this means God's Word is enough to give you confidence and assurance to move forward.

So . . .

What are you waiting on? Live like it *is* so, because . . . it is!

Actionable Intel

Write down my dad's quote, word for word, on a card or piece of paper that you can tape up alongside some of your handwritten prayers. It'll help reinforce what you're praying about.

It's Who You Are

We have redemption in Him through His blood . . .
according to the riches of His grace. —*Ephesians 1:7*

Recon

You are completely forgiven. Of all your sins. You are blameless before God. He loves you and has blessed you with a bountiful inheritance in Christ. You are rich beyond your ability to fathom it. You're a child of the King.

You've been given His Holy Spirit, who right now dwells inside you. He's changed you from someone with no hope beyond this lifetime, someone with no real control over anything, to someone who will live forever with Him, cared for by the One who controls absolutely everything.

You were once separated from His love, lost and alone. But now He's adopted you into His family, seated you with Him in heavenly places, and ensured that you will always belong to Him. He has created you with a plan, personalized to your life, that He can accomplish with great power and perfect timing.

You are saved. And you are safe. Launch your fight today from this position of strength.

Actionable Intel

These words you've just read describe your helmet of salvation. Put it on.

Big Problem

I am weary from grief; strengthen me
through Your word. —Psalm 119:28

Recon

Ever have any problems? Of course you do. *Everybody*
does. And I'll bet you can think of one of these problems—
one or two, or maybe even three or four—that don't just
bug you, they drive you crazy. Maybe one of them makes
you furious sometimes. Occasionally scares you to death.
Hardly a day goes by that you don't struggle with them,
or get frustrated by them, or feel embarrassed because
of them.

Again, you're not the only one who feels this way.
All of us do—about *something* or *someone*. I sure do. So
the issue isn't that you *have* a big problem. It's *why*. Why
is that issue a part of your life? Because although some
problems (and problem people) are unavoidable—even
useful, in fact, to help keep us growing and humble and
trusting in God—other problems seem to be there only to
hurt us and frighten us.

There is a true enemy behind these kinds of struggles.
An enemy that you have the power to defeat.

Actionable Intel

Think of the most difficult, overwhelming, upsetting
situation in your life right now. What does it specifically
do to you? How does it make you feel? What goes through
your head when you think about it? Pray today's verse for
your life. Ask God to strengthen you through His Word.

Game, Set, Match

He disarmed the rulers and authorities and disgraced them
publicly; He triumphed over them. —Colossians 2:15

Recon

Christ already has the victory. And therefore anyone (like
you or me) is victorious because of Him. Let's take a couple
of days to be a little more specific about what this victory
looks like.

The Bible says Jesus has "disarmed" His enemies, that
He's taken the power of their weaponry away. Stuck His
finger in their rifle barrels. Reduced all their firepower to
pop guns.

And not only has He disarmed them (which is a big
problem for someone who's trying to appear threatening
and dominating in battle), but He's "disgraced" them.
Embarrassed them. Didn't just take charge but—took 'em
to the woodshed.

This is your enemy's vantage point. While you face
life's struggles from a perspective of strength and victory
in Christ, the enemy operates from a position of insecurity,
weakness, and helplessness. He already knows his
weapons against you can't succeed, so he's just trying to
discourage you, hoping you'll forget about what Christ has
already done.

Yeah, good luck with that. Right?

Actionable Intel

Take ten minutes to write down some words that describe
the defeated perspective of your enemy. Use some terms
from today's devotional, or ask an adult to help you think
of some. Post this list in a place where you (and the enemy)
will always be reminded how weak he really is.

Overruled

*Far above every ruler and authority, power and
dominion, and every title given, not only in this age
but also in the one to come. —Ephesians 1:21*

Recon

Have you ever seen one of those courtroom dramas
on television? The lawyer for one side is standing up
questioning a witness, trying to drag out a confession or
build a case for why his client is innocent. The opposing
attorney, perhaps seeing his competitor getting close to
digging out the truth, jumps up, pounds the table in front
of him, and shouts, "Objection! I object!"

But the judge, the one with full authority under the
law to determine what's allowed in his courtroom, calmly
sits there and answers back—"Overruled."

Be quiet, in other words. The attorney's argument
doesn't have a leg to stand on.

Jesus' victory at the cross *overruled* the competition.
In reality, of course, no one has ever actually posed a threat
to Him, even though the bloody torture that temporarily
stopped His heartbeat certainly made it appear so. But
Jesus' rank is "far above" that of anyone who might object.
That's why you can now object to any argument that says
otherwise.

Because the One with all the power is on your side.

Actionable Intel

Look up Psalm 119:165 and Philippians 4:13. Use them to
overrule the enemy this week whenever he tries to tempt
or discourage you. See if you can memorize them.

Get Up and Go

Gird up your loins . . . and go. —*2 Kings 9:1* NASB

Recon

The actual language of Ephesians 6 doesn't really call the belt of truth a *belt* at all. It just says, "Stand firm therefore, having girded your loins with truth" (v. 14 NASB). But we can deduce Paul's meaning by what we know of the Roman soldier's attire, because the belt was how a soldier "girded" himself in battle.

In Bible times, "girding up" was what a person did when he needed to go somewhere in a hurry. He would gather up the lower part of his garment—often a long-flowing robe or toga—and tuck it into his belt or sash, freeing his feet from becoming tangled in his clothing as he ran.

How interesting, then, to see this imagery attached to truth . . . because most people tend to think of truth as something we just sit around thinking about and studying. But, no, the Bible says it's much more active than that. Truth helps us stand. Truth helps us move. Truth helps us run and chase and pursue, defeating our enemy as we go.

Truth is built for the road.

Actionable Intel

What would be a modern take on "girding up"—a technique that helps a runner or athlete be able to go faster or compete more effectively? How could being guided by the truth serve the same sort of purpose?

Perfection

*Your righteousness, O God, reaches to the
heavens, You who have done great things; O
God, who is like You?*—Psalm 71:19 NASB

Recon

God our Father is completely perfect. "His way is blameless"
(2 Samuel 22:31 NASB). "He is righteous and true"
(Deuteronomy 32:4).

God. *IS*. Righteousness.

So it can be easy to think that when Paul told believers
to put on the breastplate of righteousness, he was telling
us we need to be perfect just like God is, that we need to
have a flawless performance every single day of our lives.
No mistakes. Never a slipup.

One of the ways our enemy deceives us is by trying
to convince us that with enough willpower, with enough
hard work, we can force ourselves to do everything right.
To be perfect. But the size and weight of that breastplate is
too big—not only for you, but for all of us to carry. Trying
to be perfect is a weight too heavy to bear.

You and I may be a lot of things. But perfectly
righteous—all on our own—is not one of them. Nor is it
supposed to be. God has a solution for that. He has offered
Himself to be our righteousness.

Actionable Intel

What are some of the areas in your life where you seek to
be perfect? What happens when you realize you aren't?

You. Are. Righteous.

Abram believed the LORD, *and He credited it
to him as righteousness.* —*Genesis 15:6*

Recon

I'm going to teach you a new word today. A new verb.
Impute. It means to give something to someone. To credit
them with it. To consider it theirs.

Back in the Old Testament, God *imputed* something
to Abraham—righteousness—based on Abraham's belief
in God's promises. And according to Galatians 3:6, that's
exactly what He's done for you as well—you who by faith
have become like Abraham's children.

God's righteousness has been *imputed* to you.

You are righteous.

That's why your enemy is on your tail. He doesn't
want you living in this unseen truth. He doesn't want you
realizing you've been completely forgiven. He doesn't want
you to know and accept what God has done for you.

Many of the battles you face with sin are caused by
your enemy targeting your righteous mind and heart.
Because if he can make you think you're *not* righteous,
he can convince you that sin is your only option. As if you
were *unrighteous.* Like him.

But you are far from that. You are a child of the King
and a warrior destined for victory.

Actionable Intel

"I. Am. Righteous." Will you say those words right now?
Out loud? It may feel weird, but do it anyway! Say it so
the Devil can hear you and be assured you're not messing
around. *"I. Am. Righteous."* Yes. You. Are.

Double Up

Show me your faith without deeds, and I will show you my faith by my deeds. —James 2:18 NIV

Recon

We all know the practical benefits of double protection. Two blankets instead of one on a cold night. Two bags for the heavy stuff you carry inside from the grocery store. Backup files in case the computer crashes or gets stolen.

Doubly safe. Extra protection.

That's what happens when your righteous heart produces righteous deeds. Not only is the unseen reality of God's *imputed* gift to you in place, but so is the seen evidence that matches up with it.

A lot of well-meaning people throughout church history have actually quivered at this passage from the book of James, afraid it might be misinterpreted to mean we're required to work for our salvation. But that's not what James was saying—not at all. Faith and grace and forgiveness are all gifts from God to us. But when faith and works team up together in a believer's life, they form the sturdy breastplate that defends against even the hardest, most high-level attacks from the enemy.

You believe in God? Good. You start to live like it? Better.

Double good.

Actionable Intel

Draw a "greater than" symbol on a piece of paper. Looks like this: (>). Remember that every choice you make to obey God makes your protection against the enemy even greater than before.

Where Peace Comes From

He Himself is our peace.—Ephesians 2:14 NASB

Recon

The spiritual armor listed in Ephesians 6 is actually just Paul's way of reiterating the teaching he'd already given in the earlier part of his letter. He was sort of saying, "Here, see if this helps you remember it." And if you underlined all the parts where Paul mentioned the pieces of armor, you'd see that his discussion about the *shoes of peace* takes up more space than any other.

His main emphasis about peace is in chapter 2, verse 14. The reason we can experience peace—true peace, lasting peace, anytime peace—is because Jesus "Himself is our peace."

Before you and I were even born, sin had already separated us from God. We came into this world stained by it. But on the cross, Jesus bridged the gap that kept us opposed to Him, the one that kept us fighting for our lives. Now we have peace. Because we have Jesus. From the top of our head to the soles of our feet.

Actionable Intel

Read Isaiah 59:1–2, which describes our biggest problem in life in the clearest detail. As soon as you finish reading it, say the following words out loud: "But Jesus Himself is my peace."

Shields Up

No weapon formed against you will
succeed. —Isaiah 54:17

Recon

Those flaming arrows your enemy is shooting at you are intentional and purposeful. Don't think for a second he's just shooting randomly and hoping for a lucky bounce. He's mapped out your most vulnerable areas. Downloaded your coordinates into his aiming device. Positioned the catapult to obtain precision arc and velocity. Hoping to achieve maximum damage. Create maximum havoc.

This is no dummy you're dealing with.

No phantom of your imagination.

But while "knowledge is power," as Sir Francis Bacon said, nothing trumps the fact that Jesus is Lord. The enemy can shoot hard, and well, and fast, and persistently. But when all shields are up—when your faith in God is an ongoing lifestyle of daring obedience—the openings to your heart become too narrow for even Satan's sophisticated equipment to strike with confidence and accuracy.

His planning may be impressive. But your shield of faith is a formidable defense.

Actionable Intel

Prayer is key to staying sharp in battle, staying aware of what's coming against you. Jump into prayer at every sign of attack, and God will help you kick your faith into immediate action.

Past, Present, and Future

The message of the cross is foolishness to those who are perishing, but it is God's power to us who are being saved. —1 Corinthians 1:18

Recon

Salvation's appeal has often been the allure of heaven. And given the alternative, it is an amazing gift for which we should always be grateful.

But in reality, salvation is much more than just a prepaid ticket to eternity. It's a past-tense, present-tense, and future-tense *experience*. All three.

Follow along here. The Bible says that God "chose us in Him, before the foundation of the world" (Ephesians 1:4), that we "were" saved in the hope of what was to come. *Past tense.*

But also, we "are being" saved. This is the process of being molded into the image of Christ, pulling away from our sins, renewing our minds, living abundantly. This transformation is happening as we speak. *Present tense.*

And, of course, we *will* be saved when we enter our eternal home—*future tense*—able to eat forever from "the tree of life" (Revelation 22:14).

Turns out we're safe in all directions.

Actionable Intel

See if you can capture this time-machine reality of your salvation in a short sentence or two or three. Write down how He saved you then, is saving you now, and will save you forever. Claim it as a worshipful prayer of thanks— morning, noon, or night. Anytime you like.

God's Power on Paper

*Jesus said to them, "Have you never read in
the Scriptures . . ."*—Matthew 21:42

Recon

I wonder how many Bibles are at your house. In ours, I can think of at least eight. I keep two on my nightstand. My husband has another. Each of our three sons has one, and then two more are on a bookshelf in the living room. If I looked around, I bet I could find more.

Printed copies are one of the ways the Bible refers to the Scriptures—the ink, the page, the physical words written out. The Greek term is *graphe*, meaning a document of writings. Your Bible—the one with your name on it—is the Word of God.

So don't take it for granted. Though Bibles are most likely plentiful in your house, each one is precious. And though you could easily go get another one if you wanted, millions of people in the world still have no Scriptures translated in their language.

Treasure your Bible. It is the gift of speech from your loving God.

Actionable Intel

How might you and some friends help provide some Bibles for people who don't have one? Think and pray about that today.

It's What's Inside

Whoever keeps His word, truly in him the love of God is perfected. —1 John 2:5

Recon

Yesterday I asked you to count how many Bibles are in your home. Whether you found just one or twenty-one, the total number doesn't matter. What matters is that you're opening it and reading it and asking God to help you understand it. Those words on the page need to come alive for you.

And they can! That's because a second Greek term that refers to Scripture is *logos*. Often translated in our Bibles as the word *word*, *logos* doesn't just mean the book itself. It means the *message* of the book. It's like going to a restaurant where you can't understand all the words on the menu, and the waiter or waitress explains to you what they mean. Hearing all those flavors described makes you hungry to dig in!

Take every opportunity to get inside the message of your Bible, so that the Bible's message can get inside of you.

Actionable Intel

Who are the people in your life who help you understand the message of the Bible? Write one of them a thank-you note today to tell them how much their time and insight means to you.

His Word to You

The word of the Lord endures forever . . . the word that was preached as the gospel to you. —1 Peter 1:25

Recon

Do you remember that when Paul described the sword of the Spirit, he said it's the "word" of God? But the *word* he used for this "word" is a little different from the two you saw in the last few days of devotions. When you're holding your Bible (the *graphe*), and you're starting to understand its message (the *logos*), God will often do something really special. He will turn it into the kind of "word" Paul was talking about in Ephesians 6:17—the *rhema*—a personal word from God, meant specifically for you.

Maybe you're just reading along, or listening to your pastor or Sunday school teacher. Then something about a particular verse will hit you between the eyes, stunning you with a truth you've never thought of before, waking you up with a soul-stirring, heart-burning desire where God seems to say, "Listen, I'm talking directly to *you* now."

That's your sword. That's your dagger. A time-stamped conviction to act on what God is saying.

Actionable Intel

Ask an adult you trust to describe for you what it feels like—what it "sounds" like—when God is speaking to you through His Word. With a *rhema* word.

Lofty Hopes

*I call to You from the ends of the earth when
my heart is without strength. Lead me to a
rock that is high above me.* —Psalm 61:2

Recon

Sitting in your room on an average day, any fears or
doubts or worries or concerns you're having can all look
pretty huge.

But what if you were to pull up Google Earth and locate
the roofline over where you're sitting. Then pull back a
few clicks. A few more. A few more. What you see now is
the huge, vast landscape of your corner of the world.

Maybe underneath your specific roofline, in your
specific room, nothing has really changed. Same troubles.
Same people. Same problems. But the God who lives above
all those treetops (which He created, by the way—without
even lifting a finger) is big enough to reach down and do
something about all those things you're fretting over. Not
just for you, but for all those other little dots and pinpoints
down there, where kids just like you are wrestling and
hurting.

Always remember that because He created *everything*,
He can take care of anything you are struggling with. He
has not forgotten you. He cares.

Actionable Intel

Write down two things happening inside your home that
you're struggling to understand or deal with. Now take a
moment to remember that God sees what is happening in
your house. And thank Him for caring and being willing to
do something about it.

How-To Lesson

The peace of God, which surpasses every thought, will guard your hearts and minds in Christ Jesus. —Philippians 4:7

Recon

Wearing the shoes of peace sounds great. But how do you put them on? The verse that immediately precedes the one at the top of today's devotion tells us how. It says this: "Don't worry about anything."

Easier said than done, of course. But in order to bring the reality of worry-free peace into your life, follow Paul's next piece of advice from the same verse: "In everything, through prayer and petition with thanksgiving, let your requests be made known to God" (v. 6).

This is the phrase that shows us how to get our shoes of peace on and laced up: "with thanksgiving."

Thanksgiving activates peace. Together they form a guard that protects your heart and mind from being weighed down by concerns that are so much more short-term and self-centered than they seem at the moment.

You want peace? Without worry? Find something to be thankful for. Trust me, there's plenty.

Actionable Intel

Today your best defense against the enemy will be gratitude. So sit quietly for a few minutes and pray, asking God to compose the list for you by bringing to your mind, one after another, all the things you should be grateful for. His peace will increase in your life as your list does.

God Is Good

You are good, and you do what is good. —Psalm 119:68

Recon

A thankful heart is what activates peace in your life. "Give thanks in everything," the Bible says, "for this is God's will for you in Christ Jesus" (1 Thessalonians 5:18).

But maintaining an "attitude of gratitude" can be very hard to do. So when you're having a hard time being thankful for . . . *this* (whatever *this* happens to be today), remember that trust is the fuel for thanksgiving. The more you really trust in God and have confidence in His power, the more you can be grateful no matter what sort of circumstances you may be facing.

Lack of trust in God is why so many people aren't at peace today and why the enemy has such an easy time stealing it from them. *They don't believe God is good.* They may think He's good to *others*, but not to *them*.

If you want peace, start by being thankful for all the blessings God has given. And if you need help being thankful, believe the truth that your God, despite any evidence to the contrary, is good.

Yes, He is.

God is good.

Actionable Intel

Look for the chance to say the words "God is good" to three people today. And every time you say it, repeat it also as a prayer of praise to Him: "Thank You, Lord, for being so good."

Looking Out for #1

*Let us hold on to the confession of our hope
without wavering, for He who promised
is faithful. —Hebrews 10:23*

Recon

Which of the following three statements best describes your perception of God:

1. I trust that God is powerful and strong and that He loves me and will take good care of me.

2. I believe He is powerful and strong, but I'm not sure He loves me and has time for me.

3. I guess I don't really believe He's all-powerful. I'm not sure He'll protect me.

Any of these three choices may honestly reflect how you feel. But you must remember that your level of faith—the strength of that shield—will always be tied to your perception of God. Until you agree with the *truth* of #1, you'll too often pull back on your faith and won't be confident charging ahead into battle.

Your enemy is desperate to keep you as far down on this list of beliefs as he can. But that's because *he* knows the truth of #1 too. And he hopes you're the last to find out.

Actionable Intel

Show these three statements to someone whose faith in God you trust. Ask them to tell you why #1 is always the place to start.

Not Guilty

You were washed, you were sanctified, you were justified in the name of the Lord Jesus Christ. —1 Corinthians 6:11

Recon

The case against you, against me, against everybody—it's pretty simple, really. Open and shut. We're guilty as charged. Guilty as sin. We're all just plain guilty.

Except for this: when God saved us, He *justified* us.

Salvation means the *justification* of our sins—a legal term that means we are *not* guilty.

Shocking difference, huh? From guilty to not guilty? And yet it's exactly what Scripture says again and again about all of us who've been saved by the blood of Jesus. We're innocent. Free to walk. *Justified* in considering ourselves saved from our sins.

So put this powerful fact under your hat today, inside the helmet of salvation that keeps your mind thinking clearly. And whenever your enemy tries to convince you what a rotten mess you are, remember the 180-degree difference between guilty and not guilty that Christ's gift has given you.

Actionable Intel

Yes, you can be guilty of committing sin. Even as a Christian. But because you've been *justified*, you have an alternative. You can repent. You can turn away from it. You can live in the reality of your "not guilty" state. If you need to repent today, do it now. Get it over. And then move on.

Flying Lessons

*"Look at the birds of the sky. . . . Aren't you
worth more than they?"—Matthew 6:26*

Recon

I found a bird's nest lying on the ground the other day.
I'd seen it up in a tree earlier in the season. We'd been
watching the baby birds for a while, and we knew they'd
made it out safely into the world.

I was intrigued by what it was made of, this nest that
had kept them sheltered and protected, safe from all kinds
of dangers and predators. Lots of different things were
woven into it—grass and leaves, bits of string from what
looked like a basketball net, even a few rounded scraps of
Styrofoam, maybe from the top of somebody's tossed-out
coffee cup. And I wondered . . .

If things like garden weeds and roadside litter can
be fused together by a literal birdbrain into something
that's strong, solid, and highly effective, how much more
can your infinitely brilliant God design protective armor
to keep you safe from any threat that could come against
you, to help you reach your full potential?

Actionable Intel

Where else in nature have you seen ingenuity at work,
little wonders that serve the needs of plants or animals?
Ask yourself: If God can do that for *them,* why wouldn't
He do way more for *us*? For *you*?

Lightening the Load

Not having a righteousness of my own from the law, but one that is through faith in Christ. —Philippians 3:9

Recon

The majority of the weight in the Roman soldier's seventy pounds of equipment and supplies he carried was contained in that heavy breastplate. It was a vital piece of protection to his upper body but—wow—talk about making you feel like you're tipping over. Thankfully, though, the way the breastplate fit into his belt helped disperse some of that weight, relieving pressure from his shoulders.

Whew.

And that's what the belt of truth does for us too. Instead of leaving us to bear the full weight of the breastplate ourselves—the breastplate of righteousness—God's truth tells us that Jesus has removed this burden from our shoulders. We can still do good and righteous things, of course. But we do them because we *want* to, not because we *have* to. This truth sets us free.

We're not on the hook for earning God's favor. He's already given it to us.

Actionable Intel

Fill up a bag or backpack until it's pretty heavy. Carry it around while trying to do your usual daily activity. How long till you're ready to take it off? Describe how it feels when you finally do.

Shortcuts

Going to Jerusalem is too difficult
for you. —1 Kings 12:28

Recon

In the book of 1 Kings, a man named Jeroboam led a rebellion among the northern tribes of Israel. The unrest split the nation in two. He became king of one half of it.

He always worried, though, that he'd lose the loyalty of his subjects since they were still in the habit of going down to the temple that was located in Jerusalem to offer their sacrifices and pay worship to God. They'd feel drawn back to their roots, again and again. So Jeroboam built religious gathering places in locations that were more convenient for his people, hoping to entice them into doing their worshiping closer to home.

Made sense, didn't it? Time saving. Easier. But since God had said that Jerusalem was the only place they were to gather to worship Him, it was an unacceptable option. King Jeroboam was lowering God's standard, changing it based on convenience. And it gave people a way of feeling good about themselves without actually being obedient to God's expectations.

Our enemy still loves making these kinds of sales pitches to us. But righteousness doesn't take shortcuts. Righteousness doesn't take the easy way out.

Actionable Intel

Can you think of a way you've bent a rule so that you were still technically obeying it, but just barely? Or not really? Why does this miss the whole point of righteousness?

Contagious Compromise

He did what was evil in the LORD's sight and
followed the example of Jeroboam and the sin he
had caused Israel to commit. —1 Kings 15:34

Recon

I told you yesterday what Jeroboam did—leading people not to take worship seriously. Another interesting part of the story is that he was the first of about twenty kings who went on to rule the northern tribes of Israel. On multiple occasions throughout the next two hundred years—before the Assyrians came down, conquered the people, and ripped them off their land—the Bible describes many of these kings by saying they "followed the example of Jeroboam." His sin of compromise became contagious.

Lowering God's standard of righteousness is bad enough. But what's worse is how one thing leads to another. The first shortcut leads to the second. And the third. And the fourth . . . until you look up some point way down the road and realize not only how far you've wandered from where you started, but how many people you've taken with you or hurt along the way.

The choices we make about following God today actually have ripple effects that will spill out into our tomorrows.

Actionable Intel

Picture yourself on a slick, rainy, muddy hillside. Which is easier: sliding to the bottom or climbing to the top? The theme of today's devotion is what's often called the "slippery slope"—how the first step downhill often leads to the next one, even *farther* downhill.

On the Move

*I will strengthen them in [the LORD], and they
will march in His name. —Zechariah 10:12*

Recon

Imagine what it would look like (and *sound* like) if a unit
of first-century Roman soldiers was marching toward
you. Picture them on one of those ancient stone roads,
wearing the gladiator-style boots with the sharp, iron
nails under the soles. They'd sound louder than a squad
of football players running across the concrete pavement
into the stadium. The clatter of those spikes against the
cobblestone road would send a loud, clear message that
the army was on its way.

Peace is like those shoes. It has a sound the enemy can
hear from a mile away. All the racket and rattle, especially
when joined with that of others alongside us, sends a
shiver up his back. That's when he knows we're not just
hunkering down, hoping to withstand whatever onslaught
he's planning against us next. We're on the move. We're
on the march. We're taking the truth, righteousness, and
peace of God out on the road. When we're wearing our
shoes of peace, the enemy knows we're coming . . . and
that we're planning a victory march.

Actionable Intel

Think of how you could assemble a team of other believing
kids, joining together on some kind of spiritual mission—
of prayer, of worship, of action, of impact. Start praying
and making plans for what God would lead you to do.

Good Goes Around

We are [God's] creation, created in Christ
Jesus for good works. —Ephesians 2:10

Recon

According to Ephesians 2, God has done some spectacular things for you through your faith in Jesus. He's made you "alive with Christ" even though you were "dead" in sin (v. 5). He's raised you up to be seated with Him in "heavenly places" (v. 6 NASB). Your future is bright, and your relationship with Him is secure. He's done it all through your faith.

But look what else He's been doing—through your faith in Christ. He's "created" you for "good works," and has been preparing you—through faith—so you can "walk in them" (v. 10)

Don't miss the connection. The faith that means you'll be going to heaven one day is the same faith that means you can obey God's Word today.

And, boy, the Devil hopes you don't get the memo on that one. But here it is! Already handed to you. So go walk out those "good works" today. You can do it by faith.

Actionable Intel

Make the next "good work" you feel led to do a priority. Follow through on it. Don't listen to any rationale for not doing it.

Jesus Is Lord

If you confess with your mouth, "Jesus is Lord," and believe in your heart that God raised Him from the dead, you will be saved. —Romans 10:9

Recon

Today's verse is probably the most clear, concise statement of salvation that appears in Scripture.

And yet like all the other elements of salvation we've talked about, this confession of faith, this readiness to believe—it's more than a one-shot moment. You *live* this confession; you don't just say it. You *continue* this belief; you don't just declare it once and then go about your life the way you had before.

Because when "Jesus is Lord"—when this is actually how you think and operate—you have a daily experience of His protection and you sense the comfort of being "saved." He's Lord of your thoughts. Lord of your habits. Lord of your choices, your work, your play, your behavior.

Lay this verse at the altar of your heart, not just the altar of your church. And celebrate being "saved" every single moment of your life.

Actionable Intel

"Jesus is Lord." Draw these words in a decorative script on one of your school notebooks or somewhere you'll see it often. It's more than a belief; it's a lifestyle.

Thought Police

Taking every thought captive to obey
Christ. —2 Corinthians 10:5

Recon

You need to get to know 2 Corinthians 10:3–5. Bookmark it and plan on spending a little time there. Because if you intend to emerge victorious on a regular basis in your everyday battles, the secrets of 2 Corinthians 10 are absolutely necessary.

It basically says that even though we are physical beings, we cannot win this war using physical weapons. Being strong is not enough. Being from a Christian family is not enough. "The weapons of our warfare are not worldly" (v. 4). They're not flesh and blood. They're mental and they're spiritual.

Only the divine weapons given by God Himself are powerful enough to dismantle destructive thoughts. When those thoughts come into your mind—and they will—they do not have the right to stay. Not in a child of God. Grab them, tie them up, and take them captive, using weapons that work. Spin them around backward until they turn into thoughts that honor Christ, until they proclaim the truth about who you are.

Actionable Intel

Work on memorizing these powerful three verses. They belong inside your helmet.

Change of Clothes

You took off your former way of life. . . . You put on the new self, the one created according to God's likeness in righteousness and purity of the truth. —*Ephesians 4:22, 24*

Recon

In Ephesian culture, one of their pagan religious ceremonies involved a person removing their old clothes and putting on new ones. In doing so, they were symbolically making a break from their former ties and beliefs, demonstrating they were now following a new spiritual direction.

The change of clothes told the story.

So when Paul talked about believers *taking off* their old habits of living and *putting on* new ones, he wasn't just talking about the routine changing of clothes for the day. He was describing a formal, deliberate, ongoing, yet permanent act that signified a shift in their internal allegiance from an idol to the one true God. We're not supposed to simply put our old stuff in the laundry hamper and wear it later. It needs to go in the throwaway pile instead. Some place where we can't fish it out one of these days and try working it back into circulation.

The only way we can "put on" the breastplate of righteousness is by "taking off" the unrighteousness that's already there.

Actionable Intel

What are some "old clothes" in your spiritual closet that need to be taken off and taken out?

Truth of the Matter

Speak the truth, each one to his neighbor, because we are members of one another. —Ephesians 4:25

Recon

Although some of the things warriors learn are complex and strategic, most of what they need to know is highly practical and useful for their day-to-day lives. And as young spiritual warriors in God's army, the same principle applies to you. A lot of what you need to know is very practical. Like the lesson in today's verse: *honesty*.

I don't need to give you a lot of deep Bible lessons before you can understand what honesty means. But it's a key area of obedience and survival for someone who wants to live with the breastplate of righteousness on every day.

Are there any ways you've been dishonest recently? Have you lied? Been sneaky or misleading? Warriors are courageous enough to tell the truth because they know that integrity and character will help them stay protected from the enemy.

Actionable Intel

I'll be giving you a few practical categories of righteousness to ponder in the next few days. List some of these areas. Begin with today's topic: *honesty*. Where do you need to make some changes so that you're wearing honesty like a breastplate?

Stop, Thief!

The thief must no longer steal. Instead, he must do honest work with his own hands. —Ephesians 4:28

Recon

I'd guess when you think about stealing, your mind automatically goes to bank robberies and shoplifting, to burglars breaking into people's houses. But those examples are few and far between compared to the many incidences of theft that occur every day, all around us.

Sometimes we're even the ones doing it.

We do it by not working our hardest. By not trying our best. By being sloppy in our habits. By being inconsiderate of other people, not thinking about what our actions may be costing them. Did you ever think of stealing that way?

Stealing is stealing, whether it's someone else's time or someone else's tennis shoes. And by taking this fresh look at your responsibilities—toward others, toward God, even toward yourself—you can be transformed into someone who not only doesn't steal anymore, but whose daily life and daily actions become a true gift to everyone around you.

Actionable Intel

Make this your second entry under examples of practical righteousness: *personal responsibility*. What kinds of blessing could flow in and out of your life if you refuse to take from others or to treat lightly the gifts God has given you?

Watch Your Language

No foul language is to come from your mouth, but only what is good for building up someone in need, so that it gives grace to those who hear. —*Ephesians 4:29*

Recon

Jesus said our eyes are "the lamp of the body" (Matthew 6:22). Their radiance (or lack of) seems to indicate what's truly inside a person. But perhaps running a close second, as far as revealing someone's true nature goes, are the words we say. For as Jesus also taught, the "mouth speaks from the overflow of the heart" (Luke 6:45).

So if being vulgar or off-color in your speech is a habit you've gotten into, there's a remedy available to you. But it's not just cleaning up your language. It's asking God to help you purify your heart, to change the way you think, to avoid a lot of exposure to people (or TV, music, and media) where foul words are as common as normal ones.

Again, what may not seem like such a big deal at first is all a part of building that breastplate. Toughening its exterior. Widening its margins. The more righteousness you're applying, the more protection you're experiencing.

Actionable Intel

Okay, item number three on your new list: *speech*. What do your everyday conversations reveal about the contents of your heart? What are some practical steps you can take to keep your heart filled with purity?

Peace

*All bitterness, anger and wrath, shouting
and slander must be removed from you, along
with all malice. —Ephesians 4:31*

Recon

In a world like ours, we could all use a little peace. I don't think anybody is too eager to be around people who often bring their unpleasantness with them. Their arguing. Their disapproval. Their snarky, cutting comments and digs.

Even though we try to be kind to them, it's hard. And we sure don't want to be like them. They are hard to live around and be friends with.

But what if this person is you? People's lives are challenging enough without anyone needing to put up with our rants, our pouts, our quick tempers, or our easily hurt feelings. That's why some of the most practical righteousness you can perform is the kindness of being patient, nice, agreeable, and encouraging.

Besides, by being easy to live with, you make yourself a much harder target for the enemy.

Actionable Intel

Item number four on your list: *peacefulness*. How difficult do you find being peaceful? Would any of Paul's warning signs in today's verse describe your usual behavior? Bitterness? Anger? Shouting? Slander? How could you be a more peace-bringing person?

Forgiveness

*Be kind and compassionate to one another,
forgiving one another, just as God also forgave
you in Christ. —Ephesians 4:32*

Recon

No matter what kind of offense may have been done to you, here's your enemy's approach for handling it: Get mad. Stay mad. Because you deserve to be mad. How dare somebody do something like that to you and think they can just get away with it?

Sound familiar?

You may or may not know what hearing from God's Spirit sounds like, but here's a little tip: It doesn't sound like *that*. It sounds more like the verse that goes with today's devotion. Why don't you read it again? Go ahead, I'll wait for you.

Yeah, *that's* what God is telling you to do. To choose kindness. To show compassion. To imagine how you'd like to be treated if you'd done something to someone that you were now very sorry about.

In fact, you don't really *need* to imagine it. Because you've already experienced it. That's what God has done for you. He's forgiven you. And we should do the same for others.

Actionable Intel

We could talk about other topics like these, and we probably will. But let's wrap up this little section by closing with this fifth area of practical righteousness: *forgiveness*. How could you put this character quality into practice, perhaps before the day or the week is up?

Night and Day Difference

Let us discard the deeds of darkness and put on the armor of light. —Romans 13:12

Recon

Righteousness is already *in you*. It is a gift from God. When Jesus died for your sins on the cross, when you trusted in Him as your Savior, the righteousness of Christ was implanted within you. *Imputed* to you, remember?

And that means you're fully equipped now to put righteousness *on you*—by practicing the kinds of things we've been talking about the last few days . . . and more. Telling the truth. Honoring your parents. Working hard at school. Playing fair.

Living out your newfound strength.

When you choose to live in a righteous manner, you're not just being a good kid. You're stripping away the unseen darkness that's trying to invade your heart, and you're strapping on the armor that enables you to stand firmly in the light—your belt of truth glistening, your breastplate gleaming bright.

Let's just see that enemy try to stop you now . . .

Actionable Intel

Try to get ready for bed tonight in your room or in the bathroom with the light off. How much harder does the darkness make it? How does turning on the light change the whole situation?

Make the Call

Let the peace of Christ rule in your hearts,
since as members of one body you were called
to peace. —Colossians 3:15 NIV

Recon

Looks like it's going to be a close play at the plate. The runner's charging hard from third. The throw's coming in from the outfield. The runner slides. The catcher applies the tag. The umpire lifts his hands and says, in a loud voice . . .

You're safe? You're out?

Which one will it be?

When Paul said to "let the peace of Christ rule in your hearts," the word he used for "rule" is similar to what an umpire does in an athletic event or contest. God's peace is like an umpire in your soul, helping you look at a close call—one that sometimes could be argued either way—and help you make a good call.

God's peace in your life is your guide for life . . . and for all of its tough calls.

Actionable Intel

If there's a decision you've been praying about recently and you're unsure what to do, ask yourself this question: Which option puts you most at peace with God's Word and most in line with what His Spirit is telling you in your heart?

But What If You're Wrong?

By faith he kept the Passover and the sprinkling of blood, so that the destroyer of the firstborn would not touch the firstborn of Israel. —Hebrews 11:28 NIV

Recon

Imagine what the children of Israel must have been thinking when God said He was going to sweep through the land of Egypt and kill all the firstborn males of Israel's enemy. I wonder if they were concerned—worried that God would make a mistake and slay one of theirs by accident in the middle of the night.

Yet instead of panicking, instead of trying to run away, they did what the Lord had told them to do: put the blood of a male sheep or goat on their doorposts. "When I see the blood," God said, "I will pass over you. No plague will be among you" (Exodus 12:13).

Sound crazy? Yeah, kinda. But it was God's word to them. And they did it. Then *He* did it—He not only spared their sons from death but also delivered the whole nation from slavery.

God's Word doesn't always make the most sense in the moment. But His faithfulness to keep it—and the faith you choose when you obey it—always makes it worth following.

Actionable Intel

What would have been your first three questions if God gave you the directions He gave the Israelites back then? How well would you have slept that night if you were a firstborn child, hearing what was happening in the homes of the Egyptians around you?

A Matter of Death and Life

*How much more, having been reconciled, will
we be saved by His life!—Romans 5:10*

Recon

The Devil has been forced to concede a major loss in how he deals with you. He *cannot*—now or ever—change the fact that through your faith in the redeeming blood of Jesus, you have been saved from all your sins. You are perfectly forgiven. You are living with Christ's righteousness inside you.

Jesus' death did that. And the Devil can't touch that.

But although Jesus' death on the cross is what changed you from an enemy of God (Romans 5:10) into His beloved child, His resurrection from the grave means you can spend the rest of your life on earth experiencing freedom and abundance. If His death saved you, just think what His coming back to life can do!

That's what the Devil doesn't want you to find out. And that's why you need the helmet of salvation so much—to make sure you find out more about what this great salvation means for you every single day.

Actionable Intel

Ask God in prayer to show you (or reinforce to you) something new every day that helps you understand and celebrate what His salvation has done and is doing for you.

Ring of Fire

*The Angel of the LORD encamps around those who
fear Him, and rescues them.* —Psalm 34:7

Recon

An enemy king in the Old Testament was angry about
something a prophet named Elisha had done. So he sent
out a regiment of armed soldiers to capture him. Elisha
had a servant who saw the attackers assembling around
the city and was scared senseless at what was coming.

But Elisha kept his composure. He prayed, asking
God to show this servant something invisible and unseen
that Elisha knew was there. God answered and allowed
the servant's eyes to see the invisible—a ring of "horses
and chariots of fire all around Elisha" (2 Kings 6:17). Sure,
the enemy army was still visible too, but not without a
fierce battalion of divine competitors surrounding them
and standing guard. The enemy army was no match for
the armies of the living God.

The next time you feel outmatched by an attack on
your mind, your purity, your courage, your character,
realize that a divine army, organized and spearheaded by
God Himself, is on your side. Just because it's invisible
doesn't mean it's not there. You couldn't be any safer. He's
got you totally covered.

Actionable Intel

Read this story from Elisha's life for yourself. It's found
in 2 Kings 6:8–17. Pretty amazing. And hopefully very
encouraging.

The Hanger

*Take up the full armor of God . . . having
prepared everything. —Ephesians 6:13*

Recon

What do you think your closet would look like without any clothes hangers in it? Everything would be on the floor. In a wad. Getting wrinkled. (When I was a kid, my closet looked like that anyway, even though it *did* have hangers in it. But that's another story.)

The clothes hanger is a simple thing. A twist of metal or a mold of plastic. But because of its well-thought-out shape and size, every piece of clothing seems to fit on it. Hangs just like it's supposed to. Looks a lot like it will look when it's hanging on *you* . . . so that when you're ready to put it on, it's in good shape. Ready to go.

The belt of truth is like your clothes hangers. Not only does it help keep your life in order and balanced, but it helps prepare all your other pieces of spiritual armor for instant, off-the-hanger use. With the truth of God's Word tidying things up in your room, you can always be dressed for success.

Actionable Intel

Study or draw the frame and details of a clothes hanger. How can something so simple be so versatile and efficient? Ask yourself: Am I seeing God's truth as more complicated than it really is?

Storm Chasers

*Those who trust in the Lord will renew their strength;
they will soar on wings like eagles.* —Isaiah 40:31

Recon

Eagles possess an inner awareness that alerts them to coming storms. It's just the way God has made them. So when they sense an approaching change in the weather, they fly to a high point, settle themselves into position, and then somehow lock their wings. This way, the wind and turbulence—rather than blowing them around—actually provide lift to their flight. The storm still rages below, but they're able to soar high over the top of it.

That's a perfect picture of what God's peace can do for you. It enables you to "soar on wings like eagles." To "run and not grow weary." To "walk and not faint" (v. 31).

"In this world," Jesus said, "you will have trouble" (John 16:33 NIV). Some trouble may come directly from the enemy or from consequences of your own sin. Other trouble can come indirectly from daily life on this broken planet. But trouble alone can never be troublesome enough to knock you to the ground. Not with your wings locked on Him.

Actionable Intel

Part of what helps an eagle master these storms is by how it prepares for them ahead of time. As you pray today, ask God through His Spirit to prepare you for the storms and pressures that are sure to be coming in the future.

Trusting in God

*Daniel was taken out of the den, uninjured,
for he trusted in his God.* —Daniel 6:23

Recon

Daniel had been caught praying to God, even after a new rule had been established, saying that prayers could only be made to the Persian king. Daniel was immediately thrown into a den of hungry, sharp-toothed lions.

But miraculously, he was spared. And there's one simple reason why: because Daniel "trusted in his God." It was because of his faith. His faith was a shield around him protecting him from the lions.

Of course there are *other* stories, of martyrs who had just as much faith as Daniel yet were not spared from pain and death. But Daniel's story reminds us that our God should be trusted. Because, plain and simple, He is able to do more than you can ask or imagine, even when the circumstances are uncomfortable or dangerous. When you trust Him and place your confidence in Him, He will make sure you are able to move forward in peace from any situation that may come your way.

Actionable Intel

Pray today for people like Daniel who—right this minute—are facing serious, life-threatening challenges for trusting in their God. Pray for their safety and pray for their families. But pray mostly that God will get the glory as He works through their faith to do what only He can.

Undivided

Give me an undivided mind to fear
Your name. —*Psalm 86:11*

Recon

Does your church or school have a big room, like a fellowship hall or a large assembly area, that is usually set up with chairs and tables, able to hold a bunch of people? Sometimes, if the space needs to be broken up for smaller meetings or classes, can they pull partitions across it— basically dividing up one big room into two, three, four, or more?

That's what the enemy wants to do in your mind—he wants to wall off parts of it where you don't allow God to go so that He is relegated to your "church" section, but not your "school" section or your "when I'm with my friends" section or your "when I'm by myself" section. The enemy wants you to be a different person in different places.

But God should be Lord over every place. In every situation. You are His, and you should be in your full armor everywhere you go.

Actionable Intel

What's one area of your thoughts or behavior where you have blocked out your relationship with God? Pray and invite God to come and make Himself at home there from now on.

Never Enough

There are some who are disturbing you and want to distort the gospel of Christ. —Galatians 1:7 NASB

Recon

Paul wrote a letter to the Christians who lived in Galatia because after he'd established a church there on the truths of God's Word, other religious people had showed up, trying to convince the Galatian believers they weren't doing enough. If they *really* wanted to consider themselves Christians, these people argued, they needed to be following a bunch of other rules and regulations. And doing it all perfectly.

That's the problem with *perfectionism*. It never stops. There's always something else. Something more. And just when we think we've finally done enough, there's even more.

So trying to be *perfect* becomes this bottomless pit of disappointment. A lot of effort, but no real payoff. Thank goodness wearing the breastplate of righteousness doesn't mean we have to be perfect. Because if we did, instead of keeping us protected, it would just be an uncomfortable burden that never seems to fit quite right, leaving us discouraged and vulnerable to enemy attack.

Actionable Intel

Have you ever had an item of clothing that didn't fit well or feel comfortable? Too tight? Too baggy? Too stiff? How rotten would it feel to wear clothes like that all the time? That's the feeling of perfectionism.

What For?

Am I now trying to win the approval of human beings, or of God?—Galatians 1:10 NIV

Recon

Science experiments help you grasp the *why* or *how* behind the *what*. When you see celery leaves turning blue after the stalk's been standing in colored water, you understand how plants absorb moisture. So when you observe a tendency like perfectionism in your life, is there a way to figure out the why? And how to keep it from happening?

Let's try a little "truth experiment."

Perfectionism is often rooted in a desire to seek *God's* approval. To earn it. Yet the Bible says we've been adopted as God's children (Romans 8:17), that Christ has "accepted" us completely as His own (Romans 15:7). Already. As we are.

Perfectionism can also be fed by a desire to win *others'* approval. To be impressive. But even Jesus didn't try to impress people. "He Himself knew what was in man" (John 2:25). He knew whatever impressed them today might not impress them tomorrow. Pleasing them was never His goal.

So ask yourself these two questions: Am I trying to earn God's approval with good behavior? Am I trying to impress others with my good behavior? Neither of these motivations is what righteousness is all about.

Actionable Intel

Read John 2:23–25. How different would Jesus' ministry have been if He had been motivated by pleasing other people?

Grading on the Curve

They disregarded the righteousness from
God and attempted to establish their own
righteousness. —*Romans 10:3*

Recon

God's standard of righteousness is beyond what we can achieve. God knows we can't be perfect and perfectly follow Him.

Do you think God might just *lower* the standard of righteousness? For us? Cut us some slack? Give us a fighting chance?

That's called "grading on the curve." Let's say the highest grade average in your class was a ninety. But the teacher decided to count the ninety as a hundred. Then everyone else's score, whatever it is, would go up by ten points as well. Based on a new standard. A lower standard.

Yet God, the Bible says, "is the same yesterday, today, and forever" (Hebrews 13:8). His standard doesn't change. That's why He gave us His breastplate of righteousness. Therefore, those who attempt to "establish their own righteousness" end up with no breastplate at all. Completely uncovered and exposed to enemy attack.

So the only way we can combat our enemy is to put on God's breastplate of righteousness, knowing that God's standard is the only standard.

Actionable Intel

Look up Romans 10:3 in your Bible. What does Paul say that those who "establish their own righteousness" are refusing to do?

Seeing How You Stack Up

In measuring themselves by themselves and comparing themselves to themselves, they lack understanding. —2 Corinthians 10:12

Recon

Trying to be perfect? Can't do it. Hoping to at least be good enough? Can't do that either. So what about just trying to be better than everybody else? Will *that* do it?

Comparison is a method we try when we realize we're not measuring up to God's standards. Sure, we may not be perfect, but we certainly aren't as bad as *that* guy or *that* girl.

The problem with this form of measurement is that it's always moving. If you're comparing yourself to someone whose behavior is fairly bad, you can start to feel pretty good about yourself. You might *not* feel so good, however, if you compared yourself to someone who's steady and strong and more of a straight arrow. Doing this will make you feel discouraged and defeated.

Comparing yourself to others can result in misleading and often depressing conclusions. So this is obviously no way to wear righteousness, not if you want to "resist" the enemy and stand firm against his attacks (Ephesians 6:13). Following God is not meant to make you feel incapable and defeated. Ever.

Actionable Intel

You might be able to slam dunk on a seven-foot basketball goal against first graders. But what about on a regulation-size goal? Against high school or college players? If other people are your only gauge, you never really know exactly where you stand.

Changed in the Exchange

He made the One who did not know sin to be sin for us, so that we might become the righteousness of God in Him. —2 Corinthians 5:21

Recon

Wearing the breastplate of righteousness doesn't happen by trying to be perfect, by lowering God's standards, or by comparing yourself to others. It's about accepting God's gift to you.

Jesus died for your sins. Your debt has been paid in full. *His* death takes the place of *your* death. But not only did His death take something *away* from you (the punishment you deserve). It also gave something *to* you ("the righteousness of God"). It's a fantastic gift.

You don't need to try being perfect anymore, because Christ's perfect righteousness has now been deposited into your spiritual account. You don't need to lower any standards or compare yourself to anybody else, because when God looks at you, He sees you wrapped in the holy righteousness of His Son. Declared innocent of all your sin.

You are free now to live. Righteously.

Not to prove anything. Not to be better than anybody. Just to be who you truly are. "In Him."

Actionable Intel

Look up 1 Peter 2:24. What does it say about why you can now "live for righteousness"? What have Christ's wounds on the cross done for you?

Seeking His Righteousness

"Seek first the kingdom of God and His
righteousness, and all these things will be
provided for you."—Matthew 6:33

Recon

Let's make today another prayer writing day—a day for composing a prayer specifically related to another piece of armor: the breastplate of righteousness.

As you think about what to write down, consider the areas of your life where you seem to be struggling—places where you're having the hardest time aligning your attitudes and behaviors with God's true and righteous standard. But don't get hung up there, on the negatives . . . because the real story is not where any of us are failing. It never is. The point is always what God has done and what God can do to keep us standing. Through Christ and through the cross, He provides full-coverage protection from every taunt and temptation of the enemy.

So ask Him today for a way to put your heart into words. Present it to Him as both a divine request and a humble expression of thanks. He is going to love—*love!*—answering this prayer, again and again, because He loves seeing His righteousness shining through you.

Actionable Intel

Remember to post your prayer in a place where you can see it and pray it often. Add to it whenever He shows you another aspect of His righteousness that you want to embody.

Sharks in the Water

Keep me safe from violent men who plan evil in their hearts. They stir up wars all day long. —Psalm 140:1–2

Recon

On the TV show *Shark Tank*, people who've been working on a new product or business appear before potential investors, making an impassioned case for why their idea could be the next big smashing success. They don't just show up hoping these billionaires will take a liking to their winning personality. They come—they'd *better* come—with a business plan.

Satan has a plan. And a big part of his business model involves stirring up trouble in your heart and your relationships. His supply chain includes things like the sins you've committed, which—though forgiven—still contain all the ingredients for hammering you with guilt and shame. If that doesn't work, he'll try stirring up a friend against you, then tempting you with unforgiveness. Or creating enough pressure on you until you feel like cracking with despair or anger.

He's actually chock-full of ideas. But because you are chock-full of Jesus—full of His truth and righteousness—this makes you a customer who never needs to buy what your enemy is selling.

Actionable Intel

A business plan basically includes two things: (1) goals and objectives and (2) strategies that will help you meet your goals and objectives. If you were to outline *your* business plan for victory in life, what would be some of the main things you'd put into those two categories?

Getting Warmer?

Just as the body without the spirit is dead, so also
faith without works is dead. —James 2:26

Recon

I really wanted a cup of hot tea one cold winter morning. So I put a kettle of water on the stove, turned the dial to activate the gas underneath the burner, heard the electricity click to ignite it, and then . . .

Watched the flame go out.

So I tried it again. *Click-click*. Nothing. Again. *Click-click*. Nothing. Again. Finally I went to check the level of gas in our propane tank outside and realized our level was extremely low.

You know what I learned that day? A full charge of electricity, plus an empty propane tank, means no hot tea for me. Because electricity without gas keeps everything in my home from operating at full capacity.

Faith is like this. You can *say* you have faith, but faith that has no action coupled with it is useless. One is ignited by the other. Real faith—Christian faith—is an *active* faith that brings the Word of God to life. In *your* life.

Faith without works is not really faith at all.

Actionable Intel

What's one thing you could do today—that you *wouldn't* do today—if you didn't have faith in God today?

Blessings All Around

Blessed be the God and Father of our
Lord Jesus Christ. —Ephesians 1:3 NASB

Recon

At the very beginning of the book of Ephesians, before Paul ever mentioned anything about the armor, he wanted to tell readers what their salvation was all about. And he decided the best way to start the ball rolling was to say this: *Blessed is your God.*

Truly, the "God and Father" of your salvation is "blessed." He is rich. He has it all. Some suggest that this word carries the idea of being "fat"—not overweight "fat," but just busting at the seams with abundance and plenty.

So when you were adopted into His family, you not only came into relationship with Someone who loves you and delights in being gracious toward you. He also has literally unlimited resources. This means beyond just wanting to do anything in the world for you—the way your *earthly* parents would—His capacity for blessing means He really *can* do anything for you.

Like when He saved you from your sins. How "blessed" is that!

Actionable Intel

When you put on the helmet of salvation today, remember it's been provided for you by your "blessed" Father in heaven. And because *He* is blessed, so are you. Blessing is in your DNA.

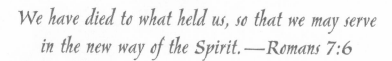

Proof of Ownership

We have died to what held us, so that we may serve in the new way of the Spirit. —Romans 7:6

Recon

The sword of the Spirit, we've seen, is the Word of God. It's active and offense oriented, rather than merely protective and defensive. But one other key thing to discover is who owns this sword. Who does it belong to? For even though you're free to use it, it's not really yours. It's the "sword of the Spirit."

The *Spirit's* sword.

And that's good—because if all the pressure were on *you* for knowing how to use it and where to point it, you wouldn't know what to do. You'd be on your own. Guessing. Flipping through the pages of the Bible with no guide showing you where to go.

But because it's the sword of the Spirit, it's the weapon He uses in heavenly places to fight for you. The reason it's so powerful is that His hand is wrapped around yours, teaching and training you the Word, making it do what He wants it to do. In you. For you.

Actionable Intel

Ask God today to show you, through His Spirit, how to use this sword. Not just in general, but how to use it *today*.

Prized Possessions

The way we know that He remains in us is from
the Spirit He has given us. —1 John 3:24

Recon

If you and I were to compare what's on our Christmas or birthday wish lists this year, we'd probably see a wide range of different things we're hoping for. But I can think of something our lists would share in common: they'd all be comprised of things we *don't already have.*

Because when you've already got something, you don't need to ask for it anymore. You might ask for something that goes with it or something that makes you able to do more with it, but you wouldn't need to ask for the same thing again.

When it comes to your spiritual armor and spiritual blessings, the same is true. You don't need to ask or beg for them. You just need to believe you've got them (because you do) and learn how to use them.

Through God's endless generosity, you already own a lot of things you probably haven't even taken out of the package yet. And unlike earthly possessions, even when you put them to heavy use, you'll find they always stay as good as new.

Actionable Intel

Ask God to help you keep from doubting, discarding, or discounting what He's already given you. Pray for ways to start putting it all into action.

Flash in the Pan

*"I watched Satan fall from heaven like
a lightning flash."*—Luke 10:18

Recon

I'm sure you've seen what it looks like when a big rainstorm kicks up, maybe as you're watching from the car window or the back door of your house. Maybe you're fascinated by the sudden streaks of lightning, hearing the sky booming with thunder. There's something both eerie *and* lovely about it. You can love it and hate it all at the same time.

And while I know there's always a chance one of those lightning strikes can crack open a tall tree or knock the power out, here's just the truth of it: Once that split-second spark of electrical energy has touched ground, it's done all the damage it can do. Show's over. All the rain and the fireworks will eventually move on, and the sun will come out. Again.

Jesus said He "watched Satan fall from heaven like a lightning flash." Yes, a flash whose power has fizzled. Don't think for a minute that your God and your enemy are coequals in some cosmic contest between the forces of good and evil, where the ultimate outcome is always in doubt. No.

Satan roars, but God reigns. End of story. Of every story.

Actionable Intel

Write down any areas of your life where you've been worried that the enemy is winning. Then draw a line through each one to remind yourself that God always has the last word.

Core Values

While bodily training is of some value, godliness is of value in every way. —1 Timothy 4:8 ESV

Recon

Any kind of exercise is good and important. Running, for example, can build your stamina and endurance. Working with weights can bulk up the power in your arms and legs. But some of the most valuable exercise is the kind that packs on strength at your *core*—the large muscle groups in the central part of your body.

Just about every motion you make runs through those core muscles. If you ever strain them or maybe injure a rib, just try lifting your backpack—or even doing something as simple as rolling over in bed—and you'll see how deeply those muscles are involved in even the most routine activities.

That's one reason why this belt of truth is so foundational to spiritual victory. Because if we can live in truth, if we can understand the truth, make decisions based on truth, and react to other people in light of the truth, we can operate from a position of strength all day long.

Actionable Intel

Ask your parents, your Bible class teacher, a gym teacher, or an athletic coach to tell you or show you some exercises that strengthen your physical core and your spiritual core. Write them down and try them both. Find out why being strong in this area is a key goal to strive for.

Lined Up

Don't turn to the right or to the left; keep your feet away from evil. —Proverbs 4:27

Recon

A car can be tuned up and in good condition—all its spark plugs firing, all its inner workings synchronized. But even a smooth-running engine, all by itself, cannot guarantee a smooth-running ride . . . not if the wheels aren't in *alignment.*

Maybe you've been riding with your mom or dad and noticed the car seeming to drift to the right or the left, out of its lane. If the car's tires were aligned properly, the driver could keep it on a straight path by making only slight corrections to the steering wheel. But if they aren't, the driver must exert steady pressure to counteract the tug, the drift. That's because one or more of the wheels is bent slightly inward or outward—probably not by much, but enough to keep the rest of the car from staying true in its forward motion.

Our spiritual "car" operates the same way. Simply knowing the truth is a great start. It can keep us running fine in the driveway. But the only way to safely get where we want to go—to victory—is to *align* our life with what we've *affirmed* in our mind and heart.

Actionable Intel

The next time you're riding with one of your parents, ask them if they'll carefully take their hands off the wheel for just a second. See if the car keeps going straight, or if it veers one way or the other. If it does, try to describe what being "out of alignment" feels like.

Peace in Your Step

The LORD gives His people strength; the LORD blesses His people with peace. —Psalm 29:11

Recon

You may be the kind of person who likes going barefoot everywhere. And that's okay—probably even good for you sometimes, letting your toes air out and breathe. But life in many ways is a long gravel driveway of sharp edges and uneven steps. And it's not going to be a peaceful walk to the mailbox every day unless you're wearing some shoes to cushion the blows.

The familiar Hebrew word for peace—*shalom*—which appears in various forms throughout the Old Testament, doesn't refer to an absence of difficulty. It's the kind of peace that leaves room for loose gravel and enemy activity. Because even with the presence of unexpected, unavoidable jabs, the peace described by *shalom* means you're able to walk steadily over the rockiest kind of terrain.

Are there some unstable things happening in your life right now? Yes, probably lots of them. Yet you can remain steadfast. Because your feet are fitted with God's peace.

Actionable Intel

The next time you find yourself on scratchy, pointy, uncomfortable ground, think of how different you would feel if you had no other choice but to cross it barefoot. Thank God for the gift of shoes—shoes for everyday life, and shoes for peace in life.

What Is Faith?

Faith is the reality of what is hoped for, the proof of what is not seen. —Hebrews 11:1

Recon

Remember that old *Sesame Street* song "One of These Things Is Not Like the Other"?

Well, maybe if you were reading today's verse, you could spot some words that don't exactly look like they go together. Underline the words *faith, hope, reality,* and *proof.* Do you see any difference between the first two and the second? *Faith* and *hope*—those are sort of wishful words, right? While the words *reality* and *proof* are more factual, more definite.

But look closer. See what's unseen. Because when God is the object of faith, nothing in this verse is actually not like the other. All the words are in the same spiritual family. Your faith in Him is a *certainty.* What you're hoping is true about Him is as sure as tomorrow's sunrise.

Never let your enemy trick you into thinking that faith is some kind of theory with no real solid foundation. Faith in God is a living, breathing reality. And if you'll make a decision to walk by faith, you'll see how real it can be.

Actionable Intel

Look up today's verse in several Bible translations. Make a note of all the different words they use in trying to capture this important truth.

DNA

[He] has blessed us in Christ with every spiritual blessing in the heavens. —Ephesians 1:3

Recon

My three boys are African American. Because that's who they are. Not because they went to African American class to learn how to be one. Not because they got a shot at the doctor's office that gave them African American antibodies. They're African American because that's what's in their genetic code. Being young African American men is in their DNA.

Well, being a believer is sort of like that. It's in your spiritual DNA. God, of course, is your Creator. The Bible says you were made "in His own image" (Genesis 1:27). But even more so, in saving you, Jesus said you were "born of the Spirit" (John 3:6). New life was encoded into you. God became not just your Creator but your Father. And nothing can ever change that. Ever.

So don't go around today wondering, *Am I still saved?* If you've received Jesus as Lord and Savior, being a child of God is in your DNA. It's who you are. It's who you'll always be.

Actionable Intel

If all the DNA in your body was unbundled and tied end to end, some people say it would stretch from the earth to the sun six hundred times. If that's the kind of care God gave to your temporary physical body, just think how carefully He can preserve your eternal spirit.

Peace with God

*Since we have been declared righteous by
faith, we have peace with God through our
Lord Jesus Christ.* —Romans 5:1

Recon

Have you ever narrowly avoided what could've been a
serious accident, where you look back and say, "Wow, just
think what might have happened"? You're safe *now*. But
it's still scary to ponder what could have been.

Well, here's another one. If not for God's loving desire
to seek relationship with us, we would be so discouraged
and devastated by our past sin, life would barely be worth
living. "All have sinned and fall short of the glory of God,"
the Bible says (Romans 3:23). And what's worse, "the
wages of sin is death" (Romans 6:23).

Yes, *death*.

"But the gift of God," this same verse goes on to say, "is
eternal life in Christ Jesus our Lord." Not death. *Life*. And
peace. "Peace with God through our Lord Jesus Christ."

So that bad feeling we talked about? If it ever leaves
you with scary doubt, you know it's being twisted by the
enemy. Because when it comes from God, it's meant to
leave you with soothing gratitude.

Actionable Intel

You are as free to interact with God right now as if you had
never committed one sin. Because of Jesus, nothing can
make you unholy and rejected in His presence. Let today's
gratitude start right there. If you need a little help, read
Ephesians 1:13–14, and turn it into a prayer of thanks
and praise.

Turtle Back

They will aim their useless arrows. —Psalm 58:7

Recon

Imagine this: An ancient war zone. Flaming arrows sailing through the air. But at the place where they're landing— on the opposing army—the arrows are clanking to the ground, their flames going out. Hurting nobody.

How?

Because of a defensive strategy called the *turtle formation*. The ancient Romans, when under this kind of attack, would sometimes soak their shields in water and hold them over their heads. Hooks on the side of the shield would help link them into each other's, creating a damp, overlapping shell of flame-quenching protection.

This strategy worked for them, and it's the same strategy that will work for you. Do you want help trying to "extinguish all the flaming arrows of the evil one" (Ephesians 6:16)? Then join together with other friends and family members who can link their faith with yours. And those arrows the enemy is launching in your direction will just fizzle out and fall away.

Actionable Intel

Tonight at dinner, tell your family what you learned today about the turtle formation. Brainstorm how you can link your shields of faith together. Turn the enemy's arrows into "useless arrows" that don't even leave a dent.

Needless Danger

*Wake up, wake up! Put on the strength of
the LORD's power.* —Isaiah 51:9

Recon

One of my sons came dashing into the house—an elbow
badly scraped, both knees bleeding. He'd had a skateboard
accident. He'd been trying to impress his brothers with a
new trick, and ended up peeling off a few layers of skin
instead.

That's about all the information I could get out
of anyone for a while as I labored to apply antiseptic
ointment and bandages to the wounded areas. But the
question I *really* wanted answered was why he wasn't
wearing the knee and elbow pads we'd bought for him—
the ones that were supposed to prevent this kind of thing
from happening.

So I asked him where they were, and he pointed to a
corner of the kitchen. Yep, there they were. Sitting there
looking all new and clean. He *had* the protection; he just
hadn't put it on. The pads can't help you when they're
piled up on the floor.

When we don't put on what we've been given for
keeping us safe, we'll find ourselves beat up every single
time.

Actionable Intel

Look again at the list of spiritual armor found in Ephesians
6:14–18. Start today making a habit of spiritually "putting
them on" every morning.

Keeping It Real

*Do not fear, for I am with you; do not be
afraid, for I am your God. I will strengthen
you; I will help you.* —Isaiah 41:10

Recon

When you've got a big project due at school, you can either (a) *underestimate* how much time it's going to take and end up slapping it together at the last minute, or (b) *overestimate* the difficulty level and perhaps worry about something that actually could've been accomplished with a lot less drama.

Or (c) you can try to be *realistic*. You can listen to what the teacher said rather than what other people said that scared you or steered you wrong. You can plan out your week or month with enough time set aside so you're not freaking out on the final weekend.

The unseen battle you're fighting in the spiritual realm is not something to play down or minimize so that you act like it's no big deal, or like it's not even real. But it's also not something to panic about as though there's no way you can win.

Take a deep breath, and then take a steady aim. You're already the victor. So you don't need to fear, but you'd better be on your guard.

Actionable Intel

Compare some of your experiences when you've either *underestimated* or *overestimated* the reality of an assignment. What could have been different if you'd been more realistic about it?

Shining a Light on Things

Everything exposed by the light is made clear. —*Ephesians 5:13*

Recon

No matter how many times I board a plane (which is often), the TSA agents at the screening desk always ask for my driver's license. Before I go through the metal detectors and on to my departure gate, they always look down at my picture and then look back up at my face to see if those two images match. Always.

But even *that's* not enough proof to verify my identity in their eyes. They then take this license of mine and run it under a special kind of light, one that can detect the subtle security layers and watermarks that are built into the card's design. If those features don't show up under the scrutiny of the light, the guards know they're dealing with a fake. A fake ID and a fake me.

They don't trust their eyes alone. They hold everything up to the light.

And whenever we're not sure what we're dealing with in life, that's what we should do too. Hold it up to the light of truth.

Actionable Intel

Where or to whom do you go when you want to find out the truth about something?

Attracting Pests

Don't give the Devil an opportunity. —Ephesians 4:27

Recon

I accidently left out a bowl of fruit on our kitchen table while we were gone for a long trip. When we came back, guess who was there to greet us? Not only some very overripe apples and bananas, but also a *horde* of pesky fruit flies.

I had not gone out to buy a sack of these bugs at the pet shop before we left and then turned them loose in the house. None of us wanted them there or had asked them to come. The only reason they *were* there was because I had created an environment that attracted them. Rotten fruit made them feel at home.

Our disobedience to God does a similar thing. It isn't only a disturbance to our relationship with Him. It is also a red flag to the enemy, alerting him that we've left the door open for him to come bother us. Since he's always looking for an opportunity to creep into the baseboards and wallboards of our spiritual house, he'll never pass up a chance to get in. And our *unrighteous* behavior does just that.

Actionable Intel

Have you ever had an invasion of ants or fruit flies or ladybugs or any other kind of household pests? Why are they easier to keep out than to get rid of once they're already inside?

Lessons from the Orchard

The fruit of the Spirit is love, joy, peace, patience, kindness, goodness, faith, gentleness, self-control. —Galatians 5:22–23

Recon

Our righteousness is symbolized by a breastplate. But one of the cool things about the Bible is how it helps us see truth in all its shapes and colors. For example, it also compares our righteousness to "fruit."

Think apples, oranges, grapes, strawberries. They all grow from trees or plants that produce their particular kind of fruit . . . and no other kind. The seed goes in the ground, the plant structure shoots up, and fruit just naturally, eventually, begins to grow on it.

So if you ever start feeling discouraged—frustrated at why you're so often falling to temptation or making bad choices, upset at how the enemy seems to be defeating you—remember you're already planted in the right place. God has made your heart the kind that can bloom with righteousness. And His Spirit is actively farming and fertilizing, renewing your mind for maximum harvest.

So quit worrying. Remember you were *made* for this. For righteousness.

Actionable Intel

Look up a picture of an orchard or a fruit tree somewhere in your family's reference books or online. Think of your righteousness as able to grow this freely, this naturally . . . because it really can.

Green Leaves, Fresh Fruit

He is like a tree planted beside streams of
water that bears its fruit in season and whose
leaf does not wither. —Psalm 1:3

Recon

Yesterday we talked about fruit. Today let's talk about leaves.

Fruit trees, of course, have leaves. And if you've ever put together a leaf collection, you know that each type of tree possesses its own unique shape and size of leaf.

But the leaves, while pretty and important and comfortable for shade, are not the main business of a fruit tree. When Jesus, feeling hungry, once came across a fig tree by the roadside and "found nothing on it except leaves" (Matthew 21:19), He made clear that leaves alone were not what He was needing.

Our "leaves" as believers represent our testimony. They identify us as Christians to the outside world. And that's good. We need to keep those leaves green and distinct. But if all we offer to people are our leaves, we keep them from being able to experience and be nourished by the fruit of our righteousness.

All leaves and no fruit is not enough. You were made for more.

Actionable Intel

Look up and read Jeremiah 17:7–8, and note Jeremiah's description of the person "who trusts in the Lord." See if you can find at least three specific blessings that come to a healthy Christian.

Less Is More

"He prunes every branch that produces fruit so that it will produce more fruit."—John 15:2

Recon

If producing fruit is good, then producing more fruit is better, right? But did you know that if you want to get the greatest amount from a plant, one of the most important strategies is to occasionally cut it back?

It's called *pruning*—cutting away deadwood or unproductive areas, as well as any branches that are getting in the way of others, restricting their growth. At first, it leaves the bush or tree looking thinner, weaker. But in the end, it makes for a stronger, healthier, more productive plant.

Or person. A stronger, healthier, more fruitful you.

Your enemy doesn't want you producing more fruit. That's why he entices you just to do whatever you feel like, to live however you want. Only a loving Father, who truly cares about your overall well-being, would be willing to clip your wings sometimes, stripping away any pockets of unrighteousness, knowing you'll be better for it in the end.

So trust God, okay? If you feel like He's telling you to "cut away" some things from your life, don't try to hang on to them. Let them go. And watch the fruit of your life grow.

Actionable Intel

Read John 15:1. What term does Jesus use to describe Himself? What term does He use to define the Father? Now read John 15:5. What term does Jesus use to describe you and me? And how does He describe our main job as "branches"? What does He say will happen if we don't do it?

Deep-Down Peace

*"Peace I leave with you. My peace I
give to you."—John 14:27*

Recon

When you think about it, the joy of being able to live at
peace with God is almost indescribable. But the benefits
of peace don't stop there. By being His child by faith, you
not only have peace *with* God, you also have access to the
peace *of* God. Throughout the day. Throughout your life.

The peace *of* God.

I mean, think how deep the reservoirs of God's peace
must be. He made everything. He knows everything.
There's nothing He doesn't control or overturn. Nothing
He doesn't understand or figure out. All the mysteries and
unknowns that make worry and dread seem like natural
options to us—He's got *none* of that.

And so because He's in *you*—and because, as Jesus
said in today's verse, He's promised to give His peace to
you, then . . .

Yes, you can live with the same kind of peace that God
possesses. No worry. No fear. No anxiety about tomorrow.

Please don't let a gift like that go to waste.

Actionable Intel

There's a little more to John 14:27. Look it up yourself, and
answer these questions: What's automatically different
about any kind of peace the world could give you? And
since Jesus' peace is so complete, how does He say our
heart is supposed to respond?

Step Wisely

Whoever listens to counsel is wise. —*Proverbs 12:15*

Recon

Yes, living by faith can often feel risky. It's *not* risky, of course, because God's Word is always true and because God Himself is always faithful. But that doesn't keep your palms from sweating when He calls you to do something that seems kind of . . . out there.

Now listen, God loves you. He knows when your heart is committed to following Him. And He knows when you're really trying to obey but are just a bit hesitant because you feel unsure. That's why He will often, in addition to what He's already said in the Bible, give you wise words of counsel from people you ask for advice.

Faith is not a pass to act foolishly. God has given you wisdom and surrounded you with wise people for a reason. So when you sense Him prompting you to do or say something (or to *not* do or say something), ask Him for confirmation from His Word and from the counsel of a person you trust. God wants you to act in the wisdom of faith.

Actionable Intel

Write down the names of three older people in your life whom you can trust and go to for advice regularly. Is there anything you are unsure about right now? Commit to talking with one of them about it.

Eternity: The Early Years

Fight the good fight for the faith; take hold of eternal life. —1 Timothy 6:12

Recon

You may not know this, but if you've been waiting for your "eternal life" to start the moment you die and your spirit is transported to be face-to-face with Jesus—or better yet, if He comes back *before* you die—you're waiting on something that is actually already happening. Spoiler alert: your eternal life has already started.

You're *living* it.

Now, it's going to get a whole lot better, of course, when you're no longer bound by the limitations of this fallen planet. It's going to be great not being hounded by the enemy anymore, not being tempted to sin anymore, not needing to wear your armor anymore because you're in the presence of the One who's ended every war forever.

But part of what it means to wear the helmet of salvation is to live every day—now—in light of the future you've been promised.

So "take hold of eternal life." Change how you live in the present by living it from the perspective of someone who's already been given a victorious life beyond it.

Actionable Intel

How do you think having an eternal perspective can help you handle problems differently today?

Deep Breaths

*All Scripture is inspired by God and is profitable
for teaching, for rebuking, for correcting, for
training in righteousness.* —2 Timothy 3:16

Recon

Inspired. It's a word that carries the idea of breathing.
(Think respiration.) In terms of the Bible, it means that
God *breathed* His message into ordinary men who wrote
down on paper what He wanted to say to His people.

It's important to remember that God didn't have to
leave us a single word on a single scratch of paper. He
could have just made the universe and left us to figure it
out on our own.

But He wanted to speak where we could hear Him. He
wanted us to know that our reality is about His greatness,
His glory, and His love for sinful people. He "inspired" the
Scripture so that we could be "complete, equipped for
every good work" (2 Timothy 3:17).

This fact alone should inspire in us a desire to read it,
learn it, and love it.

Actionable Intel

Your enemy will be breathing down your neck today. Make
sure you start the day by hearing what God is breathing
out instead.

Appearances Are Deceiving

Satan disguises himself as an angel of light. —2 Corinthians 11:14

Recon

"Please? Can we keep him? Please please please please please?"

When you are begging your mom and dad to keep the stray puppy you found, you see yourself running down to the creek with your new pet, laying your head on his back in the soft grass on a summer day. What you don't see, however, is . . .

Property destruction. Vet bills. Pooper scoopers. Cold, rainy nights and mornings when the last thing you'll feel like doing is taking him and his muddy paw prints out for a walk.

Not everything is as fun, exciting, or innocent as it first appears. And not only is this true of puppy dogs and kitty cats, it is also true of the temptations that the enemy sends your way. They don't quickly bare the white teeth of troublemaking potential, not until they've taken a big bite out of your peace of mind.

Just because something makes your face light up and seems like it'll be all fun and games doesn't mean it won't come with enormous responsibilities that will cost you more than you ever imagined. The enemy's temptations always have consequences that he hopes you overlook. Don't take the bait.

Actionable Intel

When was the last time you bought something or tried something that turned out to be nowhere near as great as you thought it would be?

Growing Up

*Then we will no longer be little children,
tossed by the waves and blown around by every
wind of teaching. —Ephesians 4:14*

Recon

Being young comes with some difficulties and restrictions. Although it does give you time to explore your dreams, pursue your passions, and enjoy the safety of a loving home before you're out on your own, I'm betting there are times when you wish you were already grown up. You're probably looking forward to finally doing some things you aren't allowed to do right now, or maybe having more courage or less fear about something in your life.

Guess what, though. By developing a love for truth, by desiring a deeper devotion to God and His Word, He can help you start avoiding the pitfalls of being young while still enjoying all its benefits. You can have a maturity far beyond your years. He can make you strong, steady, and powerful.

You may need to wait a little while before you can drive or vote for president or get married or have a family. But living by truth can start getting you ready for all the good, big things of adulthood. Today.

Actionable Intel

Look again at today's verse. What kinds of things make you feel "tossed" around and unstable? Ask the Lord to give you strength and wisdom so you can face those challenges, today and as you grow up.

Yum!

"Blessed are those who hunger and thirst for righteousness, for they will be filled."—Matthew 5:6 NIV

Recon

I don't about you, but I like to eat.

I like warm bread, straight from the oven, topped by a nice smear of soft butter. I like ice-cream cones and ice-cream cups and those mountainous brownie desserts they serve with two spoons at sit-down restaurants. I also like healthy things too, don't get me wrong, but you know what I mean. Eating is just good. Being full is just . . . ahh!

And thankfully, God understands this about you and me. He knows we don't like being hungry, that we crave the experience of sitting back and being satisfied. And although we may not be able to eat all the things we most enjoy being filled with every single day, we can certainly pig out on following Him and serving Him and delighting Him with our obedience.

Because when we do, He's made us a promise. We will "be filled."

Actionable Intel

If you were allowed to go the pantry or refrigerator at home and just get whatever you want right now, what would you want? Can you imagine wanting righteousness with this same intensity?

Peace and Love

Those who love Your law have great peace, and nothing causes them to stumble. —Psalm 119:165 NASB

Recon

Reading a Bible verse that says something like, for instance, "Love your enemies and pray for those who persecute you" (Matthew 5:44) can be unsettling. I don't know about you, but I don't always like this instruction. Depending on the day, and depending on what someone is doing to harm me, it could make me a little upset that He even expects me to love and forgive someone who has hurt me. It makes me wonder if He will really take care of the person and problem as well as I think I could do on my own.

But if I choose to simply obey, the outcome will be a sense of peace about the whole situation. If I would approach His instructions each day with the supernatural capability we've each been given by Christ—to genuinely love His Word—I will find His peace filling every area of my life.

In today's verse He's promised us "great peace" if we follow His Word. And a guard against the enemy's attempts to make us stumble.

Actionable Intel

How many of the places where you're feeling anxiety today are the result of not obeying His Word?

Falling Forward

When he saw the strength of the wind, he was
afraid. And beginning to sink he cried out,
"Lord, save me!"—Matthew 14:30

Recon

Remember the story where Jesus was walking on water? Peter always ends up looking like the bad guy in this narrative. Jumping in without thinking. Then getting scared. Starting to sink. Impulsive old Peter.

But this story shows us that even faith that falters and wobbles a little bit is surely better than faith that won't even get out of the boat. None of Jesus' other disciples apparently even entertained the notion that He might want them to come out there to meet Him. They were much too afraid of this "ghost" on the water (Matthew 14:26) to let Jesus show them just what His power could accomplish in them if they only believed.

I wouldn't worry if Jesus sometimes needs to reach down and help you up, after you've tried to do exactly what He's asked you to do but things have gone slightly awry. I'd worry more if you let the enemy keep you too scared to ever walk on the water at all.

Actionable Intel

Don't be afraid of falling today . . . as long as you're falling forward in faith.

Living for a Reason

Let us draw near with a true heart in full
assurance of faith. —Hebrews 10:22

Recon

Your enemy wants you to operate entirely by how you feel. Because if you "draw near" to God only when you feel like it, you won't be doing it very often. Not enough to make a difference.

Your salvation, however, is not just a feel-good story. It's anchored to a grounded faith. A logical faith. There's a *reason* why you draw near to God, and it's not just because you need a little pick-me-up now and then.

Notice in your Bible that Hebrews 10:22 is actually the last part of a long sentence, beginning in verse 19. The first two verses set up why we, as believers, should constantly seek out and remain in God's presence. It's because of the "blood of Jesus." Because of the "new and living way" that He's given us to live. Because He's become our "great high priest," approaching the Father on our behalf.

You don't need to feel like "drawing near" to God. Just come on. You'll feel better when you do.

Actionable Intel

Take time also to read the *last* half of Hebrews 10:22 in your Bible. Why else are we invited and able to stand in God's presence? How should this insight affect how you live today?

Repeat Performance

*Endurance produces proven character, and proven
character produces hope.* —Romans 5:4

Recon

One of the most valuable truths to learn, not only about
your unseen warfare, but also about your spiritual success
in life, is that you can't earn what God does for you. You
can't be good enough, can't be holy and righteous enough.
He just gives you Himself because He loves you enough and
is *already* enough.

But . . .

Every little forward step you make is still important.
Every time you trust Him, obey Him, believe in Him, and
love Him, you push back against the darkness and win
a new victory for your faith. Your choice makes you a
person of character who is filled with hope about the
future. Your decision snatches one more disguise from
the enemy's prop closet and one more instrument off his
tool belt. The courage and endurance of a single person—
in a single moment, in response to a single situation—
sways the balance toward victory. When you choose truth
and righteousness, God gives you hope that you can do it
again . . . and again.

Actionable Intel

Think of an area in your life where you haven't been
doing the right thing, whether out of fear or laziness or
whatever your excuse. Right now, make a resolution that
the next time the opportunity presents itself, you will
make the right choice. Then just step up and do it. And
see how a sense of hope will rise up in you.

In Tune with Truth

*Hold on to the pattern of sound teaching that
you have heard from me.* —2 Timothy 1:13

Recon

When you tune a guitar, you start with the bottom string—
the thickest one, the deepest one, the heavy E string—
and make sure its tone matches up with what a low E is
supposed to sound like. Once that string is correctly on
pitch, you can then move on through the other five (A, D,
G, B, E), building their individual sounds by comparing
them to the bottom one. If the first E is accurate, you can
make everything else sound beautiful.

Truth, then, is like our E string. Truth makes the whole
instrument sing.

As you keep growing, you'll work toward certain
goals and desires. You'll be faced with various kinds of
decisions and choices to make. You'll experience a range
of different thoughts and feelings. But as long as your "E
string" is tuned correctly, all of these other things will
come together to form the song of your life.

Actionable Intel

Do you know how to play the guitar or some other musical
instrument? What else have you learned from making
music that could apply to your spiritual life?

Light Year's Difference

"Let your light shine before men, so that they may see your good works and give glory to your Father in heaven."—Matthew 5:16

Recon

Like most kids, you probably don't want to be thought of as "different." I mean, who does? The pull of popularity and acceptance can be pretty strong, enough sometimes to make you do things and act in ways that make you feel like you're fitting in, even if you're uncomfortable doing them.

But you may already be discovering that being different from the normal, cookie-cutter model can actually be fairly refreshing, freeing, and even fun. It's a fantastic adventure that only some people are courageous enough to go on.

It is an adventure, just being yourself. And being okay with it.

Sure, people might make some cutting comments to you or about you if you choose to be righteous. Others will keep struggling to know who they really are. But over time you'll find that by being different, you're becoming more secure, year after year, in how God is using you and transforming you.

Actionable Intel

Don't get upset when people make fun of those who are choosing to follow God's Word. Save your anger for the enemy who is working through difficult people to get at *you*.

Winners and Losers

Who is the one who conquers the world but the one who
believes that Jesus is the Son of God?—1 John 5:5

Recon

Loser. That's one of the enemy's words for you. He makes
it worse, of course, by leading you to think you're the only
one he chooses to call that name, but really he tries it on
all of us, hoping to make us feel and live like losers. But
I've got a name for him too . . .

Liar. That needs to be one of your words for the Devil.
Because truth be told, he knows very well that you're not
a loser. It worries him that you're actually a victor—in
Christ—and he is desperate to keep you from operating in
the peace of that eternal reality.

So don't let him. Let the victory that comes from knowing
Jesus and the assurance you have as a warrior lead you to a
consistent, day-by-day experience of God's peace.

Loser? Ha! I don't think so.

Victor. That's who.

So who's the loser now?

Actionable Intel

I don't know what kind of insulting names or notions the
enemy has put in your head. But today's a good day to
write some of them down on a piece of paper and then
pray that the Lord will help you replace them in your
thoughts. When you're finished, ball up the paper and put
those words in the garbage—where they belong.

Go for It

Go wash seven times in the Jordan and your flesh will be restored and you will be clean. —2 Kings 5:10

Recon

Naaman was a tough military guy who got leprosy—a gross, flesh-eating skin disease. Life as he knew it was over.

But the prophet Elisha had a promise from God for him. *Go dip in the Jordan River, and you will be healed.* The promise was there; Naaman just had to go get it. But would he?

Most of the time, God doesn't just plop His promises in your hands. He places them within your reach. They're waiting at the end of a set of instructions to obey, at the intersection where faith and action mix together with the mighty power of almighty God.

The enemy will try to make you think it's not fair of God to do this, and that God ought to just give His promises to you without any responsibility on your part. But God is actually doing you a favor. He's giving you the *privilege* of participating with Him in the experience of His promises, so that by faith you'll have the confidence to go after the next one. And the next one.

Actionable Intel

What have you observed about kids who get everything they want without working for it? What kind of person might you become if God gave you gifts without any responsibility?

Watch Your Head

*Protect me from the trap they have
set for me. —Psalm 141:9*

Recon

I saw a video clip recently of a boy in China (probably
five or six years old) who somehow got his head stuck in
a fence. Not just a wire or wooden fence, but a concrete
structure artistically cut out with little geometric shapes.
One of those shapes apparently looked a little too tempting.
The boy was able to get his head *in* . . . but not *out*.

I know how foolish it sounds. "Why would anyone do
that?" you might ask. Yet God has given us a special piece
of armor knowing we *often* do that. We get our heads
stuck in places they have no business being—in lies, in
sinful temptations, in things that people said to us to hurt
us or shame us—and we can't seem to get unstuck.

The helmet of salvation can keep your head—your
mind, your thoughts—on the right side of those traps so
you don't get stuck where you don't belong.

Actionable Intel

Get in the habit of talking about your most upsetting
thoughts with people you trust—your parents, older
relatives, a favorite teacher, or someone at church. You
can keep your head out of a lot of trouble if you ask wise
people to help you keep your thoughts on track.

Tooth and Nail

*Let the exaltation of God be in their mouths and a
double-edged sword in their hands. —Psalm 149:6*

Recon

The "edge" in the Hebrew word for "double-edged" carries
the idea of "teeth"—like the teeth on a steak knife, like the
jagged teeth on an animal. They can leave a real mark.

I wonder if the writer of Psalm 149 used this word
on purpose in this particular statement from Scripture . . .
because the worship of God, formed in our mouths, creates
another sharp weapon in our arsenal.

Praise and worship are your opportunity to glorify
God for His power, His love, His mercy, His grandeur, His
never-ending patience—all the things that make you stand
in awe of Him. But the same words that are music to your
Father's ears are nails across your enemy's chalkboard.
Make it a *double-edged* set of nails. It's a sound that grates
on him all the time.

Actionable Intel

Worship the Lord loudly and strongly today. Make such
a joyful noise that your enemy won't be able to get the
sound out of his head.

This Means War

For our battle is not against flesh and blood, but against the rulers, against the authorities, against the world powers of this darkness, against the spiritual forces of evil in the heavens. —Ephesians 6:12

Recon

Apparently we don't need to know exactly how Satan's armies are organized or God would've told us in greater detail. But God does say enough in the Bible to make it clear that we're facing a full-on offensive from the enemy. From his central command, Satan is trying to create waves of confusion and chaos in our lives.

So I'm just assuming our mission must be important, or else the enemy wouldn't use so many resources to fight us. There must be something extremely valuable at stake, even in just trying to trick you into cheating on a test, or arguing with your sister, or not wanting to read your Bible or talk to God more often in prayer. Your and my demise is such a big part of his purposes that he has taken pains to assign a whole army of his forces to the job.

If slowing us down is *that* important to Satan, maybe we ought to wonder why—and make it our business to be sure he never gets the victory in our lives.

Actionable Intel

If the enemy has an organized strategy against you, what do you think you could do to organize a strategy of prayer against him? What could that begin to look like in your life?

Lie Detector

"When he tells a lie, he speaks from his own nature, because he is a liar and the father of liars."—John 8:44

Recon

Another reason why you should think of the belt of truth first among the pieces of spiritual armor (and why Paul likely chose to include it first in his listing from Ephesians 6) is because of how it relates to doing battle against your enemy . . . whose first way of attacking you is through *deception*.

He's a liar. He is anti-truth. He zeroes in on the things he knows about you and then tries deceiving you with half-truths and whole lies that can oddly start to add up and make sense in your head if you're not careful.

The belt of truth is what keeps you careful. Careful not to leap to conclusions. Careful not to trust your feelings and first impressions. Careful not to take credit for things that actually belong to God and have only been loaned to you.

Truth fights back. Against the lies.

Actionable Intel

Circle any of the following lies that the enemy has tried to use against you: "You are not special." "You're a failure." "God doesn't love you." "You should be afraid." "You are not worthy." Can you think of any others? What truths from God's Word can combat these lies?

God Is Just . . .

Won't the Judge of all the earth do
what is just?—Genesis 18:25

Recon

Just.

We tend to use this word a lot. (As in, "I was *just* kidding. *Just* forget it.") But when we talk about God being just, we're talking about His perfect sense of fairness, His heart for *justice*.

In fact, the reason that our salvation required a cross is mainly because our God, while merciful, is also just. He demands justice.

For instance, you may think that because Jesus has died for your sins on the cross, God has decided to overlook your sins. But no. They're not overlooked. They're *paid for*. Big difference.

To overlook them wouldn't be fair. It wouldn't be just. You and I would still owe . . . with our lives. But because Jesus Himself, the perfect Lamb of God, "bore our sins in His body on the cross," His death is full payment for them (1 Peter 2:24 NASB). Our sins haven't been forgotten; they've been bought. So we don't have to pay for them ourselves.

This is where our righteousness begins. This is how wearing the breastplate is even possible.

Isn't that just amazing?

Actionable Intel

In your prayers today, thank God for making sure your sins—all of them—have been completely paid for by the blood of Jesus.

Clearer Heads

May the Lord of peace Himself give you peace
always in every way. —2 Thessalonians 3:16

Recon

The Lord, according to Scripture, is not the "author of confusion" (1 Corinthians 14:33 KJV) but is the "God of peace" (Romans 15:33) who, as today's verse says, wants to "give you peace always in every way."

Think of the times when you're most confused. When you don't know the answer. When you can't figure something out. When people are telling you to do things you're not sure you should be doing. You're trying to make sense out of all of it, but you're just confused.

Here's what you need to remember the next time you feel that way. Your enemy is invested in *keeping* you there, but God is able and eager to lead you *out* of there.

Confusion is a signal to raise your hand, raise your head, and ask God for the answers and direction that can lead you to understanding. Out of the woods and into the clearing. Out of confusion and into peace.

Actionable Intel

Raising your hands almost naturally raises your head as well, while confusion makes you hang your head in frustration. The next time confusion is getting the best of you, find a quiet place where you can raise both your hands (and your head) in trusting prayer to the "Lord of peace."

Pick It Up

We must be serious and put the armor of faith and love on our chests. —1 Thessalonians 5:8

Recon

A nurse wears her scrubs to work every day. That's her uniform. But all throughout her shift, she's always picking up and using the different instruments she needs. Stethoscope. Thermometer. IV needle. Heart monitor.

An auto mechanic wears a shirt with his first name on it to work every day. That's his uniform. But with every car in his shop, he's always reaching for different tools and auto parts. Torque wrench. Battery tester. Brake shoes. Drive belts.

Faith is something you carry around internally with you all the time—your belief in God, your trust in His Word. But at any moment you could be called on to pick up that faith and put it into practice.

In the nurse's case, using her tools makes sick people well. In the mechanic's case, it makes sick cars run better. In your case, it makes your faith stronger.

Actionable Intel

Can you think of another example that illustrates today's devotional message?

Equipment Repair

Discretion will watch over you, and understanding
will guard you. —Proverbs 2:11

Recon

I've learned this interesting fact about football: whenever a player's helmet comes off—even if it gets knocked off during the action, like while he's making a tackle—he's forced to go sit out for a play. If he wants to get back in the game, he needs to go to the sidelines, check his equipment, tighten his chinstrap, be sure nothing's loose, reposition the thing on his head, and then—*then*—he can reenter. Not *before* then.

I think we need to apply this same rule to ourselves as participants in spiritual battle. If you're out there in the middle of it today, and you realize you're not thinking the way a saved person should be thinking, don't try to keep playing without your helmet. Even if you can't get to the sidelines, lift up an immediate prayer, get your head right, and *then* go back in.

Protected.

Actionable Intel

Think of something you could carry in your pocket or keep on your phone to always remind you that you belong to Jesus and that He leads you as your Lord. Always.

Praying on Purpose

"My house will be called a house of prayer."—Matthew 21:13

Recon

Prayer is so important—which is why our enemy works so hard to lure us away from it, to make us think it's kind of optional. Take it or leave it. Mostly leave it.

But prayer is vital to fighting and winning as a warrior child of God. We can't just treat it like it's something to do when we feel like it or to mark off a list. Because it's not just words. It's not just something to do—you know, hoping to make God happy with you for checking in. No, prayer is a *gift* He's given you. It's your opportunity to communicate anytime directly with the One who holds everything in your life together. And not only that, it's a crucial way of staying plugged into God's heart and being vividly aware that you are personally connected to Him. What's more, it constantly reminds you of the tools and weapons He's given you to battle with.

Prayer keeps your spiritual armor activated and your enemy at bay.

Actionable Intel

Before you run off to do anything else today, take just a minute or two to stop and pray—thanking God for His blessings, asking for His help, trusting Him to be your Ultimate Fighter.

Abracadabra

*By his cunning he shall make deceit prosper
under his hand.* —Daniel 8:25 ESV

Recon

Sometimes the concept of *deception* is a little hard to grasp. In thinking about the enemy's strategies against you, maybe a word like *illusion* would, uh . . . do the trick.

You know, like magic. Magic tricks. Pick a card, any card. Nothing in my hand, see? Nothing up my sleeve. And yet no matter how amazing the illusions get, there's always a secret behind them. Something you didn't see. Something the magician hid so well or did so fast, your eye just wasn't able to keep up with it.

But if you knew how the trick worked, if you knew the truth, it would completely change the way you felt about what was happening on stage. You wouldn't be so surprised and shocked. You'd be different from others in the room who didn't know, who couldn't tell. You wouldn't fall for it like they would. The magician wouldn't be able to fool you any longer. Not with that trick anyway.

Because you'd know the truth. You'd know that even the magician's (or the enemy's) best tricks are only illusions.

Actionable Intel

Do you happen to know any magic tricks? Have you been able to fool people with them? What do they not see? What do they not know? But how often can you keep doing your trick once they've figured it out?

Up for a Field Trip?

The fruit of righteousness is sown in peace by those who cultivate peace. —James 3:18

Recon

Think of a person you know—whether a grown-up or someone more your own age—who just seems to radiate *peace.* They're a calming influence on others. You know you can count on them to be there, under control, and to stay the same no matter what is happening all around. People go to them with their problems and concerns, and this person just seems to know what to say (or *not* to say) to steady the situation and make others feel better.

Know anybody like that?

My challenge for you today is to go find that person. See if they'll meet with you. Tell them you'd like to talk. What you really want to do, though, is *listen.* Find out what makes them able to stay in such a calm place, levelheaded, free to give and care and show people God's peace.

I've done this very thing. And I promise you—you'll learn something from it.

Actionable Intel

Be sure to process what they tell you. Write down any takeaways from your conversation—even if it's just *one* memorable thing they told you—that can change the way you live.

Cool It

A gentle answer turns away anger, but a harsh word stirs up wrath. —Proverbs 15:1

Recon

Ray Kelly, former New York City chief of police, started out as a street cop. One night he found himself face-to-face with a pack of twenty high schoolers who were fist fighting and throwing rocks. He was all by himself in the middle of this group of kids who really wanted to hurt each other.

"It took a few minutes, but I managed to calm everyone down," said Kelly, a former Marine and Vietnam veteran. He'd discovered through life experience that keeping his cool and keeping his head, even in tense situations, was the best way to calm others down as well. "Calm," he said, "like anxiety and uproar, is almost always contagious."*

The enemy's advice to you in tense situations is to give back as good as you're getting. To keep the bad feeling going. Level it up. Don't hold back. To be louder and harsher than *they* are. But the wise words of Scripture, dating back thousands of years, work not only in the Lower East Side but everywhere else. Keep your cool, and you can put out the fire.

Actionable Intel

When could you give a "gentle answer" to someone today? What relationship in your life needs one the most?

---

*Ray Kelly, *Vigilance* (New York: Hachette, 2015), 53.

Power You Can Feel

I pray that He may grant you, according to the riches of His glory, to be strengthened with power in the inner man through his Spirit. —Ephesians 3:16

Recon

Many of the lines that the enemy uses against you are meant to target your insecurities. To make you feel fragile, like a failure is about to happen. He tries to convince you that you're not good enough. You're not prepared enough. Everybody else is better. You don't belong here.

Ever felt anything like that?

The only reason lies like these can hit their target so squarely is that you've got your shield down. The power that God is waiting to turn loose in you doesn't come to you *before* you act on His Word and His promises. It comes *while* you're acting on them.

So don't wait until you *feel* the confidence inside you before you obey what God asks you to do. Get your faith in gear, and His confidence will come find you. Then you'll feel it. And then you'll want to feel it again and again.

Actionable Intel

You won't know you can do something until you try it. That's how faith works. That's how you work off those silly, yet suffocating insecurities. What can you do in the next twenty-four hours to act in faith and ward off the attacks of the enemy?

Given in Trust

Guard, through the Holy Spirit who lives in us, that good thing entrusted to you. —2 Timothy 1:14

Recon

God doesn't give us things just to give them. They're "entrusted" to us, almost like seeds or young plants, so He can keep growing them within us.

I remember, for example, a verse God kept drawing my eye toward as a young person: "It was for freedom that Christ set us free" (Galatians 5:1 NASB). This "freedom" Paul talked about—freedom from needing to perform, freedom to follow God and overcome my enemy—spoke to me at such a deep, heart level. Being *saved* by Christ meant that I was *free* in Christ. Free to live.

Learn to "guard" moments like these, when God's Spirit speaks so personally to you. Write them down. Reflect on them. Don't just say, "Oh, that's nice," and then keep moving on with your day. Start looking for *why* God showed you this and *how* you can use it.

It's not a gift to play with; it's a gift to put into action.

Actionable Intel

If you don't already have one, look and listen for a verse of Scripture that could be your life verse, like Galatians 5:1 has become for me. If you *do* have one, repeat it often as a reminder of who God is and how He provides for you.

Turning the Tide

"With God all things are possible."—Matthew 19:26

Recon

In one of the most exciting endings to a college football game ever, the University of Alabama lined up to try a 56-yard field goal with one second left and the game tied—in the final game of the season. If they made it, victory. If they missed it, overtime. Their opponent, the Auburn Tigers, lined up on defense.

Except for one person, who lined up in the end zone. On offense.

The field goal was barely short. The Auburn player caught it in the air. Instead of settling for a defensive stop, he took off running. And 109 yards later, he had scored the winning touchdown. He could have just let the missed field goal bounce away, a failed attempt by the other team. Instead he saw a way to turn it into something more. And, boy, did he ever.

That's how a warrior thinks. Play defense, yes, but always look for a way to take more ground, to move forward, to advance and win.

Actionable Intel

You'll wear yourself out if you're just trying to keep bad things from happening. But you'll feel energized by making good things happen instead. How could you do that today?

Plugging In

*Our inner person is being renewed day
by day.* —*2 Corinthians 4:16*

Recon

Cell phones are nice things to have if you want to text a
friend or you need to tell your parents what time to pick
you up. But one of the responsibilities involved in carrying
a cell phone is making sure it stays charged. If you don't
remember to plug it in, that *low* battery signal soon
becomes a *no* battery signal, and you're stuck needing to
borrow somebody else's or just doing without.

Without a charge, you're out of luck. Out of juice.

And you can expect the *same* sort of feeling—
spiritually—if you don't stay regularly plugged into
God's Spirit through prayer, through reading the Bible,
through worshiping at church, and through being around
Christian friends. None of us is designed to be our own
little power plant, able to keep ourselves fully charged
without receiving some outside input.

Spiritual armor and Christian confidence are always
available, but you need to plug in if you want to access
them.

Actionable Intel

What kinds of things keep you most "plugged in" spiritually?
Have you done any of those things today?

Early Decision

Tell them, "This is what the Lord God says," whether they listen or refuse to listen. —Ezekiel 3:11

Recon

You're smart. I can tell. Anybody who would make it a priority to read about such important stuff when they're young is smart.

Because let me tell you what happens every time you take in truth. The power of living in truth as a young guy, as a young girl, is that it builds up an early resistance to deception. Like a vaccine shot for the chicken pox. Instead of having to actually *get* the chicken pox, and having to go through the whole experience of being sick and scratchy and uncomfortable, the vaccine you get as a little kid builds a lifelong shield against the disease.

And that's what you're doing. Right this minute. The chance of you becoming like the people in today's verse who "refuse to listen" to "what the Lord God says"—that person won't be *you*. Because *you* are living in truth. Already. Guarding against the enemy's lies. Already. Learning how to match that belt of truth with every outfit. Already.

You, my friend, are going to be ready for anything.

Actionable Intel

When you think of yourself being a year older, five years older, ten years older, what are some of the good habits you want to be part of your life then? List two or three of those. What could you start doing today to begin preparing for a lifetime of living with those habits and getting better at them?

The Power of Peace

There is no Jew or Greek, slave or free, male or female; for you are all one in Christ Jesus. —Galatians 3:28

Recon

I'm sure you've seen footage of modern riots and mass demonstrations, of angry protestors violently expressing hatred for other groups of people. But trust me—the deep-seated, historical hatred that existed between Jews and Gentiles (non-Jews) in Bible days was extreme too. When Paul told them that the gospel was powerful enough to unite Jews and Gentiles in love and shared purpose, he might as well have been talking about the dogs and cats in your neighborhood. *Nothing can ever make them get along. Nothing.*

But it can if it's truly God doing it.

This gospel you've believed—the gospel of Jesus Christ—is not just a sweet little church story. It is a radical, earth-shattering, shape-bending, mind-blowing mission.

And that's the kind of power—the power of almighty God—that came into your heart when you trusted your life to Jesus. The reason you can live in peace with God, with others, and with yourself in any situation is that peace has come to live inside of you.

Actionable Intel

Think of two people (or two groups of people) who hate one another about as much as anyone possibly can. Now imagine them being friends who'd do anything in the world for each other. Write down their names and pray specifically for them to experience the peace of God. How can you help?

Just a Pinch

"The kingdom of heaven is like a mustard seed."—Matthew 13:31

Recon

It doesn't take much. Little is big.

Step on a honeybee in the backyard, in your bare feet, and tell me that little things can't have a big impact.

Doesn't this truth play out all over the Bible? David kills *Goliath*? Young Mary gives birth to *Jesus*? Five loaves and two fish feed *five thousand*?

It's God's way. His preferred way. The *only* way, really. Because without Him, "you can do nothing" (John 15:5). Even with more faith you can still do . . . nothing.

The issue isn't how much faith you have; all that matters is how *big* God is.

And because God's power is so great, all it takes is a "mustard seed" of faith to turn *nothing* into *anything* He wants it to be . . . into absolutely *anything* He wants to do through you.

Actionable Intel

Look up Luke 17:5–6. What was the apostles' request of Jesus? And how did Jesus answer them? What would have been a better request for them to make?

Swimming Lesson

Let the fish of the sea inform you. —Job 12:8

Recon

Sharks are dangerous, just like your enemy is dangerous. But I learned something about sharks while watching a television show one day.

A group of researchers put tracking devices on a number of great white sharks so they could monitor their movements and see how they captured their prey. The sharks would dive deep in the ocean, wait for the right moment, then zoom up at full speed to the surface to grab an unsuspecting seal. Their success relied on the element of surprise.

But in the same episode, researchers also watched sharks that were swimming near the surface. With the sharks in sight, the seals swam around them with ease and even appeared to *tease* the fierce predators at times. The sharks didn't even try to catch them. Because without the element of surprise, they knew they had no chance to grab hold of these swift swimmers. By being wise to their attackers' intentions, the seals had the upper hand.

And so do you. By knowing your enemy is there and not allowing him to take you by surprise—you've won!

Actionable Intel

Write down the names of a couple of good friends who can be your team of Navy SEALs. Commit to watch out for each other, alerting one another to the enemy who may try to catch you unaware.

Joy and Peace

Consider it a great joy, my brothers, whenever you experience various trials. —James 1:2

Recon

Joy appears early in the list of what Paul called the "fruit of the Spirit" (Galatians 5:22–23). Joy is confident hope that comes from trusting in God's goodness. It lets you remain calm, grateful, and forward-looking, even when everything around is screaming from anger and despair. Being *happy*, or all smiles, may not be possible in the moment. But being *joyful*—staying bigger than the problem—is always possible.

It's no accident that "peace" follows directly after "joy" in Paul's list. Because that's how it happens in real life. Hard times come. Storms blow in. Challenges outnumber and overwhelm us. But when we choose to truly consider it "joy," even when we're walking through a tough thing, that's when peace begins to flow like a river. God's Spirit gives us power.

Satan wants to separate you from joy at every opportunity. And yet every situation in life—no matter what—remains an opportunity for joy. That must really drive him crazy.

Actionable Intel

Ask God for joy today, especially in the areas of your life where there's really no reason you should have it. And expect to receive it from Him.

Bear Up

*Put on a heart of compassion, kindness, humility,
gentleness and patience; bearing with one another, and
forgiving each other. —Colossians 3:12–13 NASB*

Recon

Sometimes love takes the form of "bearing with one another," like today's verse says. "Bearing with one another" means grinning and bearing it.

I'm glad the Bible is so real. I'm glad Christianity is not just some imaginary, feel-good religion. Instead, it comes down to earth and actually works when you're at school and other places where life actually happens. I'm glad God understands love isn't the same thing as being best friends with everybody, but that we can sometimes best express His love simply by being patient with others.

In Paul's list of the fruit of the Spirit in Galatians 5:22–23, "peace" follows "joy." But the quality that follows "peace" is "patience." God's Spirit can enable you to be patient with someone even when he or she is trying to make you upset. You can just take your stand on the peace that is deep within your soul. The armored boots of peace will hold you steady and strong and keep you patient with others.

Actionable Intel

The ability to love others with God's supernatural peace and patience comes from realizing just how much God loves us. Read Ephesians 3:17–19, and realize you've been given enough love to share.

Cool Under Pressure

*We always carry the death of Jesus in our body,
so that the life of Jesus may also be revealed
in our body.* —*2 Corinthians 4:10*

Recon

Cool under pressure. That's how we like our movie heroes. When pushed to the edge, surrounded by the enemy, and seemingly all out of options, they're still able to think on their feet, answer the challenge, keep their cool, and stay in control.

How do they do it?

The apostle Paul said we can *all* be like that. "Pressured in every way but not crushed . . . perplexed but not in despair . . . persecuted but not abandoned . . . struck down but not destroyed" (2 Corinthians 4:8–9). That's not because we're in the pretend world of make-believe movie stars, but because we've actually received Christ and His gospel into our hearts. He is the "treasure" inside these "jars of clay" (that's *us)* that gives us the cool-under-pressure power of His peace and confidence (v. 7 NIV).

The gospel in you—the "life of Jesus" in you—can make others look at you and think, *How does he do it? How does she do it?*

It's only because of what *God* can do.

Actionable Intel

Read 2 Corinthians 4:6, which comes directly before some of the verses in today's devotional. Notice how the power God uses to save you is the same power He used when He created the universe. So never think there's *anything* your God cannot do in you.

Hold On Tight

Even there Your hand will lead me; Your right
hand will hold on to me. —Psalm 139:10

Recon

If you saw someone falling to earth from a moving airplane, you'd expect to hear screams of raw panic. In reality, however, that's not what usually happens, even with first-time skydivers. Instead their reactions are usually either silence or shrieks of exhilaration.

The reason for their reaction is simple. They're strapped to a skilled instructor who knows *exactly* what he or she is doing. So the first-time jumpers have *peace*.

Spiritual peace comes from spiritual confidence too. And spiritual confidence comes from knowing that even if the worst is happening—even if you're scared to death from what you're seeing, sensing, and feeling—you're being guided and held steady in God's capable, all-wise hands.

So inch those shoes of peace to the edge of the launch point. Enjoy the thrill of what awaits you. Be ready for the chance to feel new waves of excitement in your spiritual journey. And jump.

Don't worry. He's *got* you.

Actionable Intel

Tell yourself today that you're not going to be held back by feelings of fear or dread. You're going to trust the arms of God that are wrapped tightly around you.

Prayer for Peace

The LORD lift up His countenance on you, and
give you peace. —Numbers 6:26 NASB

Recon

As with the other pieces of spiritual armor and weaponry, I want you to join me in praying—specifically, strategically—that God would fit you snugly in the boots of peace and that you'll remember to walk in them proudly every single day of your life.

Today's verse from Numbers 6 is a good place to start. It's the closing line to a short, three-line blessing that God instructed the Israelite priests to pray over the people. It goes like this:

"The LORD bless you, and keep you; the LORD make His face shine on you, and be gracious to you; the LORD lift up His countenance on you, and give you peace" (Numbers 6:24–26 NASB).

He's already done all this for you through the sacrifice of Jesus and the gift of His Holy Spirit. But you continually need Him to do all this—day in and day out—so you can stand against the tricky temptations and discouraging attacks of the enemy.

So you can walk in peace.

Actionable Intel

Personalize this prayer for yourself, for your family members, for your pastor, for your friends. Or create another prayer, based on other Scriptures and what you've been learning about God's peace.

Sending the Right Message

His intent was that now, through the church, the manifold wisdom of God should be made known to the rulers and authorities in the heavenly realms. —*Ephesians 3:10* NIV

Recon

Have you ever seen a commercial on television and not even known what it was about? Maybe the images looked pretty or exciting, but you still couldn't tell what product was being advertised.

Christians who can't get along are probably the most confusing commercial message that could ever be presented to the world. We say we're loving and caring and compassionate and Christlike, and yet we're fighting with each other. We say we love God, but there is no love expressed one to another.

When we truly live out the gospel with one another, when we allow His Spirit to lead us into peaceful unity and forgiveness, we not only paint a much clearer picture for the world to see. The effects also reach into "heavenly realms" and force our enemy to see the power of God turning enemies into friends, turning arguments into fun and family dinners.

Let's have our own fun by making him sit down and watch that.

Actionable Intel

Think of another Christian you know who, for whatever reason, just hits you the wrong way. As an act of grateful worship to God—and as an insult to the enemy—try doing something on purpose to befriend and be nice to this person.

Like Some More?

*He kept giving them to His disciples to set
before the people. —Mark 6:41*

Recon

I would love to have been there the day Jesus fed five thousand people with a little boy's sack lunch. And, actually, there were five thousand *men,* the Bible says, "besides women and children" (Matthew 14:21). So there might have been ten thousand, fifteen thousand, or *more.*

But although we can't *be* there, let's allow today's verse to take us there. When Jesus said His blessing over the five loaves and two fish, it wasn't as though—*poof!*— two mini-mountains of bread and sea bass just magically appeared. The people would have mobbed it! What actually happened is that Jesus just kept "giving them" more, as they needed it. And there was always enough. More than enough.

When you step out on God's Word by faith—to obey Him, to follow Him—you can be sure He will keep giving His power and provision to you. As you need it. And there will always be enough. More than enough.

Actionable Intel

See it for yourself today. Choose to be obedient to what you know to be true from His Word, even if it makes you look funny, even if you don't feel like it or think you can do it. Watch Him give you what you need to do it . . . while you're doing it.

Foundation Matters

*If anyone builds on that foundation with gold, silver,
costly stones, wood, hay, or straw, each one's work
will become obvious. —1 Corinthians 3:12–13*

Recon

My husband and I recently got a new bed. And unlike our
old one, which stood way up off the ground, this new bed
frame is built a lot lower. On our high bed we didn't need
box springs to keep the mattress raised. Now we do.

The first night, we couldn't get a good night's sleep.
Even though the mattress was the same, something about
adding the box springs—changing the foundation—changed
the way it felt to sleep on it. We didn't think changing what
was *under* the mattress would matter, but it did.

Foundation matters.

The habits and activities that form the "foundation"
of your lifestyle change your ability to function well in all
areas of your life. Right now, for instance, you've chosen
to make reading devotions a regular part of your life. Keep
doing this no matter where life takes you, okay? Because
reading the Bible, talking to God, and obeying Him will
keep you from the things that make people's lives feel
restless and without peace. Be careful not to change these
foundations. They matter. They impact your life in more
ways than you can imagine.

Actionable Intel

What are the foundational anchors you intend to keep
in your life each day? Write them down, and commit to
keeping them faithfully. Ask someone to help hold you
accountable to them.

Nothing but the Truth

Continue in what you have learned and
firmly believed. —2 *Timothy 3:14*

Recon

From the minute you wake up and walk out the door every morning, lies are swirling all around you. Lies about your appearance, your significance, and your value. Lies about what's best for you to think about and concentrate on. Lies about the way certain people feel toward you and how you're supposed to interpret what they say or do. Or what they don't say or don't do.

Lies.

That's why you always need the truth. The truth of what the Bible says.

So sometime between that minute when you wake up and the minute when you walk out the door, start off each morning with a truth from the Bible—a breakfast of wholesome, great-tasting truth that'll stick to your ribs, making you not quite as eager to bite at the first deceptive thought that floats through your head. A few early doses of the Word will help you be better prepared for the whole day.

Actionable Intel

It's not as important how much of the Bible you read as how much of an impact it makes on you. So you can choose one passage per week—or even per month—to write down, think about, and pray over each day so you can receive the truth you need.

Stand Up Straight

*He said to me, "Son of man, stand up
on your feet."—Ezekiel 2:1*

Recon

Has your mama ever told you to stand up straight? To
stop slouching? To sit up? To hold your head up? To put
those shoulders back and not slump around all draggy
and droopy?

The main part of your body that helps you do that
(you *are* going to do that, aren't you?) isn't really your
head and neck and shoulders. Those are merely the end
of the chain. They are just the upstanding result of what
actually begins somewhere else in your body. The real
energy behind a straighter, stronger posture comes from
your core. Remember us talking about your core? It's
your gut. Your stomach muscles. Flex those into action,
and that's what makes you stand out with a nice, strong,
confident, noticeably different kind of posture.

The belt of truth works the same way. Buckle it
around your middle, and every other area of your life will
naturally grow taller and stronger.

Actionable Intel

Practice standing up straighter in front of a mirror. Why is
just lifting your head not enough? What do you feel, and
what do you see, when you tighten those core muscles?

Well Within Reach

*I have set before you life and death, blessing
and curse. Choose life so that you and your
descendants may live. —Deuteronomy 30:19*

Recon

As the children of Israel were preparing to enter the land
of Canaan, Moses told them what they could expect in
this new place. More important, he told them about the
war they could expect within their own hearts. A war of
choices. Whether to obey the God who had given them
this promised land, or to follow their natural desires into
laziness, sin, and idolatry.

The enemy wants you to think you *have* no choice.
Or that the choice to follow God is way more trouble and
effort than you should expect of yourself.

But, no, Moses said: "This command that I give you
today is certainly not too difficult or beyond your reach"
(Deuteronomy 30:11). They didn't need to do anything
heroic or superhuman. In fact, this choice was simple,
achievable, and well within their reach as God's children.

Righteousness is always a choice you can make by the
power of God's Spirit who lives in you.

Actionable Intel

Write down the one or two main areas where you struggle
most with sin. Under each, list two or three very practical,
very specific choices you can make to turn this sin into
obedience. Ask God to help you put these ideas into
practice—one choice at a time.

Keep Building

By faith Noah . . . built an ark to deliver
his family. —Hebrews 11:7

Recon

The odds were stacked against Noah. First, the thoughts of those around him were "nothing but evil all the time" (Genesis 6:5). Second, God had told him to build an ark—an unknown object that would take 120 years to complete. Third, the reason for needing an ark in the first place was that God intended to bring rain. Rain? Noah had never seen rain. No clue what it was.

So try to get into Noah's mind and consider what he must have been thinking, out there hammering day after day, year after year. Think about how discouraged and doubtful he may have felt on some days, wondering whether or not following God's command was really worth all this trouble.

Living a life of faith is often like this. But when you choose to trust God anyway and do what He says despite the discouragement and doubt the enemy may heap on you, you'll reap the benefits just like Noah and his family did.

So keep building that boat, my friend. The next generations are counting on you.

Actionable Intel

Ask an adult for permission to look online for a scale model of what Noah's ark might have looked like. Let it remind you—in large detail—just how much power God can give a person to stay faithful to His Word.

Unpacking

With your minds ready for action . . . set your
hope completely on the grace to be brought to you at
the revelation of Jesus Christ. —1 Peter 1:13

Recon

Recently I was looking for a particular T-shirt and couldn't find it anywhere. Not in my dresser. Not in my closet. Not in the laundry pile. Nowhere . . . until I looked in the suitcase I hadn't unpacked from my last trip, and— *voila!*—there it was. Think of the hassle I could've avoided if I'd only unpacked.

Now I realize the wise thing to do when you get home from a trip is to unpack your bags and put everything away. But you know what? My family and I don't always do that. Just sayin'.

And honestly, many people don't do it with their salvation either. They drop it off on their way in the door from church on Sunday, and then don't go looking for it again until the following week.

Save yourself some frantic searches for peace and confidence. Keep the truth of your salvation unpacked, easy to reach, quickly remembered, ready to wear.

Actionable Intel

Consider doing a ten-, twenty-, or thirty-day trial, where every day you discover *one* thing in the Bible that has to do with salvation and tell your parent or a sibling what you've unpacked today. (Ephesians 1 is a great place to start your search.)

Precision Attack

I will attack him while he is weak and weary,
throw him into a panic, and all the people
with him will scatter. —2 Samuel 17:2

Recon

King David's son, Absalom, had risen up in full revolt against his father. He was determined to bring him down and seize the throne of Israel by force. But David, though a little past his prime by this point, was still a mighty opponent. He couldn't be defeated easily.

Absalom's advisors told him if he planned his attack for a moment when his father was "weak and weary"—too tired or unprepared to fight back—then he'd have a fighting chance.

The same strategy is used against you. Why else do you think your worst temptations tend to strike when you're the most vulnerable—when you're tired, when you're loaded with homework, when you're upset with someone or disappointed about something? Just a lucky guess on your enemy's part? I don't think so.

His attacks against you (and the timing of them) are not mere coincidence. That's why your prayers for God's protection and your awareness of the enemy's strategy need to be just as deliberate.

Actionable Intel

Try charting the usual circumstances when you feel the most tempted toward sin. What patterns do you see? What kinds of situations ought to make your spiritual antennas go up?

Still Here

Then the word of the LORD came to
Jonah a second time. —*Jonah 3:1*

Recon

You remember Jonah? Jonah and the big fish? Jonah was a guy who didn't want to hear the truth. Didn't want to do what God said. Didn't like how God had chosen to do things or what He was inviting Jonah to do along with Him.

So he paid a dear price for his refusal to buckle himself into the ride God wanted to take him on. He spent a three-day nightmare inside the stinky digestive tract of some big, hungry fish.

But when Jonah miraculously (and quite grossly) was set free from his watery grave, guess what was there to meet him on shore? The same truth of God's message, spoken to him "a second time." As in, *Why don't we see if we can try this again, Jonah? Without the fish?*

God's truth doesn't change. His Word stays the same. We either get on board with it, or we go overboard without it.

Actionable Intel

Compare Jonah 1:1 (pre-fish) with Jonah 3:1 (post-fish). Notice what's exactly the same about God's message both times. If anything's changed, we hope it's Jonah, right? And we hope it's us too.

Alien Landing

Beloved, I urge you as aliens and strangers to abstain from fleshly lusts which wage war against the soul. —1 Peter 2:11 NASB

Recon

"Aliens?" Is that what he called us?

Peter wasn't talking about, you know, *alien* aliens. But I guess it's sort of true. We actually *do* come from another place. That's why our lives can look different compared to people whose only home, whose only real choices, are stuck in this visible world.

So I say, embrace the strangeness. Let them wonder. When they see you standing up for another kid at school, when they see you refusing to participate in things that are wrong and harmful, let them wonder what planet you come from. Let them see the difference—the kind that shows up in your actions. Let them see the look of a fighter who isn't intimidated by things that "war against your soul."

People pay good money to go to the movies and see aliens on the big screen. How about letting them see one who sits in the desk right next to them every day?

Actionable Intel

What are some things you could do today that would be "alien" to this culture?

Come Clean

You will not be able to stand against your enemies until you remove what is set apart. —Joshua 7:13

Recon

Israel had conquered mighty Jericho when the walls came tumbling down. Next on their list was the sleepy little town of Ai. With Jericho in ruins behind them, Ai should have been a piece of cake.

Instead, the men of Ai ran the Israelites out of town, killing them as they went. We find out later exactly why: one of the Israelite men had disobeyed the Lord. During their march through Jericho, he had snatched some prize possessions to keep for himself rather than dedicate them to God. He'd hidden them in his tent, but now his secret had come to light. There would be no peace among Israel—and no victory over even their puniest enemy—until peace was restored through confession and repentance.

The same truth holds true for us. God has made peace with us. He has given us power and armor and the promise of His protection. But holding on to our sins will always keep us from fighting and winning the way we could.

Actionable Intel

The enemy talks us into believing that secret sins don't matter and that no one will ever really know. But he's wrong. Throwing out the garbage makes room for blessing. Today, ask the Lord to forgive you for the sins that you may have been trying to keep hidden. If there is someone else you need to come clean with, do it as soon as you can.

Good Morning

*Satisfy us in the morning with your faithful
love so that we may shout with joy and be
glad all our days.* —Psalm 90:14

Recon

The reason God demands faith from you is really because
He loves you. His power is unending, and the potential
He's put in you is huge. He can do so much, but He wants
you to experience it *with Him.*

The enemy tries to make a life of faith look like a
problem instead of a gift. *He's* the one who makes it feel
like a chore, or a burden, or a big hassle.

But really faith is not demanding something of you
that will make life harder. It's an invitation to make life
better. More rich and full and satisfying. Faith is how God
calls you out the door of mundane living and into the
joy of truly knowing Him. He calls you to walk in unseen
places that can take you to great accomplishments and
abundance every day for the rest of your life.

Actionable Intel

Tomorrow morning, when you wake up, ask God to help
you use today's verse and today's thought to make faith
not look frightening or boring or unimportant. Ask Him to
help you see it as a joy and privilege.

In-House Treasure

*That you may know the hope to which he has
called you, the riches of his glorious inheritance
in his holy people.* —*Ephesians 1:18* NIV

Recon

Being a Christian means you are a child of God. Which means you've been given a "glorious inheritance." A new identity. Divine power. God-given strength. Hope. Grace. Forgiveness. Everything. All of it. It's all yours.

And yet one of the Devil's deceptions is to make us think of ourselves as nothing more than slaves. Working for a distant, detached owner who doesn't really want a relationship with us and who's probably angry with us most of the time. The Devil wants to convince you that your Father isn't really interested in your well-being—just in what you can do for Him.

So let's clear the air here with a fresh breeze of gospel truth. You're not a sniveling servant who has to work hard to gain approval, hoping someday to be accepted as more. You're already a child of God who's been given the promise of incredible blessing. You can walk into every day with confidence, knowing that you are already enough and that you are already loved.

Actionable Intel

Create a blessing jar, where you collect specific, written reminders of God's goodness toward you. Add to it as you learn new things about your salvation or as you experience His blessing in your life. Enjoy taking the written blessings out and looking at them. Enjoy your treasure.

Sole Supplier

Who do I have in heaven but You? And I desire
nothing on earth but You. —Psalm 73:25

Recon

I've often wondered how anyone survives who doesn't have Jesus as his or her Savior. I think *you* have probably lived long enough already to know that what we can get on this earth—what is *seen*—is simply not enough to keep us at peace. Without real trust in God that provides us with *unseen* storehouses of peace for the visible needs of life, this journey will be long and hard and nothing else.

The world promises us peace—from achievement, from popularity, from dangerous habits and the need for new stuff. But this hole in our hearts—in *all* of our hearts—can only be filled by relationship with Jesus Christ.

Nothing else is shaped to fit.

Save yourself some time.

And stop looking for it.

Actionable Intel

"If I could only have . . ." What? What are the two or three fill-in-the-blanks that most commonly complete this sentence in your life? You can *pray* for them. There's probably nothing *wrong* with them. But if God chooses not to give them, you apparently don't need them.

Could We Do This Later?

We've worked hard all night all night long
and caught nothing! But at Your word,
I'll let down the nets. —Luke 5:5

Recon

Peter was tired. And probably upset. All night, no fish, and now nothing to sell. There was nothing to like about this whole situation.

But this man—this Jesus—had told him to "put out into deep water and let down your nets for a catch" (Luke 5:4). And somehow Peter trusted Jesus' word more than his own knowledge of the sea or even his own craving for breakfast and sleep.

Peter trusted Jesus enough to dirty up the nets he'd just cleaned. He trusted Him enough to demand his sore, aching muscles to row out from shore to a place where he knew the fish weren't biting. And in the end, he trusted Jesus enough to follow Him from that point forward, wherever He might lead, for the rest of His days.

When faith tells you to push through your tiredness, you never know what God might do next.

Actionable Intel

Read the rest of this story in Luke 5:6–11. Why would going home and going to bed (and ignoring what Jesus had told him to do) have been the biggest mistake Peter ever made?

Prayer Without Words

We do not know how to pray as we should, but the Spirit Himself intercedes for us with groanings too deep for words. —Romans 8:26 NASB

Recon

I've got a few friends who have bubbly, outgoing personalities, and they enjoy talking to others as much as possible. But sometimes, when life is tough, even the most talkative people can clam up when it's time to pray. They just aren't sure how to pray or what to pray. Even though they try, they can't seem to come up with the right words to say.

But when you really need to pray, and yet you don't know what to say, you're actually in the perfect place for God to hear you and respond—because the Spirit of God, who came to live in you when God saved you, takes the silent words of your heart and translates them into words that only God can understand.

So don't worry when you are struggling through your prayers. When they come from a heart that trusts in, depends on, and calls out to God, it's everything He wants to hear.

Actionable Intel

When you pray today, don't get hung up on the words. Just talk to Him from the honest, open depths of your heart. The Spirit will do the translating.

Two Places at One Time

Set your minds on things above, not on earthly things. . . . Your life is now hidden with Christ in God. —Colossians 3:2–3 NIV

Recon

I love Skype. Just flick on a computer, push a couple of buttons, and you can talk to *and see* the people you love. When I'm traveling for work and my sons are back at home, we use Skype a lot. I dial them in . . . and there they are! They're not *here* with me. I'm not *there* with them. But still, we're together. Through this amazing technology, we're in two places at one time.

And that's sort of what being saved is like. We're here. On earth. We've got things to be responsible for, work that needs doing. But through salvation, we can dial into heavenly places and receive all their benefits. Our salvation allows us to be with Jesus in heavenly places. Physically we might not be at home—in heaven—but we have access to all that our real home offers us, and we can remain consistently connected to our Savior. We're always closer to Him than we think.

Actionable Intel

Every time you stop to pray today, don't let your enemy convince you that your words aren't going anywhere. Remember what God's Word says: you and Jesus are right here together.

The Whole Truth?

It is not the one commending himself who is approved, but the one the Lord commends. —2 Corinthians 10:18

Recon

Paul, as you may remember, had been a bitter foe of Christians before he became a best friend of Christians. People often treated him with suspicion. Or thought he was bossy. Or told him he was wrong. Some even wanted him dead.

So in 2 Corinthians 10—as in other places among his writings—he was trying to defend himself against people who claimed he was a pretender, a manipulator, a liar, or worse. But in the end, he basically said, "Look, it doesn't really matter what I say; it doesn't really matter what you say; all that matters is what God says."

All that matters is the truth.

Your worth is never based on what somebody else says or thinks, whether behind your back or right in front of your face. You are loved, accepted, and approved by the same God who created all the galaxies in the entire universe.

So who cares what anybody else thinks? And that's just the truth.

Actionable Intel

Read Ephesians 1:3–6. How much stock do you need to put into what other people say or think about you?

Keep the Line Open

*If I had cherished sin in my heart, the Lord
would not have listened.* —Psalm 66:18

Recon

Sin has many terrible consequences that the enemy tries
to keep you from knowing about until it's too late. And
maybe the worst thing, of all the bad things, is that sin
creates distance in your relationship with God.

Not because *God* puts it there; our sinful nature puts
it there.

Your praying is where you really feel the gap between
the two of you. God wants your conversations with Him
to be open and encouraging. Comforting and uplifting.
Helpful and relaxing, with you knowing there's nothing
standing between you. But as long as sin is given room to
nestle in our hearts, it causes a wall. We're not as free to
talk. We're hiding things that we don't want Him to see.
(As if we really could.)

Among the great tricks of sin is that we think we can
keep it up without paying a price. But when sin leads us
to hang back from staying as close as possible to God, it's
costing us something we can't live without.

Actionable Intel

Come before God in prayer today with nothing to hide.
Tell Him all about your sins so that you can enjoy free-
flowing relationship with Him. He is "faithful and
righteous to forgive us our sins and to cleanse us from all
unrighteousness" (1 John 1:9).

Smile!

In any and all circumstances I have learned the secret of being content—whether well fed or hungry, whether in abundance or in need.—Philippians 4:12

Recon

When I was sixteen, I went on a mission trip to Haiti. A group of local kids were always hanging around our work site, and I was overcome by what I witnessed. I'd never seen such poverty. Their clothes—what little clothes they wore—were old, torn, and shabby. They had bugs in their hair. They were obviously underfed. Starving. But they were almost always . . . smiling.

I made a special connection with one of them, a girl named Manette. Years later, in fact, after a devastating earthquake struck their island nation, I worked through various contacts to try to find her, to see if she'd survived. Finally I received an e-mail, along with an attachment of a current picture, confirming she was alive and well. Before the image of her face even fully loaded on my screen, the first thing I noticed—again—was that wide, beautiful smile of hers.

Manette's smile still reminds me that joy is not dependent on money, security, good health, or anything else. A smile is just a simple testimony of a deep-rooted faith and trust.

Actionable Intel

No matter what you face in life today . . . *smile*.

The Case for Church

Let us be concerned about one another in order to promote love and good works, not staying away from our worship meetings. —Hebrews 10:24–25

Recon

At the time when this verse was written, not everyone saw much need or use for church activity. But the reason for being in church back then—like the reason for being in church now—is not because we *ought* to. It's because we *need* to.

The church is made up of people who not only *have* faith but who want to *live* their faith. And that makes the church sort of a shield-building factory and fix-it shop. We come together with all our nicks and bruises—we share and sing and worship and pray—then we send each other back out into the world with our shields reinforced and ready for action. Loved, encouraged, and ready for "good works" of faith.

The enemy wants you to think that church is too boring or stuffy or time-consuming, that you have better stuff to do and you won't really get anything out of it. Because he knows that without it, your shield will never be any stronger than you can make it and keep it yourself.

Actionable Intel

Call and talk to somebody who goes to your church (or some other church). Ask them what they think are the most important benefits they get from being a part of their local church.

Written on Your Heart

Weren't our hearts ablaze within us while He was talking with us on the road and explaining the Scriptures to us?—Luke 24:32

Recon

To some people, the Bible is just a book. But that's not how two men traveling to the ancient town of Emmaus would describe it—not after meeting Jesus out there and hearing Him speak. As He talked to them about the Scriptures (Luke 24:27), they realized something was happening inside. They felt inspired. They felt enlightened. Their hearts burned. They began making connections between stray thoughts and questions that had never fit together before.

The Bible says you have been given an "anointing" through the Holy Spirit and through the gospel to understand what God is saying in His Word. "His anointing teaches you about all things and is true and is not a lie" (1 John 2:27).

So when you read the Bible, you aren't just reading words on a page anymore. God's Spirit brings them to life so you can live them in *your* life.

Actionable Intel

The more you read your Bible, the more you'll experience this. God will strike you with the truth of a word, phrase, or idea that matches up *exactly* with something that's going on in your life. Be watching for it. And when it happens, be sure to write down what He shows you.

Coming into Wealth

Now if we are children, then we are heirs—heirs of God and co-heirs with Christ. —Romans 8:17 NIV

Recon

I was visiting in the home of a couple who, for many years, have worked as Christian camp counselors. It's not exactly the kind of job you choose if you want to make the big bucks.

But their home—it was stunning. Beautiful. Positioned on the banks of a scenic lake. Large and roomy. Crafted with quality detail.

They told me during my visit that this gorgeous home wasn't something they could afford, not on a camp salary. But one of their parents had left them a sizable inheritance. That's why they were able to live there and keep doing the work they loved. All because of a special gift they'd received.

As a child of God, you too have been given an inheritance from your Father. A spiritual inheritance. Rich and grand. More than you can imagine . . . so that even while you're living here, doing what you do here, you can *think and live* like someone who's been given eternal riches.

Because you *have*.

Actionable Intel

Go into this new day realizing you've received an enormous inheritance of blessing from your heavenly Father. How does this one thing change everything?

Sitting Pretty

"Sit at My right hand until I make Your enemies Your footstool."—Psalm 110:1

Recon

In ancient times, being "seated" was the symbolic position of a king whose army had already been victorious in battle. Instead of standing, pacing, worrying himself to death, he would park himself on his throne as a visible statement of his complete and utter triumph.

He sat down . . . because victory was already his.

Think of what this means for you! The resurrected Jesus—your King—is *sitting* beside the Father in heaven. This is not an image of His disinterest in your struggles or His unwillingness to get up and come help. It's simply the contented confidence of Someone who's already beaten His enemies and is just waiting for them to finally get the message.

So even better than realizing you're spiritually present with Christ in "heavenly places" is knowing what He's doing up there. *He's sitting.* "After making purification for sins, He sat down at the right hand of the Majesty on high" (Hebrews 1:3).

He has sat down . . . because He's already won. And now you are "seated" with Him (Ephesians 2:6).

Let's be sure we give our enemy that message loud and clear, every day.

Actionable Intel

Twenty-four-hour challenge: For the next day, every time you feel the enemy tempting you or causing division or stirring up chaos, sit down in a chair (or anywhere) as a symbolic reminder—both to yourself and to the enemy—of the victory that is yours in Christ. At the end of the day, come back here and record how many times you chose to sit.

Wraparound Vision

I have chosen the way of truth; I have set Your
ordinances before me. —Psalm 119:30

Recon

All of us know what we look like from the front. We can see this much in our bathroom mirror. What we can't do is stand outside ourselves and see what we look like from other people's perspectives.

But maybe you've played around before in one of those full-length, triple-panel mirrors, like the ones that are sometimes in the dressing rooms or far corners of department stores. You can look to your right, look to your left and, hey, there's a side view you don't usually see of yourself. With a mirror *behind* you, you can even get the complete 360-degree version of what that new shirt and pair of pants actually look like, from every angle. Because the more mirrors around you, the clearer perspective you get.

Truth is like a good mirror. The more truth around you, the better view you can get on everything.

Actionable Intel

How can you keep reflections of truth in more places all around you?

Help Is on the Way

You are being renewed in the spirit of
your minds. —*Ephesians 4:23*

Recon

In Romans 7, the apostle Paul said this: "I do not understand what I am doing, because I do not practice what I want to do . . . For I do not do the good that I want to do, but I practice the evil that I do not want to do" (vv. 15, 19).

Can you relate to ever feeling that way? Wanting to do what's right, but (doggone it!) still doing what's wrong?

You want proof of the unseen war that's circling around you? There you have it. When you and I deep down *want* to do something, but we strangely feel tugged *away* from doing it, there's no other explanation than the presence of an outside force causing the struggle.

But it's okay—because by putting on the breastplate of righteousness, you can start to see the battle changing in your mind. When you're not sure you can do it, the Holy Spirit is telling you different. Yes, you can—because He is here. Because He is changing you.

Actionable Intel

Praise God in prayer today for being your hero, who comes to your rescue when you're drowning. Not only does He rescue, but He keeps renewing you with the strength to stand taller this time than you stood before. He's your year-round, all-around supplier of righteousness.

Eyes Up Here

You will keep the mind that is dependent on You in perfect peace, for it is trusting in You. —Isaiah 26:3

Recon

"Look at me! Look at me!"

Have you ever heard a kid say that? Or at least *act* like that? Wanting all the attention? Maybe they felt jealous or ignored, so they tried really hard to get people to notice them, whether on the monkey bars or making a long basket during basketball practice. "Watch me! Watch me!"

It can be annoying, right?

The Devil is like that too. Apparently, he's never outgrown the need for attention. He craves the spotlight in your life. He constantly tries to take your attention off God and put it on *him*. In fact, he'd like you fixed on him all day long if he can get you to do it. But in return, he'll do nothing but rob you blind.

God wants your attention as well, but not because He craves it or needs it. The reason *He* wants your attention is because He knows what *you* need—the "perfect peace" He gives to those whose minds stay fixed on Him.

Actionable Intel

Every time you're alone with your thoughts in the next twenty-four hours, deliberately shift your thinking away from what the enemy would want you to think about, and place your thoughts on God—who He is, what He can do, and the relationship you have with Him as His child. This will guarantee you a life of peace.

Do What the Sign Says

*Help me understand Your instruction, and
I will obey it. —Psalm 119:34*

Recon

No Running.

Could it be any plainer? You know what "no" means. You know what "running" means. You know what both words mean when you put them together. It means do anything—walk, sit, or just stand there. Anything but running. *No Running.*

But spend a nice summer afternoon at the family YMCA or community swimming pool, and how many times will you hear the lifeguard's whistle? Followed by some version of these words: *Stop. Running.*

Lots of believers say they want to know God's will, and they wonder if they've got the faith to do it. But enormous faith isn't really required for most of the things God is calling you to do. It's just choosing to be obedient to plain, simple instructions that are spelled out in His Word. Plain as the nose on your face. Plain as the two feet on the end of your own two legs.

As you read God's Word, you'll receive His instruction and guidance. Choose to obey. And God's Himself will empower you to follow through with it.

Actionable Intel

What's something you *know* you shouldn't be doing, but you *are* doing? Instead of continuing to fight with it and fail at it, talk to someone today who can help you with it— someone who can lovingly hold you accountable for being obedient to God.

Let's Move

Determine in your mind and heart to seek the
LORD your God. —1 Chronicles 22:19

Recon

David was old. But his message to the leaders of Israel in 1 Chronicles 22 was based on a truth as new as this morning's sunrise.

God had given the nation "rest on every side" (v. 18). Israel was great in the world, and its future looked bright with David's son Solomon preparing to become king. But even with the rest and peace the people were experiencing— like the rest and peace we've been given in Christ—David challenged them to act decisively and proactively. Instead of lounging and loafing around in their comfort, this was their opportunity to get their minds and hearts in gear to follow hard after God.

Your enemy wants you to adopt the "take it easy" line of thinking. *Sit back. Don't sweat it. What's the big rush here?* But salvation is actually a charge to get busy. To get with it.

Don't sit around, young warrior. Time is short. Set your mind, focus your heart, and pursue God's purpose for you. You'll be glad you did.

Actionable Intel

Read all of 1 Chronicles 22:19. What was David telling the people to "get started building" on? What kind of new building project do you think God is leading *you* to tackle, building on the foundation of your salvation?

Take a Knee

At the name of Jesus every knee will bow—
of those who are in heaven and on earth and
under the earth. —Philippians 2:10

Recon

"In heaven and on earth and under the earth." That pretty much covers everybody, doesn't it? If someone's not *on* the earth, and they're not *above* the earth, and they're not *under* the earth, there's a fairly good chance they don't really exist, right?

So when the time comes, one day in the future, for everything unseen to be peeled back and exposed for exactly what it is, the Bible says not a single knee will be able to support anyone's claim that Jesus isn't Lord of all. And not only will their *knees* bend, but also their *tongues*, pushing out words that some of them never thought they'd be forced to say, confessing that "Jesus Christ is Lord, to the glory of God the Father" (Philippians 2:11).

Jesus might bend down to serve and heal and wash a follower's feet—all because He's so loving and caring and compassionate. But in matters of mastery, He doesn't bend a knee to anyone. On, above, or under the earth.

Actionable Intel

You can pray, of course, in any kind of body position. But find a time and place today where you can drop to your knees, look up from your location "on earth," and praise your God in heaven. In fact, *right now* is as good a time as any!

Truth at All Times

I did not hide Your righteousness in my heart . . . I did not conceal Your constant love and truth. —Psalm 40:10

Recon

When does truth feel the most uncomfortable to you?

Is it when you're under pressure to cave or conform to what somebody else wants you to do? You know what's right. You know what you shouldn't do. *You know the truth.* But it currently seems to be costing you popularity points that you're not sure you want to give up.

Is it when you're on the spot for declaring your loyalty to Christ? Maybe even your Christian friends are backing down, leaving you standing there alone. Why should you be the only one to stand out and be different?

Is it when you're going through a hard time? You're frustrated and upset. You just want to react. To feel sorry for yourself. Not to care. To quit trying. *But you know the truth.* You know God can still make something good come from all this.

Yes, that belt of truth may be pinching you a little, or even a lot. But the reason you wear it is for moments like these. It'll hold you together when you're afraid that you might come apart.

Actionable Intel

When was the last time your faith and belief in God's truth put you in a sticky situation? How did you handle it? What do you wish you would've done differently? What did you do right?

Perfect Makes Practice

You were once darkness, but now you are light in the Lord. Walk as children of light. —Ephesians 5:8

Recon

"Practice makes perfect." Ever heard this phrase? There's actually a nugget of truth in there. The harder you work at something—whether it's playing the piano, perfecting a dance routine, or hitting a fastball—the better you become at doing it.

But in your relationship with God, things are often different. For instance, you don't practice your way to perfection with Him. Since He's already declared you perfectly righteous through your relationship with Jesus, His *perfection* can now inspire you to be better in *practice*.

So in Him, perfect actually makes practice. See the difference?

It's one little difference that makes a huge difference.

Actionable Intel

Do you have a hobby or team sport where you put in a lot of practice? What if you were already perfect at doing it? How different would your practice be?

Peacemakers

"The peacemakers are blessed, for they will be called sons of God."—Matthew 5:9

Recon

The first words of Jesus' Sermon on the Mount (found in Matthew, chapters 5–7) are called the *Beatitudes*. This English term comes from a Latin word meaning "happy" or "blessed." The beatitudes tell us how children of God can experience the good life.

One of those ways is by *peacemaking*. Peacemakers "will be called sons of God." That's because through peacemaking—valuing relationships, being forgiving, loving others—you bear the family resemblance, an unmistakable likeness to God Himself.

Maybe people have told you before that you look like one of your parents, that they see your mother's eyes or your father's smile in you. When you seek to keep the peace with others, you're following in the footsteps of your heavenly Father, who made a way for sinners to be reconciled to Him, "having made peace" through the blood of Jesus' death on the cross (Colossians 1:20).

You rarely look more like God than when you're making peace.

Actionable Intel

Read 2 Corinthians 5:18–21. What "ministry" does Paul say you've been given because of what Christ has done for you? What is one way you can take this ministry seriously in the next twenty-four hours?

No Fear

God has not given us a spirit of fear, but of power and of love and of a sound mind. —2 Timothy 1:7 NKJV

Recon

Fear is one of the enemy's favorite weapons of choice, because fear will make you want to drop your shield and run away.

I'm not talking about healthy fears, the kind that lead you to be careful when necessary, like locking the door when you leave home. I'm talking about *fear.* Constant worry. Can't-sleep-at-night anxiety. Stuff like that.

But God knows this tactic of your enemy's. And He knows it's a bunch of hot air. That's why more than three hundred times in the Bible, He tells His people not to be afraid. "Fear not." "Be ye not afraid." "Do not fear." Look it up. It's everywhere.

You know those times when you're searching high and low for just one verse to tell you what God wants you to do? Well, here's about three hundred of them. And they're all saying the same thing.

Don't. Be. Afraid.

Actionable Intel

Ask your parent if they'll purchase you a plain white pillowcase. Then look up some verses about God's power over fear, and write them in marker on the case. When you lay your head down to sleep at night, you'll be sleeping on God's Word.

What Are You Thinking?

The mind-set of the flesh is death, but the mind-set of the Spirit is life and peace. —Romans 8:6

Recon

Nobody likes to think about death. It's upsetting. It's depressing. Who wants to go around thinking about sad things? Let's think about happy things. Nice things.

And yet every time we think like an unbeliever, we're actually thinking about death. Without realizing it. Every thought that's driven by selfishness—every thought of worry, dread, and unworthiness—every thought of pride or fear or insecurity—even a lot of the thoughts that make us feel good for a little while but are really just satisfying a sinful urge . . .

They're thoughts that lead to death—the death of our joy and our peace. They're death thoughts disguised as normal thoughts.

But you can turn them into thoughts of "life and peace" by setting your mind on the Spirit, by thinking about your salvation.

Why think about death when you can think about the beauty and bounty of life with Christ?

Actionable Intel

Look up Philippians 4:8. List the things that this passage says your mind should be focused on.

Reading Between the Lines

*The word of God is living and effective and sharper
than any double-edged sword. —Hebrews 4:12*

Recon

A lot of people write good books. I'm sure you've got some
favorites yourself. Maybe you've even got a *real* favorite
that you've gone back and read again and again—a second
or a third time. And every time you do, you see new things
in there. You notice details that deepen the story and add
to why you like it so much.

But no other book is like the Bible. Because you don't
just *read* it. It reads *you*. The Holy Spirit is so active within
the Word that He can speak directly to your life through
it. Hebrews 4:12 says it's almost like a surgeon's scalpel,
sharp enough to cut through tight places where nothing
else can reach.

Sometimes you may not like where it's going, what it's
opening you up to hear. But the goal is to bring healing,
not harm. Everything the Spirit drives home is meant to
draw you closer to God.

Actionable Intel

Reading Hebrews 4:12–13, you can feel kind of scared
at what God is looking for by examining you so closely.
But read on through verses 14–16, and you'll see how
He actually just wants to help you live in the freedom of
complete openness with Him.

Never Say Die

Jesus also shared in [flesh and blood], so that through His death He might destroy the one holding the power of death—that is, the Devil. —Hebrews 2:14

Recon

I don't imagine you think about death or dying very often. You're still pretty young. It probably doesn't seem like something to spend time worrying about right now. But whether you've noticed or not, every day's newspaper contains two or three pages of write-ups about the local men and women—and sadly, yes, occasionally even the kids—who've died in the last couple of days.

That's just reality. That's life on a temporary planet. I know it's no fun to hear, but it's the truth. Death really happens.

But Jesus really crushed it—by crushing Satan, the one who thought he could make us be so afraid to die that we'd do anything he wants. And maybe we *would*, if nothing was stronger than death. But Jesus is stronger than death. His love for you is stronger than death. His power in you is stronger than death. And when we (or someone we love who's a Christian) close our eyes on earth, we immediately open them in heaven. So death isn't a disaster after all, like our enemy was hoping it would be.

Actionable Intel

Heaven is real. And death, while sad for those of us who are left behind, is really just a transition to another place. Have you lost a loved one through death? Have any of your friends? How can you make them feel better by gracefully and compassionately sharing the news from today's devotion?

Trust Yourself?

Trust in the LORD *with all your heart, and do not rely on your own understanding.* —*Proverbs 3:5*

Recon

I know what the Disney movies say about "believing in yourself." They're telling you not to feel limited by average expectations. They're telling you to shoot for your dreams, even if everything seems to be working against you. That's good. I can see why we'd all want to cheer for that. Fair enough.

But if "believing in yourself" is all you're going to believe in, you'll have a major problem. Because this "self" we're talking about, both yours *and* mine, is not a hundred percent trustworthy. We sometimes don't even have our *own* best interests in mind. Too often our only concern is the short-term, instant-fix, want-it-now variety.

So without telling you not to keep your hopes and dreams alive, I'm just saying (like the Bible says) not to "rely on your own understanding" . . . except to the extent that *your* understanding is grounded in *God's* understanding.

Actionable Intel

Think of a movie you've seen that champions this "believe in yourself" theme. What are the healthy parts of that message? But what are the problem areas that come from believing only in yourself?

Inside and Out

"On the outside you seem righteous to people, but inside you are full of hypocrisy and lawlessness."—Matthew 23:28

Recon

Here's a little intel for you. If the enemy starts to realize you're beating him on the righteousness front and that the temptations he's trying to trick you with aren't working as well as he planned, he may decide to launch a different kind of attack strategy.

For instance, let's say you've been doing a better job lately of completing your chores without needing to be nagged and reminded, but you're often mad that you have to do them. Maybe you're even making a little extra clanging noise with the garbage cans or the spray bottles, just to be sure everybody knows how you really feel about the whole thing.

Attitude. If Satan can't stop you from doing the right thing and obeying God, he'll at least try weaseling his way into your heart to mess with your motivations and attitudes.

The breastplate you're wearing protects your heart from even *this* devious trick. And as the Holy Spirit, who lives in you, molds you more and more into the image of Christ, you'll find your attitudes becoming more and more like those that honor God.

Actionable Intel

Confess to God in prayer that sometimes you only obey because you know you're supposed to, not because you truly want to. The best way to beat the Devil is by putting these unseen shortcomings out in the open, inviting God to change you on the inside.

No "Go" Shoes?

"You must be dressed for travel, your sandals on your feet, and your staff in your hand."—Exodus 12:11

Recon

During a vacation we took with several other couples, the wives were noticing how much more we'd packed compared with our husbands. One of us said, "I brought so many nice pairs of shoes to match my outfits that I forgot to pack a pair of tennis shoes!" To which one of the men responded, in puzzled amazement, "All those dress shoes? And no go shoes?"

As far back as the exodus of the Israelites from Egypt, God has wanted His people prepared to move into action at His call. To be ready. In our "go shoes."

That's what the "shoes of peace" from Ephesians 6 are designed to be. They're not dress shoes we've been given for the purposes of impressing people. They're working shoes. Action-oriented shoes. They're get-dirty shoes. They're designed to take us into places where peace is missing—where Jesus is needed—and bring His love and peace wherever we go.

Actionable Intel

Where do your spiritual "go shoes" need to take you today? Are you ready?

Cross the Bridge

Underneath are the everlasting arms.
—Deuteronomy 33:27

Recon

Between our home and our ministry office is a rickety little bridge that crosses a deep ravine. Whenever people drive up to it, they nearly always slow down and creep across, afraid it might just fall right out beneath them.

But not me. I sail across it in my heavy car with full confidence. Why? Because I've seen big delivery trucks go back and forth across that bridge almost every day. And if *they're* not heavy enough to collapse it, then what does *my* little car need to worry about?

Living by faith is sort of like crossing a bridge—from the known of *this* side to the unknown of the *other* side. And the truth is, sometimes that bridge of faith can appear pretty shaky.

But our faithful God has been carrying the weight of His promises throughout all of history, so we never need to wonder if He can handle the pressure of our total trust. We can just have faith and move. With no worries. He'll always hold us up.

Actionable Intel

Turn to Deuteronomy 7:9. Write it on a separate piece of paper or in the journal at the back of this book. You might want to memorize it too. It's one of those verses you can carry throughout your whole life.

Big Baby

Don't be childish in your thinking, but be infants in regard to evil and adult in your thinking. —1 Corinthians 14:20

Recon

I'm glad you're taking more responsibility for yourself. I'm glad you're maturing in a lot of ways. I'm glad you're making a commitment to read this devotional and spend time with God in His Word and in prayer.

That's really grown-up of you. I hope there are some people in your life who are celebrating that.

But there's one area where God actually *wants* you to be a baby. And to *stay* a baby for life. He never wants you to grow up in your knowledge of sin and evil.

Babies can't read. *So don't read about it.* Babies can't talk. *Don't talk about it.* Babies can't walk. *Don't walk toward it.* Babies can't process a lot of information. *Don't get curious about it.*

If you're going to be ignorant somewhere, just be ignorant about sin. It'll be one of the smartest decisions you'll make every day.

Actionable Intel

Is there something you know more about than you should? What can you change about the people you're hanging around, or maybe the music and media you access, that will keep you from going any deeper into sin?

Worked Up for Nothing

*The Son of God was revealed for this purpose:
to destroy the Devil's works.* —1 John 3:8

Recon

Let's review just a second what we've learned about the Devil in our devotional so far. Our enemy—disarmed, disgraced. Our enemy—utterly overruled. Our enemy—completely mastered. Our enemy—his main weapon (death) rendered powerless by Jesus' eternal life.

Wow. That's some total domination right there. I'd say the sound you hear rising from the enemy camp—the noise he hopes will strike fear in your heart—is actually a veiled cry for help. He's whipped. And he knows it full well.

Because that's why Jesus came to the earth: "to destroy the Devil's works." And what Jesus comes to do, Jesus *does*. Make no mistake about that.

So while your enemy is working hard to suffocate you with sin, with insecurity, with fear, with doubt, with despair, always remember he's getting worked up for nothing. His works are no good here. Jesus has worked it so that nothing can ever defeat you.

So don't give the enemy the pleasure of taking you for even a short ride in the car of rebellion or lies or discouragement. Say no to him, and keep your eyes on Jesus.

Actionable Intel

Write down the things you'll need to be prepared to say no to Satan about in the next twenty-four hours. After you make your list, ask the Lord to give you the courage to follow through on it.

Calm Down

Don't let the sun go down on your
anger. —Ephesians 4:26

Recon

Have you ever heard this verse before—about not letting "the sun go down on your anger"? What you *might* think when you hear it is that God is telling you never to get mad. But if you'll get out your Bible and read the first part of the verse, you'll see where it says, "Be angry and do not sin." *Be angry?* Am I hearing that right?

Yeah. There are things to be angry about. Not everything, but getting mad can sometimes be okay. It can even be the best, right response under the circumstance. (Bet you didn't expect to read *that* in your devotions.)

But when anger simmers and lingers and stews overnight—over days—that's how it stops being a potential jolt of reality that helps correct an unfair situation. Instead, it becomes something that divides us from each other, breaking relationships and crippling our hearts. And no child of God needs to be down with that.

Actionable Intel

God gives us a number of pictures in the sky that help remind us of His truth. And one of them—the sunset—can be our reminder to end each day with our anger put to bed. When you see the sun go down tonight (or tomorrow), what else do you need to send over the horizon with it?

Controlling the Traffic

Do not be conformed to this age, but be transformed by the renewing of your mind, so that you may discern what is the good, pleasing, and perfect will of God. —Romans 12:2

Recon

Thoughts constantly run through your head. All day and even all night. Ideas, opinions, suggestions, little imaginary conversations.

Some of those ideas are coming from your enemy. He's trying to direct you toward sin, toward selfishness, toward wasting your time and being irresponsible. He's hoping to convince you that taking God seriously is more than anyone should expect of you, that it will only end up making you look weird or cause problems you don't really want.

But you can quiet those confusing, condemning thoughts—by surrounding yourself with the truth of Scripture and by always obeying what it says. The more you listen to God's Spirit inside you, the easier you'll be able to tell where all these negative transmissions are coming from.

Listening and following. It's how spiritual warriors keep their minds sharp and focused.

Actionable Intel

Every time you notice a thought today that sounds like a lie or feels like temptation, turn it into a prayer, asking God to take full control of what's happening in your mind . . . so that He can have full control of your heart.

All-Terrain Vehicle

*Therefore we will not be afraid, though the
earth trembles and the mountains topple into
the depths of the seas. —Psalm 46:2*

Recon

You and I cannot always control the kind of ground we're forced to walk on.

One of your parents or grandparents, for example, maybe even one of your siblings or best friends, might become sick and need serious surgery or medical treatment. Your family, whether through a job change or financial difficulty, might need to move to another neighborhood, another city or state—a whole new world of change and starting over.

None of these kinds of changes are easy to deal with. They're hard on your emotions, on your relationships, on your faith, on just about everything. The only two things you can really count on at times like these is that, one, your enemy will try to take advantage of the situation, hoping to worm his love for chaos, doubt, bitterness, and hatred into your heart. But two, God's faithful love and care is always there. He will hear your prayers and be there to help you make it over any bumpy ground you travel in life.

Actionable Intel

Think of God's peace as being an off-road vehicle, a four-wheeler, able to navigate the bumpiest, bounciest terrain. The shock absorbers of peace keep you moving forward even when the road gets tough. Today, ask the Lord to give you His peace throughout everything you'll face.

Come On In

Let us approach the throne of grace
with boldness. —Hebrews 4:16

Recon

I don't know what your typical mood or temperament is. You might be quiet, calm, and level-headed. Or maybe you're loud, extroverted, and headstrong. But no matter what your general personality may be, there's *one* thing— and *one* place—where all of us can afford to be **BOLD**.

And that's in *prayer*.

When Jesus came into your heart, He came bringing "boldness and confident access" to God, made available to you through your "faith in Him" (Ephesians 3:12). The Devil, of course, works hard convincing you that you're too sinful and too unimportant to think you can just walk into God's presence and expect Him to hear you. But not only are you welcome to enter, you can also be sure (according to the rest of today's verse) that you can walk out of there with new mercy and grace and all the help you need for all the things you face.

Actionable Intel

When you pray today, pray with the boldness He's given you. It's what He wants from you. That's the kind of faith He can do something with.

Brain Change

As he thinks within himself,
so he is.—Proverbs 23:7 NASB

Recon

Scientific discoveries of the brain are catching up with what God's Word has said all along: the way we think creates ripple effects that stretch deeply into our lives.

One particular scientist I know—a neuroscientist—can use brain scans to prove how a person can change his actual brain tissue by thinking healthier thoughts. Dark, little toxic branches can be corrected and reformed within the person's brain when he regularly purifies his thought patterns.

Pretty amazing stuff. But really no surprise to those who've gotten in the daily habit of wearing their helmet of salvation.

If you're not happy with what's been running through your mind lately, reach for a solution that could retrain your brain. Strap on the Word of God and the truth of what He's done for you in Christ, and you'll feel like a whole new person.

Actionable Intel

Retrain your brain. Choose three truths that align with God's Word that you will intentionally center your thoughts around today.

Power Nap

*Knowing the time, it is already the hour for you
to wake up from sleep.* —Romans 13:11

Recon

I love to sleep, don't you? Take a rainy Saturday morning, after being up late on Friday night. Maybe you hear your mom or dad awake, starting the coffee, frying some bacon in the skillet. You think about getting up, but the covers are so warm and your eyes are so tired, and the next thing you know . . .

It's two hours later.

That's totally fine for rainy Saturday mornings or holidays, but we must not ever take a break or a day off from standing guard against the enemy. Stay spiritually sharp and alert, even on the weekends. In fact, the enemy is banking on the probability that he can catch you napping, not noticing he's around.

His tricks and temptations work best when you're not suspecting him. So, yes, get your shut-eye. Take a vacation from homework or sports practice. But make sure you never take a vacation from God's Word, from prayer, and from staying watchful for the Devil's activity. He needs to know you've always got an eye on him.

Actionable Intel

What or who helps you get up in the morning for school? Your parents? Your alarm clock? Who can you ask or what can you use to help you stay *spiritually* awake?

The Fine Print

Doesn't the ear test words as the palate
tastes food?—Job 12:11

Recon

When I was a kid, there was this company that offered to send you twelve of your favorite handpicked record albums (big vinyl LPs, which I see they're starting to make again)—all for a penny apiece. Twelve cents. Plus shipping. For more than a hundred songs.

Good deal, huh? Except that as part of the offer, buried in the fine print, you were also signing up for a two-year contract where you were required to buy *more* records—*from them*—at much higher prices than you could buy in the store.

Wasn't such a good deal after all.

The stuff your enemy tries to sell you is a lot like that. Sounds good. Sounds *great*. Big fun. Low cost. No obligation.

But always read the fine print. Expose every point and paragraph to the light of God's Word. You'll see why you can't afford to give the enemy even a penny of your time and attention.

Actionable Intel

See if you can locate an advertisement or software agreement or something that lists several lines of fine-print disclaimers. Why don't we like to read those? What are we risking by not?

Natural Growth

I pray this: that your love will keep on growing. —Philippians 1:9

Recon

When you were a little baby or toddler, did you make yourself grow? Did you wake up every morning, thinking, *How can I make myself stronger today? When will I ever learn to walk? If I don't concentrate harder, I'll never grow out of this crawling stage.*

No, you grew because God was *causing* you to grow. The food you were eating, the love you were receiving, the desire for adventure He'd given you—all of it added strength and health to your body. So growth was a natural outcome of being healthy.

Spiritual growth is really no different. If you want God's righteousness that's already inside you to grow into new behaviors and attitudes, don't focus on *them*. Focus on *Him*. Make sure you are healthy and strong spiritually, and then He'll make sure those changes start happening. Naturally.

It's a lie of the enemy to make you think following God is something you need to force upon yourself. When your heart and mind are set on Jesus, you'll simply grow. Don't worry about it.

Actionable Intel

Look back at some of your baby pictures and early childhood pictures, and see how your body and abilities were changing through the years. Now write down some examples of the *spiritual* growth you've seen happen in the past year of your life as you've focused on God.

The Missing Peace

When I considered all that I had accomplished and what I had labored to achieve, I found everything to be futile . . . nothing to be gained. —Ecclesiastes 2:11

Recon

Learn this lesson early in life: *things are just things*. Nothing more, nothing less.

New things get old.

Thrills eventually come to an end.

Fun things lose their excitement over time.

It's fine to have a new gizmo, gadget, or toy. But take it from an Old Testament king named Solomon, whom history remembers as one of the wealthiest (and wisest) individuals of all time. He said, "I increased . . . I made . . . I constructed . . . I acquired . . . I owned . . . I amassed . . . I gathered . . . I became great . . ." (Ecclesiastes 2:4–10).

And yet in the end . . .

He was disappointed. Dissatisfied. It was still not enough.

Good things often come to those who just wait, but peace never comes to those who just want.

Actionable Intel

Look through your toy box or game shelf or rec room closet, or wherever you and your family keep most of your fun stuff. How much of what's in there looks like much fun anymore? Where did the fun go? Why didn't it stay? Ask the Lord to help you place more value on eternal things than on temporary things.

Otherworldly

The world was not worthy of them. —Hebrews 11:38

Recon

Have you ever seen an image of planet Earth from outer space? It's beautiful, isn't it? Our big, blue world.

But I think a better view of the cosmos is the one you might be able to get from your back porch tonight. You don't need to be in a rocket ship or even stand behind the lens of a telescope to take in the unbelievable landscape of the universe. And when you see those stars and the huge, deep, inky night sky, remember that you, like the faithful heroes in Hebrews 11, have been called by the One who created everything you're looking at.

Sure, this earth is nice. It'll do while you're here. But what it offers is not worthy of you—someone who's been made for *unseen* places, someone who answers to a King whose kingdom includes all that exists.

Your faith may be small. But your faith is in Someone huge. Don't let *anything* on this earth scare you into thinking that you can't do *everything* Jesus asks you to do. Here, there, and everywhere.

Actionable Intel

When you look up into the sky tonight, don't just see the moon and stars and clouds. Let it remind you of the One who created it. See the One you've placed all your faith in.

Marvelous Mystery

"The wind blows where it pleases, and you hear its sound, but you don't know where it comes from or where it is going."—John 3:8

Recon

Today's verse is how Jesus described the Holy Spirit. I realize that the Spirit can be a bit of a mystery, even to those of us who are part of the family of God. Old-timey Bibles call Him the "Holy Ghost," which certainly doesn't make us want to cozy up to Him much.

But the Holy Spirit is God, and He's the best friend you'll ever have. His power is what has changed you into a person capable of faith and courage far beyond your natural abilities. He shows you the right paths to take, while warning you of other paths that are harming you. The godly things you do, the wise decisions you make, the times you stand up for what's right—people don't always know where that's coming from. But *you* do. It comes from the Holy Spirit who's been given to you.

As you learn to hear how He speaks, and as you respond to Him in obedience, He will do what He came to do—give you the power to live an outrageously victorious life that honors and glorifies your heavenly Father.

Actionable Intel

Ask God in prayer today to reveal more and more to you about His Holy Spirit. When you see Him mentioned in Scripture, pay close attention. Listen for Him. He will lead you like a Friend.

You'd Pray? For Me?

"I have prayed for you that your faith
may not fail."—Luke 22:32

Recon

Jesus saw in Peter a man whose faith was fixed firmly on Him—the way He wants yours and mine to be. But this didn't mean Peter was perfect. In fact, a few verses later, Jesus came right out and told him that before the night was over, Peter would "deny three times that you know Me" (v. 34).

Knowing Peter's weakness, knowing Peter would fail Him, Jesus was already praying for him. Praying that Peter wouldn't lose his shield. Praying he'd be brave enough to pick it back up, even after dropping it so badly.

The enemy cannot take your shield away from you. All he can do is try to convince you not to use it. But every time you realize you've been trying to live without it, you can be sure that Jesus Himself is praying to the Father for you, eager to help you get your shield of faith back.

He doesn't do it because you're perfect. He does it because you're His.

Actionable Intel

Someone in your life today needs the encouragement of knowing someone's praying for them. Tell them that one of those people is you. And tell them—even better—that one of them is Jesus.

Ever Faithful

The virgin will become pregnant and give birth to a son, and they will name Him Immanuel, which is translated "God is with us."—Matthew 1:23

Recon

The Messiah had been promised for centuries—way back when the prophet Isaiah wrote, "A child will be born for us, a son will be given to us" (Isaiah 9:6). He was to come through the natural line of Abraham, through the priestly line of Judah, through the royal line of David, and through the miraculous power of God. And as soon as Jesus belted out His first cry as a baby, He was already the faithful fulfillment of Old Testament prophecy.

If he could accomplish all of that as a newborn baby, think how much more He accomplished more than thirty years later, when He cried out from the cross, "It is finished!" (John 19:30). He accomplished everything. Perfectly. According to plan. And all according to God's faithfulness.

The shield of faith in your hand reflects the continuing light of Jesus' ministry. It reminds you that God's love has always provided for His people. It's connected to a flawless and eternal promise. So raise your shield up in triumph. Your battle has been won.

Actionable Intel

Worship God today for His legacy of faithfulness. He has never faltered a single time, not through an eternity of faithfulness.

Above and Beyond

*Now to Him who is able to do above and beyond
all that we ask or think . . .—Ephesians 3:20*

Recon

God is just "above and beyond." It's his natural M.O. When He created water, He didn't just create small drops; He went ahead and created whole oceans. Wasn't the brilliant heat and radiance of one star impressive enough? Did He really need to go and create entire galaxies—so immense that most of them no human eye will ever see?

Couldn't birds have been just yellow? Or black? In a standard size and shape? Why create thousands of different types and species? Big ones, little ones, cute ones, even funny ones.

He didn't just make hills. He made the Rocky Mountains and the Himalayas. He didn't just make the sun. He made sunrises and sunsets.

He's just "beyond"—*way past* what we'd already consider to be *way past.*

So when you're thinking your shield of faith isn't much to look at, remember the One who gave it to you. He can take your little bit of faith and make it go "above and beyond" in standing against the enemy.

Actionable Intel

Think of some other examples, in addition to the ones I gave you, that show how God has proven Himself "above and beyond."

A Working Faith

We always pray for you that our God will . . . fulfill every desire for goodness and the work of faith. —2 Thessalonians 1:11

Recon

I've got a job for you.

I'm pretty sure you've heard your parents say something like this to you, just before putting you to work on a household chore, an outdoor project, or some other kind of task that called for team effort. But your heavenly Father does the same thing—not because *He* needs your help, but because *you* need to see your faith at work.

Faith that sits around doing nothing is missing out on the whole reason it exists. What's the point of that? What's even the *fun* of that? We can only goof off so long before we end up feeling lazy, icky, cross-eyed, grumpy. And that leads to feeling bored, tired, and dull.

Well, with faith, there's *always* something to do. Something to learn. Something to dig up. Something to cook or create or hammer on. "The work of faith" is your chance to see what faith is really for. It sets the stage for the adventure of a lifetime. So live it. Act on it. Right away.

Actionable Intel

How can you put your faith to work today? What kind of "job" can you give it to do?

Praying for Faith

Build yourselves up in your most holy faith and
pray in the Holy Spirit. —Jude v. 20

Recon

The power of strategic prayer comes from focusing on your biggest need for spiritual improvement and then asking God for help with it. By putting your prayer ideas in writing, and by returning to them on a regular basis, you keep your head in the game. You're able to see His answers coming at you in surprising ways—often at surprising speed.

Today I challenge you to pray a specific prayer, asking for strength in your shield of faith. Remember that your faith itself doesn't need to be huge as long as it's completely focused on the supreme power, love, wisdom, and faithfulness of almighty God.

Your prayer for faith may be only a line or two. That's okay. Just be sure you're asking God to lead you in what to pray. To show you what you truly need. To fill you with the kind of faith that can put out all the fiery arrows of the enemy.

Pray for faith.

Actionable Intel

Tape up your prayer on a wall or mirror where you will see it regularly. And start praying it today.

Warrior God

Truth is missing. . . . The LORD saw that there was
no justice, and He was offended. —Isaiah 59:15

Recon

Surprised to read a verse that says God can be offended? What might surprise you even more is that what offends Him most is not that folks like you and me need as much forgiveness as we do, but that we are being badgered all day long to turn away from Him, to believe things about Him and His Word that aren't true.

He's mad at your enemy and at sin. Not at you.

He's offended that "truth is missing."

That's why He's done something amazing. He Himself has strapped on His armor and leapt to our defense. He has lashed out as a Warrior against the enemy of His people. He has swooped into battle as the Defender of terrorized sinners and has declared Himself the Redeemer of those who turn to Him.

God realizes we're no match for spiritual danger without Him. He knows we need a Fighter on our side. And He knows how to fight and win.

Actionable Intel

Read Isaiah 59:16–20. I've had you look at these verses before, but read them again. What do you see God doing? What do you think this image would look like? Write down what you think your enemy feels when He sees God armored up.

Well, That Depends

*As for me and my house, we will serve
the* LORD. *—Joshua 24:15* NASB

Recon

Do you know the term *relative truth*? It means, sure, there might be a right way and a wrong way of doing things. But it sort of depends. On the circumstance. On the timing. Or simply on the person or people involved . . . because there's *your* truth and there's *my* truth. And those two truths may or may not go together with each other.

Uhhh . . . no.

There's not *your* truth and *my* truth. There's just *true truth*. Like in Joshua's statement to the people of Israel in today's verse. He said to them, basically, "Look, you decide. You can worship the Lord, or you can go play around with the various idols and false gods of the land. But for me, and for mine, we're standing right here with the Lord." Period.

The choices you and I make every day—they don't *depend*. Because truth—God's truth—has already been *defined*.

Actionable Intel

Try starting a conversation with your family at the dinner table one night about the question of whether truth is absolute.

Acquired Tastes

Taste and see that the LORD *is good.* —*Psalm 34:8*

Recon

I'm sure you have your favorite foods, as well as the ones you just almost can't stand. But you'll be amazed how your taste buds can change over time. Some of the vegetables I never liked when I was a kid are some of my favorites now. I promise, you will eventually learn to enjoy some of these once-unlikable things.

So let me encourage you today with this thought: You might have a hard time staying motivated to worship, or pray, or spend time in the Word, or even to read this devotional. (It's okay. I don't take it personally.) But the more experiences you share with God, the more your tastes will begin to change and develop. Instead of being content with a steady diet of empty calories offered by the world, you'll start hungering for things that show just how much God loves you . . . and how much you love *Him* for the changes He creates in you.

Taste and see. He's really that good.

Actionable Intel

Can you think of one or two foods you didn't know you liked until you tried them? Why did you avoid them before? How did they end up surprising you? Now, what are one or two new things you could try this week with the goal of developing a deeper relationship with God?

Tying It All Together

*Above all, put on love—the perfect
bond of unity.*—*Colossians 3:14*

Recon

You've got the belt of *truth,* the breastplate of *righteousness,* the shield of *faith*—things like that. You probably wouldn't expect any of your spiritual armor to be something like *love*, would you? Doesn't sound too warrior-like.

But slipped inside your shoes of *peace* is an Odor Eater of *love* that helps you battle one of life's most unpleasant problem areas—the sour, smelly smell of broken relationships.

Hopefully you don't have too many of those in your life—whether at home with your parents or siblings, or at school with your teachers or classmates. But wherever they exist, or wherever they may threaten to crop up, the warrior in you has an answer for that. The *perfect* answer, in fact. Love is "the perfect bond of unity."

No matter how weak it may sound at first, *loving others* takes a huge amount of power that only God can give you. I actually think you look even stronger with it on.

Actionable Intel

Are you currently in any kind of disagreement with someone? What if you laid down any other weapons you've been using and approached the problem with love today? What would that look like?

Your Faith Place

By faith Abraham, when he was called,
went out to a place . . . not knowing where
he was going. —Hebrews 11:8

Recon

One of the reasons God gives us so many real-life stories to read in the Bible is to let us see what He can do when we actually trust Him.

Abraham was willing to leave his home and resettle in a land he didn't even know existed. But when he went to the place where faith would be required, God made him the father of a new nation.

Esther risked her life to approach the king and ask him to save her native people. But when she went before the king in faith, God changed the decisions of a God-less empire and spared the Jews from death.

The men Jesus called to follow Him as His inner circle of disciples walked away from careers and other paths they expected to take in life. But by trusting God in faith, they became the first to carry Christ's message to the world.

There's no telling what God could do through you if you went to your faith place too.

Actionable Intel

Where's the "faith place" He wants you to go today? Will you go there? Wouldn't you like to see what He plans to do for you there?

The Indirect Route

Make Your ways known to me, LORD;
teach me Your paths. —Psalm 25:4

Recon

Every time I visit Washington, DC, I'm more lost than the time before. The maze of complicated streets is hard to navigate, even with a map. In fact, from what I hear, even the locals can sometimes grow frustrated by how the city is laid out and the traffic issues it creates.

But in reality, this haphazard grid of angles and diagonals was arranged by design. The city architects wanted to prevent easy access to the White House so that any potential enemy, if trying to attack, would have a hard time finding a direct path to their target.

I know how the patterns of your life can be confusing, frustrating. They don't seem to make any sense sometimes. But part of God's wise reason for leading you down what looks like too twisty of a path is to keep your mind sharp, your heart trusting . . . and your enemy baffled because he doesn't have a straight shot at you.

Actionable Intel

Thank God in prayer today that He does what you and I would *never* do—walk us right into a difficult path, knowing it's the most direct route to keeping us safe and protected.

Want To

It is God who is working in you, enabling you both to desire and to work out His good purpose. —Philippians 2:13

Recon

I'll let you in on a little secret. *I don't always feel like doing the right thing.*

Actually, it's no secret. It's how all of us feel from time to time, and we're better off just admitting it than trying to act like it's not true.

So, sure, I'll confess that my "want-to" doesn't always "want to." But the *real* news is that God already knows this little tidbit about me (and about you too), and has promised to give us the "want-to" if we'll ask Him for it.

Maybe you're like me and don't always want to be kind to your little sister or obey your teacher or be respectful to your parent. But God can actually help you want to. Really! He can!

If He only cared that we did good things, He could have just given us the power to obey Him and nothing else. But this God of ours wants us to *enjoy* obeying Him. He wants us to get the full experience of feeling His passion in our hearts. So He even gives us the desire for it. What more could we want?

Actionable Intel

If you've been having a little trouble lately in the "want-to" department, make your struggle a reason for praying today. Ask God specifically to give you the "want" to do what's right.

Courage

> *"Haven't I commanded you: be strong and
> courageous? . . . for the LORD your God is
> with you wherever you go."*—Joshua 1:9

Recon

One of the main characteristics of any true warrior is
courage—the courage to do the right thing, at the right
time, for the right reasons, based on what God's Word
says is right.

As long as "truth" can be whatever we want it to be—
based on how we're feeling at the moment, on whether
it's sunny or cloudy, or on our friends' opinions—then no
one needs to be "strong and courageous" enough to go
against the tide and take a stand. Instead we can just hide
behind our personal likes and dislikes (even if they are
wrong) and feel fine about doing it.

But when we realize that the truth—God's standard—
is not going to budge, no matter how we twist its words
around to fit what we want them to say, we must make a
choice. We can choose to be courageous in a world full of
cowards.

I believe you're courageous enough to make the
right choice. Because you're a warrior. And that's what
warriors do.

Actionable Intel

Try to think of a current event or a television show where
you saw someone choose courage over compromise. What
did you learn from it?

Fashioned for Righteousness

He will purify the sons of Levi and refine them like gold and silver. Then they will present offerings to the Lord in righteousness. —Malachi 3:3

Recon

A sculptor was working to complete his latest creation, a lifelike stallion chiseled from a big hunk of rock. A friend who was in his studio that day, admiring the artist's work, finally asked the one question all of us wonder: "How do you do that?" To which the sculptor simply said, with his chisel raised in the air: "I just chip away at everything that doesn't look like stallion."

In the same way, God chips away at everything in your life that doesn't look like Jesus.

The enemy, of course, wants you to resist this process. It hurts. It can seem harsh and unfair. But God knows that in knocking things loose from where they don't belong, He's helping you wear a sturdy breastplate of righteousness that will keep you protected. He's turning you into someone who not only looks more like Jesus on the outside but is actively living in purity and holiness on the inside.

This stallion in you is not just a chunk of carved rock. You're a living, breathing war-horse for Jesus.

Actionable Intel

Turn to Ezekiel 36, and read verse 26. Part of being shaped into the image of Christ comes from not being so hard and stony to begin with. Ask God to give you a tender heart that's more easily shaped by righteousness.

Unlikely Companions

*God proves His own love for us in that while we were
still sinners, Christ died for us!*—Romans 5:8

Recon

Most of us gravitate toward people who are similar to
us. People who like the same things, the same music, the
same subjects, the same kinds of conversation. That's
normal behavior for most people. And there's nothing
wrong with that.

But what makes the gospel so extraordinary is that
God is nothing like us, yet still chose to be in relationship
with us. Think about it—He's perfect; we're imperfect.
He's holy; we're unholy. He's unlimited; we are very, very
limited. But He still sent His Son for unworthy sinners
because of His "love for us"—so that we *could* become like
Him, by His power at work in us.

That's what love does, when it's the love of God.
It reaches out. It ignores differences. It looks for
relationships. It seeks peace where peace doesn't just
naturally exist.

It puts on its shoes and goes out looking for people to
befriend. In Jesus' name.

Actionable Intel

Sometime this week, make a point of seeking out one person
who's not exactly your type—who wouldn't ordinarily
hang with you. And maybe eat lunch with him or her in
the lunchroom. Do something to get to know that person.
Not because you *should,* but because love just does.

No Laughing Matter?

"Why did Sarah laugh, saying, 'Can I really have a baby when I'm old?' Is anything impossible for the LORD?"—*Genesis 18:13–14*

Recon

When the Lord announced to Abraham that his wife, Sarah, would be giving birth to her first child at the ripe old age of ninety, she couldn't help but let out a little chuckle of disbelief.

And yet according to her write-up in the "Hall of Faith"—chapter 11 of Hebrews— she's described as someone who believed God entirely, who boldly "considered that the One who had promised was faithful" (Hebrews 11:11).

So which account is the right one?

Well . . . both. Because not every single moment in your journey is the kind of material that would appear in your spiritual highlight reel. Even spiritual giants, if caught by the right camera angle at the wrong time, can give off the look of a spiritual weakling.

You are more than what each individual snapshot reveals. You are an entire body of work—one that you are working out day by day, little by little, up and down, all the time.

Actionable Intel

What grade would you give yourself for the level of faith you've practiced today? If you're not too happy with it, guess what? You can start your day all over right now. And a brand-new one starts first thing in the morning.

Shatterproof

"My salvation will last forever, and My righteousness will never be shattered."—Isaiah 51:6

Recon

Ever broken a glass on the kitchen floor? Then you know what a mess it can be to clean up. The sharp, jagged pieces must be carefully swept into the trash to keep anyone from getting cut. Even then, little bits and beads of shattered glass can escape the broom or vacuum, meaning you'd better not go barefoot in that area until you're sure there's nothing to cut yourself on.

When the Devil tries planting doubts in your mind, one of his goals is to get you thinking of God's love and faithfulness (and therefore your salvation) like a fragile piece of glass that can shatter at any moment. One wrong move and—*crash!*—your relationship with God is broken. And once it's done, you'll never be able to put it back together again. You'll need to walk on eggshells around Him, hoping He'll forget what you've done.

This is a lie, so don't believe it. Your salvation, like God's righteousness, is shatterproof.

Actionable Intel

Know anyone who needs to hear this truth today? Look for an opportunity (maybe at lunch) to tell that person about your shatterproof salvation.

Done Deal

Thanks be to God, who gives us the victory through our Lord Jesus Christ!—1 Corinthians 15:57

Recon

What if you had a big game coming up on Saturday? A tough one. Against a tough opponent. But somehow—for reasons you couldn't really explain—you knew beyond a shadow of a doubt that your team was going to win no matter how well they played. My question to you is this: How would this knowledge change your approach to the game?

I know how some people might think. They'd say, "Well, if I knew we were going to win, I'd kick back and have fun, just hang out and claim the prize." Yeah, but that's not a warrior talking. A warrior wants to win, sure. But a warrior also wants to do their best at all times. Wants to face the challenge and overcome it. Certain victory wouldn't change a true warrior's desire to *work*. It would just take away the need to *worry*.

That's what Jesus' victory means for you. The outcome is already decided. No need to worry.

Actionable Intel

Approach your next big challenge with this same kind of mind-set—total confidence, backed up by sold-out effort.

Say What?

He did what was right in the LORD's *sight . . . he did not turn aside to the right or the left.* —2 Chronicles 34:2

Recon

I just happened to notice that my fingers had drifted a full keystroke to the left while I was typing today's devotion. I was trying to type, "You must make the choice to align yourself with truth," but when I looked up to the computer screen, it said, "Tiy nyar nJW RGW XGIUXW RI kufb tiyeawkd qurg reyrg." It was immediately clear that something had gone horribly wrong.

I mean, just look at it. Does that sentence sound even remotely like the one I was trying to type? Is there a single word in there that makes a lick of sense? I even hit the caps lock button at one point, and—see what happened? Suddenly I was typing in TALL SCREAMING CAPITAL LETTERS instead of nice, calm lowercase ones.

Just because I was one space off. Less than an inch. That's all it took to create such confusion. That's why "making the choice to align yourself with truth" is so critical. It doesn't take much of a drift to make a real mess.

Actionable Intel

Type a nonsense line like mine, and print it out where you can stick it on your wall. If someone asks what it means, tell them, "That's to remind me what happens if I don't follow the Word—word by word."

Back on Your Feet

Though a righteous man falls seven times,
he will get up. —Proverbs 24:16

Recon

Three of the pieces of spiritual armor from Ephesians 6 are specifically connected to the command written in verses 14 and 15—telling you to "stand"—so you can "stand firm against the schemes of the devil" (v. 11 NASB). "Take your stand," Paul said, with the belt of *truth* in place, with the breastplate of *righteousness* secured, and with the sandals of *peace* on your feet. These three—together—provide stability that *all* of us need if we hope to fend off the attacks of an enemy who's trying hard to take us down.

So whenever you feel tripped up—whenever you feel like you've lost your spiritual sense of balance—check the status of those three items first. Because one or more of them has likely slipped out of place.

Are you faithfully feeding yourself from the *truth* of the Bible? Are you consistently choosing *righteousness* over sin? Are you living at *peace* with God and with the people around you?

Sometimes you'll stumble and fall. We all do. But God has provided you a way back up.

Actionable Intel

When fixing a broken appliance or computer, repairmen often perform a set of "diagnostics" to help locate and isolate the problem. Write down today's trio of key words—*truth*, *righteousness*, and *peace*—as a trusted method of *diagnosing* a heart that's not in good working order. Pray about the state of each of these in your life today.

Really Good News

I am not ashamed of the gospel, because it is God's power for salvation to everyone who believes. —Romans 1:16

Recon

The gospel of Jesus Christ—the incredible love of God that sent Jesus to die for us so that we could live with Him by faith—is *good news*. That's a general definition for what the word *gospel* means. "Good news." (And boy, is it ever!)

But while the Greek word we translate "gospel" appears dozens of times in the New Testament, it's actually not a word the Greeks used very often. Because it didn't just mean "good news." It meant something even more— "good news that's too good to be true."

Because that's exactly what the gospel is—news that is *so good* it almost sounds unbelievable and unthinkable. The fact that someone else would give His life for you sounds unreasonable, right? But it's true. Waking us up every morning. Singing us to sleep every night.

And if it's that good, then it's too good to keep to ourselves. Because when you and I go out telling it to others, that's the worst news your enemy will get all day.

Actionable Intel

This week, ask the Lord to give you an opportunity to talk with someone about what Jesus has done—for you, and for that person. Be praying, looking, and ready to tell the good news.

Something to Lose?

"If anyone wants to be My follower, he must deny himself, take up his cross, and follow Me."—Mark 8:34

Recon

If somebody ever tells you that being a Christian won't cost you anything, don't listen to them. You might even want to run hard and fast away from them.

Worth it? Yes. But easy? No.

People were often coming up to Jesus, telling Him they wanted to be His followers. They wanted to be part of the excitement of hanging around Him. His words made them feel good. His miracles amazed them. His Spirit drew people toward Him, out of their ho-hum, mundane livelihood.

But once they realized that following Jesus was a full-time job, most of them found a convenient excuse for backing out. As do many today. They want *Him*, but they still want all their other stuff too.

The enemy says you can have it all. Jesus says you can have even *more*—by denying yourself and following Him.

Actionable Intel

Read Mark 10:28–30. What does Jesus promise to those who give it all . . . to go with Him?

Not Bad?

Joy and gladness will overtake them. —Isaiah 51:11

Recon

How are you doing today? Good?

Or just "not bad."

Technically speaking, these two terms say roughly the same thing. Good is the opposite of bad. If something's not bad, it's good. But just hearing them, one answer sounds upbeat and positive and the other sounds sad and sort of Eeyore-ish.

I've discovered that when most people think about the benefits of salvation, the first ideas that pop to mind are often the "not bad" type—no hell, no eternal punishment. But often when the word *saved* is used in the Bible, it doesn't just refer to people escaping death, like a nation being saved from a hostile enemy. It means they're entering into a positive, blessing-rich state of health, wholeness, joy . . . goodness. It wasn't just about what they *weren't* getting; it was more about all the great things they *were* getting.

So what'll it be today, as you think about what God has done for you? A not-frown? Or a nice smile?

Actionable Intel

Anytime you hear yourself saying or thinking negative things today—even just some not-so-positive things—spin those thoughts around on their heads. Be extremely thankful today for God's good things.

Freedom

"You will know the truth, and the truth will set you free."—John 8:32

Recon

Think of a soldier in action. He's moving right, moving left, dodging enemy fire, fast on his feet. Uphill, downhill, on any type of ground. If he didn't have the belt, he'd have nowhere to tuck in his extra gear and loose ends. He'd be an accident waiting to happen. Maybe even a victim of war. If he didn't voluntarily *restrict* certain parts of his uniform or equipment to that strap around his waist, he would severely limit his freedom of movement.

Our lives always come with new battles and challenges, and being able to move through them successfully often requires restricting something. Giving something up. Even if only temporarily. Making a certain kind of sacrifice. In return, however, we enjoy the ability to fight today's battle at full strength, at full speed.

Whenever you feel restricted by the truth, remember it's actually a shortcut to freedom.

Actionable Intel

If you thought God was instructing you to give something up—not anything bad, just something that's maybe taking a lot of your time or interfering with more important things—would you do it? What would it be? What might happen to your spiritual freedom of movement if you did?

Shake It Off

"My covenant of peace will not be shaken."—Isaiah 54:10

Recon

Our sense of peace usually rises and falls with the day's events and feelings. Made a ninety-five on a tough math test? *Peace.* Your name on the board for talking? "See me after class?" *Not peace.* Getting a smile across the room from that person you sort of like? *Peace.* Being told during afternoon practice that you won't be starting next game? *Not peace.*

But while all this drama is taking place down here, remember you're actually living in a larger kingdom, in a bigger world. It's an unseen place where the Lord Jesus reigns over all, and where your spiritual shoes form-fit around every life event. They're able to keep you always level and balanced. Always at peace.

The visible world never stops being a bouncy house of highs and lows, hills and valleys. But the covenant of peace, made by the Prince of Peace (Isaiah 9:6), means that nothing can ever steal your peace.

Actionable Intel

Has this been an up day? A down day? A middle-of-the-road day? Ask God to break through and make it a *peaceful* day, no matter what kind of day it turns out to be.

Skin in the Game

We were pleased to share with you not only the gospel of God but also our own lives. —1 Thessalonians 2:8

Recon

Part of the process of building or buying a house is signing a contract. You put your name on the bottom line, declaring your intentions to go through with what you've said.

But just signing your name is not enough. The builder or seller typically asks for *earnest money*—a "good faith" payment—a deposit that obligates you even further.

Writing your name on a contract is technically binding, but also easier to back out of. Tear up that piece of paper, and the deal's off. But if you've given the other person a fairly large chunk of cash, you'll think long and hard before trying to weasel out of it because now you've got some skin in the game. Backing out will mean losing more than just a little time and effort. You could lose some big money.

Jesus put His skin in the game by dying on the cross for you. He did more than just talk about redeeming you. He laid down His life for you. So what kind of commitment should His sacrifice inspire from you?

As little as possible? Or some "good faith."

Actionable Intel

What are some "good faith" payments you could make in your relationship with God? What are some practical ways that you can put some "skin in the game" and deepen your level of commitment and faith in God?

Dying to Change

"Unless a grain of wheat falls to the ground and dies, it remains by itself."—John 12:24

Recon

Let's say that there are twenty-five bags of grass seed available for purchase at your local Home Depot. Twenty-four of them are purchased, and the owners open the bags and spread the seeds across their lawns.

But what about the one bag that never left the store? If you opened it at the end of the summer, what would be inside? Seeds, that's what. It wouldn't have become grass like all the other bags of seeds because there's only one way that grass seed knows whether to turn into grass.

The difference is in the *dying*. When grass seed enters the earth, the combination of water, nutrients, pollen, and other things cause its outer shell to peel away. To open up. To send out roots. To sprout. To grow. If it won't stop being grass seed, it can never be grass.

Salvation, in a similar way, also requires letting some things die. Things you may enjoy being and doing. But only in giving them up—in letting them die—can you truly become what God created you for.

Actionable Intel

Read the next verse—John 12:25. What are some of the "loves" that may be causing you to "lose" some opportunities as a believer in Christ?

What Goes Around

"Shouldn't you have had mercy on your fellow servant just as I had on you?"—Matthew 18:33 NIV

Recon

Jesus told a parable about a man who owed his king an enormous amount of money. Impossible to pay. Even if the man did nothing else his whole lifetime than to work at it, he still couldn't pay it off. And yet this king, in an act of mercy, forgave the man his full debt.

Nice story, huh? Except the next thing you know, this same man whose heavy burden had been lifted off his shoulders went out looking for another guy who owed *him* some money. Not a lot of money; just a *little* money. You'd think he'd want to pass along the forgiveness, right? That's the way I was hoping the story would end. But instead . . .

Well, let's put ourselves in his place, shall we? Let's say we'd been forgiven a debt we could never repay, the way Jesus has forgiven us from all of our sins. And let's say somebody did something to hurt us or make us mad, and we refused to forgive them or be their friend anymore.

See where this story is going?

Actionable Intel

Turn to Matthew 18, starting in verse 21, and read the rest of that chapter. Just fifteen verses. Ask yourself if there's anyone you need to forgive. Try to let them know about it today.

Run

How beautiful on the mountains are the feet of the herald, who proclaims peace . . . who says to Zion, "Your God reigns!"—Isaiah 52:7

Recon

I'm not exactly what you'd call a runner. You might call it jogging, or barely-not-walking, or looks-like-she's-dying. But out there in the morning, in my baggy sweatshirt and sweatpants, I'm picking 'em up and putting 'em down. So I'm a runner. Kind of.

The Bible paints the picture of God's people as *runners*. Up on the mountain ridges. Breathing the crisp air. Bringing news from one place to another—from the unseen world to the visible world.

And even if some of us (me) aren't the most natural runners like other people (like you maybe), *all* of us runners look "beautiful" when we're wearing the shoes of peace, when we're pumping in stride with God's truth and righteousness. Then our lives are continually saying to others, in one fluid motion, that *our God reigns.*

Actionable Intel

Do you know somebody who really needs to be reminded today that *our God reigns?* May I suggest that you "run" and tell them as fast as you can?

Nothing to Worry About

"If that's how God clothes the grass of the field . . . won't He do much more for you— you of little faith?"—Matthew 6:30

Recon

Outside your window, you might hear the sound of wind in the treetops. Might hear a dog barking. Might hear a police siren in the distance or a car door shutting in the neighbor's driveway.

What you *won't* hear are the moans of fretful anxiety coming from the grass in your yard—worrying that Saturday is probably mowing day (oh dear!), or that the blades might lose their color in the bright sunlight, or might get trampled the next time you and your friends are running around in the yard. No, they don't worry. God simply takes care of them.

Obviously a blade of grass doesn't have the ability to worry, but you do. And the enemy wants to take advantage of this. He wants you worried about *everything.* But Jesus tells you not to worry about *anything,* since "your heavenly Father knows" what you need (Matthew 6:32).

Learn a lesson from the "grass of the field." They just let God be God.

And I think He does it beautifully, don't you?

Actionable Intel

Rate your level of worry today on a scale of 1–10, and then write down exactly what you're most worried about. Then talk to God about what you've written down.

Good Work

Work out your own salvation with fear
and trembling. —Philippians 2:12

Recon

Many people have gotten the idea that Christianity shouldn't require any work. They think that God should not only save us but also fix all our problems. Turn every temptation into a softball. Not give us any responsibility to fit into the rest of our schedule.

I thought this was supposed to be a gift! we often think.

Yes, it is—the gift of being able to team up with His Spirit on the quest of a lifetime. Something we could never even have a hope of doing otherwise. The fact that He allows us to be actively involved in it—even though we did absolutely nothing to deserve it—is because He's *giving* us the thrill of watching Him do incredible things through us and for us as we partner with Him in His purposes.

So expect to work. Hard. Being a dedicated Christian is not easy. But it's the best work you'll ever find, with the best payday you can ever imagine.

Actionable Intel

Do something hard today, something you'd usually shy away from. It won't make you any more saved, but it'll give you another piece of evidence for what He can do in a hardworking, hard-believing heart.

Breathe In, Breathe Out

Based on the gift each one has received, use
it to serve others, as good managers of the
varied grace of God. —1 Peter 4:10

Recon

Have you ever heard about active voice and passive voice? Maybe you learned about it in your grammar class at school. *Active voice* is when the subject of the sentence is doing something. ("He ran to help his mom with the groceries.") *Passive voice* is when something is being done to or for the subject of the sentence. ("He was given a free home-cooked meal for his trouble.")

Kind of weird that I'm talking about grammar during devotional time, huh? But the truth is that each day of your life is a constant mix of both the active and the passive. Doing things and receiving things.

Success in your spiritual life works the same way. You *receive* things from God (power, confidence, health, all kinds of blessings), and then you *actively* put them into practice—by working hard, by caring about people, by standing up for what's right.

It takes both to win the unseen battle.

Actionable Intel

Write down some of the things you've received (and continually receive) from God. Now here's your challenge: determine one or two things you will actively do today in response to what He's given you.

True or False?

Christ has liberated us to be free. Stand firm then and don't submit again to a yoke of slavery. —Galatians 5:1

Recon

Some lies of the enemy are so old and stale, you'd think we should be able to see through them by now. Take this one, for example: "God's forgiveness is not enough. He's still not satisfied with you. Try a little harder, kid, and maybe He'll learn to be happy with you someday."

That's a lie. The lie of *legalism*—the idea that His love and approval depend on your performance, that you still need to earn them. Satan's been spouting this one for centuries, and lots of Christians live every day with this doubt and disapproval swinging over their heads.

And it's Just. Not. True.

"You were called to be free" (Galatians 5:13). "No condemnation now exists for those in Christ Jesus" (Romans 8:1). "You are saved by grace through faith, and this is not from yourselves; it is God's gift—not from works, so that no one can boast" (Ephesians 2:8–9).

Put *that* in your belt and run with it.

Actionable Intel

I want you to remember this exact location where you're reading this devotional. Look around you and make a note of your surroundings. Then every time in the future when you hear this lie—the lie of legalism—think back to this precise place and time. Remember the truth.

Sanctification

From the beginning God has chosen you for salvation through sanctification by the Spirit and through belief in the truth. —2 Thessalonians 2:13

Recon

Let's do a quick Bible study today. On this Bible verse. Take a pen or pencil and underline the words *salvation* and *sanctification*.

"Salvation," we know, means being redeemed by God's grace from the death sentence we deserve so that we can live forever with Him, perfectly forgiven.

But "sanctification"—now *there's* a new word for you, most likely. *Salvation* is the once-for-all-time, *permanent fact* of Christ's righteousness being given to you. *Sanctification,* however, is the ongoing, over-time *process* that takes this righteousness and changes your life to match it. Just as a person grows from baby to child to teenager to adult, God grows us by *sanctifying* us— transforming us, little by little.

He does this through "the Spirit." And He does it through your "belief in the truth." Because when Spirit and truth come together in your life to create a righteous lifestyle, that breastplate of yours begins to cover up more and more attack points where the enemy wishes to harm you.

Sanctification keeps saving you.

Actionable Intel

Look up *sanctification* in a regular dictionary. Then look it up in a Bible dictionary. (If your family doesn't have one, ask to look it up online.) Write down several things from these definitions that stand out to you.

Ready or Not?

*From the Simeonites: 7,100 brave warriors
ready for war. —1 Chronicles 12:25*

Recon

First Chronicles 12 is probably not what your pastor is preaching on this Sunday. Like a lot of the chapters in this Old Testament history book, it's filled with lists of people with Dr. Seuss-sounding names like Mishmannah and Ishmaiah.

But beginning in verse 23, we come across a list of the armed troops who arrived in Hebron to see David crowned king of Israel. And among them are soldiers identified as coming from the tribe of Simeon: "brave warriors ready for war."

Ready. For. War.

Being a warrior is great. Being armored up is impressive and necessary. But not every fighter in this unseen battle is "ready for war"—strong in the Word, active in prayer, pure in heart and mind, listening for the sound of the Commander's voice, ready to snap into action at His first marching order.

Every new day is a new opportunity to prepare yourself to be the enemy's worst nightmare. Be on the alert and girded for action every single day.

Actionable Intel

Write out the disciplines that you intend to maintain each day—not just so you can check them off your list, but so that you can be "ready for war."

Superlatives

LORD, Your faithful love reaches to heaven, Your faithfulness to the clouds. —Psalm 36:5

Recon

Superlatives (suh-PURR-la-tives) are what you call adjectives or adverbs when they're in their most extreme form, usually indicated by the suffix –est at the end. It's how great becomes *greatest*. Quick becomes *quickest*. Bright becomes *brightest*. You get the idea.

Well, this whole idea of superlatives is why your faith, though necessary, doesn't necessarily need to be big. Or bigger. Because *God* is already the biggest of all. And when your faith is completely in *Him*, it's already as big as it needs to be.

That's because with even a little faith, you can trust in love that "reaches to heaven"—to faithfulness that goes up into the clouds. His righteousness is like "the highest mountains"—His wisdom and judgment like the "deepest sea" (v. 6). Everything God is, He is the best at being. Everything He does, He is the best at doing.

Why should even a single ounce of your faith be anywhere else?

Actionable Intel

"God is the ____-est." "His ____ is the ____-est." How many different words could you use to fill in these blanks?

That's Not Me

Do not fear disgrace by men, and do not be shattered by their taunts. —Isaiah 51:7

Recon

School was hard for me sometimes. I was really only accepted by a small group of friends. Some of the other groups I tried to be part of—through sports and other side interests—never truly welcomed me. They never seemed to want *me* as much as I wanted *them*.

Most of us can relate to feeling rejection at one point or another in our lives. And because this feeling is so widespread, our enemy sees it as a great opportunity. He attaches himself and his lies onto the coattails of these negative experiences, and then tries jamming this sense of rejection into the center of your mind, where you can't get around it—where it's all you can see or think about.

There's really only one solution to this common problem, and it's already available to you right now. The helmet of salvation—the truth that you belong in Christ—is the satisfying, comforting answer to every rejection.

Actionable Intel

Today, find a kid at school who is usually left out or who you suspect might feel rejected, and do something to make sure they feel the love of God. Go ahead. I dare you.

Heads Up

*Be serious! Be alert! Your adversary the Devil
is prowling around like a roaring lion, looking
for anyone he can devour.* —1 Peter 5:8

Recon

The enemy would be much happier staying under radar.
Stealing from you in ways you don't notice until it's too
late, until you look down and realize you're missing
things. But one of the reasons for reading the Bible is to
discover insights about the Devil that he doesn't want you
to know.

Like this "roaring lion" business. The Devil is a
prowler. He's a stalker. His innocent "I would never do
anything to hurt you" look disguises his angry, aggressive,
attack-mode mentality.

Smart warriors, however, can use this information
against him. By staying alert. By taking him seriously. By
realizing this unseen lion could be waiting to strike at any
time, from any corner of the room. The only way he can
"devour" you is if you're not watching . . . if he can convince
you that spiritual knowledge and spiritual awareness are for
spiritual sissies. There is nothing wimpy about developing
spiritual eyes to spot spiritual lies.

Actionable Intel

Look up 1 Peter 5:8–9 in two or three different Bible
translations. Make a note of the action verbs you're told
to apply to this lion sighting.

Lion with a Capital L

Look! The Lion from the tribe of Judah, the Root of David, has been victorious. —Revelation 5:5

Recon

All this talk about lions makes me think of a scene from *The Lion King*. Remember when young Simba and Nala are being chased by the hyenas? Backed into a cave, Simba tries desperately to fight back, squeaking out a puny little roar that makes the hyenas laugh at him, daring him to try it again. But the next time he opens his mouth, the roar is deep and ferocious—but it's not *his* roar this time. It's the roar of his father, Mufasa, coming to the rescue.

The Bible says that Jesus is a lion as well—"the Lion from the tribe of Judah." His dominance over evil is real and victorious. His reign is eternal. He lives forever. So when you fight back against your enemy, the roar you're able to work up from inside you is more than just your one little voice. It's the roar of your Rescuer—your Savior—echoing all the way from heaven and back.

Actionable Intel

Read as much of Revelation 5 as you can manage today. See if the image of Jesus as the Lion of Judah gives you reason to worship Him, just as it did for the people in Scripture.

Doesn't Add Up

The men who had gone up with him responded, "We can't go up against the people because they are stronger than we are!"—Numbers 13:31

Recon

The Lord had instructed Moses to pick twelve men to go "scout out the land of Canaan I am giving to the Israelites" (Numbers 13:2). The land *I am giving* them. Did you get that? God was *giving* them the land, and they just had to go and get it.

So now, go back and read the verse at the top of this page, which represents the majority report from those Israelite spies who were sent out. What do you think? If the truth is that God was "giving" them this land to occupy, then what do you call these fears the men were expressing?

When God makes promises in His Word, but we're afraid to act on them . . . when God makes promises in His Word, but we don't see how they apply to somebody like us . . . we're believing lies. And believing lies is how Christians allow the enemy to trick them into living outside of their promised land.

Actionable Intel

Turn to Numbers 13. Read verses 27–29 to hear more specifics about the spies' concerns. Then read verse 30, where one of them has a little different take on the situation. Who sounds like a warrior to you?

Hearing Is Believing?

Be doers of the word and not hearers only,
deceiving yourselves. —James 1:22

Recon

You hear that? It's God's Word, speaking to you and me just as clearly and plainly as possible. "Do not merely listen to the word," as one translation puts it—"Do what it says" (NIV). Two steps.

Plain. And. Simple.

Some of what causes us to be deceived is that we're not even doing the *hearing* part. We're not listening or paying close enough attention to what God tells us in the Bible. But when we fail to be "doers" of it too—when we resist God's efforts at helping us line up our actions with the truth of His commands—we become the ones who are actually "deceiving" ourselves.

So be sure you're hearing the Word—hearing it preached, hearing it taught, hearing it everywhere and as often as possible. But remember that your sense of hearing is only as effective as the changes that happen by *doing* what you've heard.

Actionable Intel

Look up the verse that comes directly before the one we discussed today: James 1:21. How does James describe the "word" that God has given us? How are you *receiving* the word in your heart?

Since You Asked

Always be ready to give a defense to anyone who asks you for a reason for the hope that is in you. —1 Peter 3:15

Recon

The gospel is the pathway (the *only* pathway) to peace—the only way to have peace *with* God, the only way to experience the peace *of* God. That's why His command in Ephesians 6:15 is that you keep your feet "sandaled with readiness" for declaring this "gospel of peace."

Ready to share it. Ready to pass it along.

Now this doesn't mean you'll always be met with a courteous reception. When Peter was writing today's verse, for instance, he was talking to people who were suffering deeply for their faith. Being a Christian in those days was scandalous and suspicious and made people subject to all kinds of suffering and persecution.

But even when the enemy uses people to be *offensive* toward you and your faith, your *defense* can be one that exemplifies peace—the same peace the gospel provides to all who receive it.

Actionable Intel

Read 1 Peter 3:16. Write down the words Peter uses to describe the kind of behavior you should show when telling people about Jesus. What does he say will happen if you do?

Track Record of Trust

I will praise Your name, for You have
accomplished wonders, plans formed long ago,
with perfect faithfulness. —Isaiah 25:1

Recon

One of the things we can't quite appreciate in America is just how old *old* is. The oldest parts of our history in the United States, with the exception of natural wonders, are only a few hundred years old. But when visiting Europe or China or Israel, you can see works of man that are many hundreds, even a thousand or more years old. They look ancient. And they are.

Yet with God, "one day is like a thousand years, and a thousand years like one day" (2 Peter 3:8). The distance between today and the moment when Isaiah spoke these words in the 700s BC—if we use the apostle Peter's math—is the distance between today and two or three days ago. Almost *no* time.

That's how awesome our God is. That's how vast and eternal His faithfulness is. Yet the enemy wants you to think that God cannot be trusted. But if God has sustained the world for all this time, from one generation to the next, how could you ever think He won't also take care of you?

Actionable Intel

Try speaking with one or two people today who are much older than you, and ask them to try telling you how faithful the Lord has been to them throughout their lifetime.

What a Difference

I received mercy for this reason, so that in me, the worst of them, Christ Jesus might demonstrate His extraordinary patience. —1 Timothy 1:16

Recon

The American poet Henry Wadsworth Longfellow could take a cheap sheet of paper, write a poem on it, and make it worth $6,000. *That's genius.* Uncle Sam can take a disc of ordinary metal, stamp an eagle on it, and make it worth $100. *That's money.* A mechanic can take material that's worth $5 and make it worth $50. *That's skill.* A painter can take a fifty-cent piece of canvas, design a picture on it, and make it worth $1,000. *That's art.*

But God can do something no one else can do. He can take a sin-stained life like yours and mine, wash it in the blood of Jesus, pour His Spirit into it, and turn us into people who are more valuable than all the possessions of all the millionaires in all the world. *That's salvation.*

And that's what He's done for you.

Actionable Intel

See if you can think of some other examples where someone turns throwaway scraps or stray parts into something of worth, beauty, and value. Recognize in these stories a small picture of what God has accomplished with you.

Born Liar

Did God really say, "You can't eat from any tree in the garden?"—Genesis 3:1

Recon

Genesis 3. Barely a single page turn into the Bible. And here's our enemy. Breathing lies already.

But don't take *my* word for it. Let's investigate. Let's back up and see if God really *did* say what Satan said He did.

Genesis 2:16–17. God said, "You are free to eat from any tree of the garden, but you must not eat from the tree of the knowledge of good and evil, for on the day you eat from it, you will certainly die."

All right, so let's see what we've got here. Satan's interpretation of this statement was that God had said they couldn't eat "from any tree." The truth was that God had said they were "free to eat" from any tree. Except one—the one that would kill them.

Here is clear-cut evidence that there is a liar among us. And you know exactly who he is.

Actionable Intel

Why do you suppose this story appears so early in the Bible? Why do you think God wanted to expose our enemy's "true" colors right from the beginning?

Weight Less

I am not ashamed, because I know the One
I have believed in. —2 Timothy 1:12

Recon

Displacement is the scientific term for the amount of liquid that's moved around when something solid is dunked in it. Example: fill the bathtub, mark the water line, then get *in* the bathtub, and mark the water line again. The reason it's gone *up* is because your body is now *displacing* an area where water used to be. See?

Spiritual armor is a *displacement* process as well. When you secure truth, righteousness, and peace in and around yourself, you displace other things that used to be there—like fear, like doubt, like insecurity—like all those things that used to make you clam up from talking about your faith because you were scared, timid, unsure, or just wanting to blend in.

So even though the armor does contain a little weight, it ends up taking other weight *off* you, which actually makes you feel much lighter and freer with it on.

Actionable Intel

Write down one thing you would do for Jesus today if you weren't afraid of what others might think. Now choose to wear your armor and move forward in faith. As you do, you'll feel fear and insecurity being displaced.

Able to Stand

God is faithful, and He will not allow you to be tempted beyond what you are able. —1 Corinthians 10:13

Recon

Many big, fat lies come together to form a sinful temptation. And one of the biggest and fattest is this: *you cannot resist it, no matter what you do*.

This lie might be true if you only had your willpower to keep you from falling for it, because, yes, the enemy is persistent and his temptations can be, well . . . tempting. But anytime he tries to lure you to cheat, to take shortcuts, to get mad, to fight—he's not just messing with *you*. He's up against your faith in a God who is irresistibly faithful. And God plus anyone—even you, even me—is always a majority.

A winning combination.

So no matter what temptations you may see coming your way today, remember that you can resist. You can win. Because the power of God is on your side.

Actionable Intel

Worship God today not only for being faithful, but also for knowing you so well and protecting you so completely that no temptation—none—can ever truly overwhelm you.

Change of Mind

How long will you harbor malicious thoughts within you?—Jeremiah 4:14

Recon

The job of the Old Testament prophet was very tough. If he was serious about giving God's Word to the people (who were typically doing things they shouldn't), it meant delivering messages that almost nobody wanted to hear—especially in Jeremiah's case. He was a man who desperately wanted Israel to respond to what God was saying, who wanted them to have "a future and a hope" (Jeremiah 29:11).

Change your thinking, he pled with them—because that's where it starts. Right thinking about God. Right thinking about ourselves. Right thinking about our sin and its cost. Right thinking about God's love and His desire to bless us for His glory.

Danger was coming in Jeremiah's day—an oppressive enemy overtaking God's people. Danger is here now too—an oppressive enemy trying to steal everything he can steal.

Change your thinking. Embrace the truth. Come experience the salvation of your God.

Actionable Intel

Write down three toxic thoughts that routinely attack your faith, your confidence, your self-esteem, your hope. Then have someone help you find three Scripture passages you can write down that overthrow each toxic thought.

Zoom in for a Close-Up

His delight is in the LORD's instruction, and he
meditates on it day and night. —Psalm 1:2

Recon

Have you ever tried (or have you ever heard of someone trying) to read the whole Bible through in a year? That's quite a goal. And a good one. I mean, we say it's the most important book in the world to us. Seems like we ought to at least have read all of it, right?

But while reading big chunks of the Bible is great—and I've certainly done it that way—my favorite way of reading the Bible is to focus on one verse at a time. Sometimes just a single *phrase* in a verse. Sometimes just a single *word*. I close my eyes, repeat it in my mind, think about it, and pray for God to help me really understand what this single line means. To me. Today.

That's because sometimes the battle secret we need right now doesn't come from knowing the entire playbook, but from truly grasping what God is saying . . . one line at a time.

Actionable Intel

Read today's verse several times very carefully, and ask the Lord to speak to you through it. Stop and pay special attention to any words that stand out to you. Ask questions about them. Think about them. You'll feel their deeper meaning start to grow in you.

Sunshine Laws

"Anyone who lives by the truth comes to the light, so that his works may be shown to be accomplished by God."—John 3:21

Recon

Every state in America has what they call *sunshine laws*. These are regulations that require certain proceedings of government to be conducted in public so that any citizen who wants to come listen can do just that. Or at least a news reporter or a video camera can capture everything that happens and keep a record of all the details of the event.

There's something about the light—or in this case, the sunshine—that helps ensure the truth is being spoken, that the truth comes out.

The Bible says that one way to know if the belt of truth is strapped securely around you is by how comfortable you feel conducting your life in public view. Truth loves the light—seeks it out, in fact—while anyone who *doesn't* love the truth "hates the light and avoids it, so that his deeds may not be exposed" (v. 20).

What kinds of sunshine laws do you need to have in *your* life?

Actionable Intel

What kinds of things do you think could happen in "backrooms" and "behind closed doors" of politics if it weren't for sunshine laws?

Up-Front Protection

*You are being protected by God's power
through faith for a salvation that is ready to be
revealed in the last time. —1 Peter 1:5*

Recon

I hope the idea of eternity amazes you. Living with Jesus, living in heaven—it'll be so wonderful. For instance, it'll never be night there, the Bible says, because "the Lord God will be their light" (Revelation 22:5 ESV). That's the kind of place we're headed, you and I, when all the grand prizes we've been promised by faith in Jesus are "revealed in the last time."

But until we finally reach that world where "grief, crying, and pain will exist no longer" (Revelation 21:4), the Lord has given us something today that's fully adaptable to the world we currently live in: *protection.* Yes, right this minute, we are being "protected by God's power."

Whatever danger, confusion, violence, and spiritual difficulty this planet may possess, His armor can protect us from being overcome by it. The same God who's waiting to surprise us with heaven one day is able to keep our enemy from ever catching us by surprise, undefended, on the earth.

Actionable Intel

Read the entire passage found in 1 Peter 1:3–9. Make note of some of the ways he describes your future. And because these future promises are so certain to come true, what kind of attitudes does he say we can freely practice already?

Sleep Soundly

A united cry went up from all of them for about two hours:
"Great is Artemis of the Ephesians!"—Acts 19:34

Recon

In ancient Ephesian culture, most people's main concern was to make sure the gods were pleased. And because there were so many different gods, you never knew which one was doing *what* to you—which one you'd offended, which one wasn't happy with you.

It was exhausting.

A poor Ephesian was never able to lay his head down at night without knowing whether or not he'd done enough to satisfy his pagan deities. This would have made for many restless nights since he depended on them for everything from rain on his fields to a roof over his head.

So do you see why the gospel of Jesus Christ would have been such good news? And why it's still such good news today? Through faith in Jesus, through the grace of God, ordinary human beings can be assured without a second thought that whatever may be going wrong, God remains our loving Father.

"I will both lie down and sleep in peace," you can say, "for You alone, Lord, make me live in safety" (Psalm 4:8).

Actionable Intel

Make this your bedtime prayer tonight. Rest in Him. Rest in His goodness and love for you.

Protecting His Good Name

*If we are faithless, He remains faithful, for He
cannot deny Himself.* —2 Timothy 2:13

Recon

Many times in Israel's history, they rebelled against God
and lived in disobedience like the pagans around them.
This meant God was always within His rights to act in
swift punishment, to destroy them.

But again and again He showed them mercy. And He
gave a specific reason for this decision: "because of My
name, so that it would not be profaned in the eyes of the
nations" (Ezekiel 20:9). So He forgave. He restored. Yes,
He disciplined too, like any good father would. But He
would not allow His love to appear too weak to handle
Israel's faithlessness. His "name" was worth more than
His rightful revenge. He chose to restore, because that's
who He is. Redeeming lost sinners is just what He does.

So live for Him, yes. Let Him strengthen you for the
fight. But when you're disappointed with yourself, when
you know you haven't been loving and obeying Him as
you should, trust His name more than your own feelings
or situation. Repent of your faithlessness. And receive His
faithfulness.

Actionable Intel

Try composing a praise song or poem that describes God's
faithfulness despite our unfaithfulness.

Never Give an Inch

The weapons of our warfare are not of the flesh but have divine power to destroy strongholds. —2 Corinthians 10:4 ESV

Recon

Imagine you're trying to get away from the strongest person you know, and you've almost succeeded. But he still has you by one handful of shirt or blue jeans. You're slapping, tugging, trying to break free. But one "strong hold" at one place is often all it takes to keep the rest of you from moving forward like you want.

That's why you've got to fight. You can't just hit-and-miss your way through and expect to experience the total victory in Christ you're after. Your enemy knows he only needs *one stronghold* to make you miserable and stunt your growth. So even letting him have *one* is one too many.

But hear me now. Any single stronghold of sin or fear or insecurity can be defeated by the weapons and armor we've been talking about. One stronghold may be enough to slow you down, but no stronghold is too strong for a true spiritual warrior.

Actionable Intel

Write down any area where you feel the enemy has a "strong hold" on you. Is there one? Today, take the battle there again—in prayer, in worship, with others' help, with all your armor in place.

Personalized Edition

*Write on it all the words I have
spoken to you.* —Jeremiah 36:2

Recon

Did you know it's okay to write in your Bible? You can make notes to yourself—right there on the crinkly Bible pages—whenever God makes one of His words become a "sword of the Spirit" word.

Imagine this: Let's say your grandfather gave you his Bible, the one he's been using for years as a faithful follower of the Lord. The verses of Scripture in there, of course, would be the same as the ones in your Bible. But what would truly make it special is what your granddad himself had written in those pages—how God had spoken to him through the years in specific ways, giving him personal directions. Your grandfather's writings would be an immense treasure to you.

So don't be afraid to underline things, highlight things, to jot down little statements in the margin that a preacher has said. Use your sword to leave marks along the trail that'll help you always find your way home.

Actionable Intel

When you're reading your Bible today, bring a pen or pencil with you as well. If something the Spirit says really registers with you, make a note of it. Right where He said it.

Our Own Worst Enemy

Each person is tempted when he is drawn away and enticed by his own evil desires. —James 1:14

Recon

We're all human. We all have bad days. Despite being victors in the overall war, not every individual battle is a smashing success. Even the best teams and players lose a game every now and then.

But what you don't want to do is to lose a match with *yourself.* You don't want the enemy sitting off to the side with his feet up and with his lunchbox open while you're falling into a hole that you dug with your own shovel.

That's exactly what happens when we allow sinful thoughts and ideas to become sinful habits. We stop questioning them. We just act on them. They become the routine way we operate. We give the enemy exactly what he wants without his having to lift a finger. We do his own dirty work *for* him.

And I say it's time we stop making this so easy for him. Don't you?

Actionable Intel

What are some of the unwholesome thoughts and actions that you most often cave to? Ask someone you trust to back you up in prayer and help you become a tougher opponent.

Making Plans

Why it is that you planned this thing in your heart?
You have not lied to men but to God!—Acts 5:4

Recon

During the early days of the church, a man named Ananias and his wife, Sapphira, sold a piece of property and then donated what they claimed to be every last penny from the sale to the church.

They weren't obligated, of course, to give *anything*. And what they gave was probably a lot. But they said they gave *everything*. Only . . . they didn't. They held back a portion of the money for themselves.

They lied.

But notice, in today's verse, where the lie started. *In the planning stages*. When lies are given meeting space in your heart, they eventually get acted on. That's why the earlier you invite truth into your thinking and planning, the less likely you'll ever be to face one of those cold-sweat, mind-spinning moments where you're trapped in a lie and trying to wriggle your way out. Always put truth-telling as item #1 on your planning agenda.

Actionable Intel

Read this full story in Acts 5:1–11. Notice in verse 11 the dramatic result from God's way of dealing with even an understated lie. Remember, lies that you tell to others are in reality told to God.

Subtle Differences

Solid food is for the mature—for those
whose senses have been trained to distinguish
between good and evil. —Hebrews 5:14

Recon

If someone were to go to their first symphony concert ever, they'd probably find the whole thing fascinating. The black tuxes and bow ties, the amazing mastery of those difficult instruments. Even if classical music wasn't really their thing, it's still impressive that anybody can play like that, right?

But what would this same performance sound like to a person who'd been going to these concerts for years—someone who perhaps can play an instrument themselves, who's trained to distinguish not just good music from poor music, but good music from great music?

One of the ways the breastplate of righteousness offers you protection is by giving you a heightened awareness to tell right from wrong, good from bad—even good from better, or better from best. You don't learn these lessons simply from going to church or reading the Bible. You learn them from being "trained," from putting the Word into practice. From putting on your armor. Day after day.

Actionable Intel

Read this quote from Charles Spurgeon, great English pastor of the late 1800s: "Discernment is not a matter of simply telling the difference between right and wrong; rather it is telling the difference between right and almost right." Discuss this idea with someone you trust, and then write it in your own words.

Red Light, Green Light

*We are asking that you may be filled with
the knowledge of His will in all wisdom and
spiritual understanding. —Colossians 1:9*

Recon

Every day comes with decisions, large and small. And God has given you a tool to help you know how to navigate them. His peace (or your lack of it) will guide you.

Sometimes you'll sense the *red light* of conviction, signaling for you to stop—now! Plowing forward could get you hurt—bad. Or could hurt someone else. Don't do it.

Sometimes you'll sense the warning of a *yellow light,* often as a thought of uneasiness or doubt. You're not sure. Best to wait, hang back, and ask some more questions before going on . . . wait until you feel more sure about it, wait until you see a . . .

Green light. The green light of peace doesn't mean the next patch of road is easy and smooth, but God's Spirit is drawing you toward it, leading you to follow. Leading you by His peace.

Leading you by those shoes of peace . . .

Actionable Intel

The next time you're riding in a car, ask whoever is driving how they handle each color of traffic light. See if you can pick up on a spiritual lesson from what they tell you.

Hand Writing

*Look, I have inscribed you on the palms
of My hands. —Isaiah 49:16*

Recon

Do you ever write anything on your hand? Maybe a friend's phone number. Maybe an assignment due date. Maybe the time of your next practice, ball game, or notes to remember what you planned to say. Maybe a one-word message of inspiration to yourself.

You put things there because you want to be sure to remember them. Or perhaps because you don't have any paper to write on. When you need the information, you'll know where to look. It'll be right there. On your hand.

Well, God doesn't need to write on His hands for *any* of those reasons. He never forgets things. He's never late to things. He's never behind or in a rush or not sure where to find a scratch piece of paper.

He writes your name there—right there on His hands—simply because you're His. Simply because He wants you close. Simply because He loves you, and you're special to Him.

Actionable Intel

You think God ever forgets about you? Forgets where you are? Forgets what you're going through? Read Isaiah 49:14–15. You're not the first to wonder. But what's His answer to your question?

His Child for Life

*"I'm no longer worthy to be called
your son."—Luke 15:19*

Recon

In Jesus' parable, the prodigal son squandered his entire inheritance after demanding it from his father ahead of time. He threw it all away. Treated it like something he could spend however he wanted. And now he was broke. Guilty and ashamed. If there's one thing he knew, he knew his father would never take him back now.

Or so he *thought*.

As a parent myself, let me just tell you, there's nothing any child of mine could ever do that would make him any less my boy. Or any less loved. *Not worthy to be called my son?* Ridiculous. And if that goes for me, just think what it means from God.

I know how it feels. To feel unworthy. To feel guilty and no longer loved. But believe me, that's not how it is. Your Father is crazy about you. Always has been, always will be.

Actionable Intel

Reread the parable of the prodigal son—Luke 15:11–24. What needed to change in how the son thought about his father? What needs to change in how you think about your heavenly Father?

Why So Forgetful?

Forgetting what is behind and reaching forward to what is ahead. —Philippians 3:13

Recon

Do you remember what you did on March 3, two years ago, between 10:30 and 11:30 in the morning? No?

Why not? Weren't you there? Were you blacked out for that hour? Taking a mid-morning nap? I doubt it. And yet for some reason—even though you were wide awake, probably in class or something, with people all around—you've got no memory of it. *How come?*

Is it because you've been working hard to forget it? Do you repeat to yourself every day, *Forget what happened on the morning of March 3.* No, the reason you've forgotten it is because you've replaced it with something else. You've scooted it off the stage of your memory by trotting something new out there instead.

That's how you get bad thinking out of your head. You don't kick lies out as much as you put truth in. You don't concentrate on the Devil as much as you focus on Jesus.

Actionable Intel

Worship Jesus today every time He comes into your mind. And just see if your enemy can get any traction inside your head.

More Than You Know

*To all who did receive Him, He gave them the
right to be children of God.* —John 1:12

Recon

The enemy says you're ordinary, nothing special. God
says you are "remarkably and wonderfully made" (Psalm
139:14). The enemy says you're unloved and unlovable.
God says He has "loved you with an everlasting love"
(Jeremiah 31:3).

The enemy says you're not worth much, that you
can't do anything. God compares you to "living stones"—
unique, unlike any other—"being built into a spiritual
house," able to offer "spiritual sacrifices acceptable to
God through Jesus Christ" (1 Peter 2:5). He says you're
part of "a chosen race, a royal priesthood, a holy nation,
a people for His possession, so that you may proclaim the
praises of the One who called you out of darkness into His
marvelous light" (v. 9).

At one time you *weren't* these things. But now you're
a child of God. "You had not received mercy, but now you
have" (v. 10).

You've been saved. And you will never be the same.

Actionable Intel

Look up and read Psalm 139:1–6. See if you don't feel
special to God when you're finished.

Helmet Safety

He is a shield to all who take refuge
in Him. —Psalm 18:30

Recon

All but one or two states in the US have laws requiring motorcycle riders to wear helmets, at least until age eighteen or twenty. In many states, *nobody* can ride without one. But even where people technically can get away with not wearing protective headgear, the smart ones still do. To some people, helmets feel too heavy, too uncomfortable, too uncool. But those same qualities are seen by others as providing them with full coverage and security. By knowing their head is protected, they're able to enjoy mile after mile of worry-free enjoyment.

Your "helmet of salvation" serves a similar purpose—keeping you constantly aware of the protection His grace provides from all enemy threats and attacks.

Too many people treat their helmet like an optional accessory. They rarely even think about it. But what they don't realize is that being shielded from harm today is the way to get the absolute most from every ride in the future.

Actionable Intel

What are some of the opinions you've heard others give as to why Christianity is too cumbersome or restricting? How do those same things make you feel protected and give you peace and joy in life?

1=1=1

There is salvation in no one else. —Acts 4:12

Recon

You are a child of God. And as a child of God, you have been given an incredible inheritance by your Father. These two realities—your identity in Christ and your inheritance in Christ—join together to form your helmet of salvation.

One equals the other, equals the other, equals the other.

When you live knowing (1) who you are, and when you live knowing (2) what you've got, you live knowing (3) the helmet of salvation is on your head, protecting your mind from enemy lies.

Today I'm asking you to go to your prayer place and write out a simple prayer, asking God to keep you daily reminded of who He's made you to be and what He's given you to work with. Pray that He would fit your mind with this ruggedly protective helmet, so that you can experience the full blessings and privileges of your salvation *right this minute.*

Actionable Intel

Go throughout your day today knowing you're being protected by the One who's added you to His family.

Working as a Team

As iron sharpens iron, so one person sharpens another. —Proverbs 27:17 NIV

Recon

In 2 Samuel 10, King David's fighting men found themselves surrounded by two opposing armies. So David's general, Joab, divided his forces and put his brother in charge of half the men while he led the other group. They each fought their own battle against one of the hostile armies.

And this is what the two brothers agreed on: "If the Arameans are too strong for me, then you are to come to my rescue; but if the Ammonites are too strong for you, then I will come to rescue you" (v. 11 NIV). Neither of them was truly alone in the fight, because if one of the brothers began to lose, the other would rush full-force to his defense.

That's a pretty good strategy for us to use as well. In fighting our own battles, we should team up with family members and friends who are willing to share in our combat.

Actionable Intel

Think of someone who could join you in this kind of mutual warfare—someone you can ask to be your partner in standing firm against the enemy. Maybe one of your siblings? One of your friends? Pray about how you could ask them to join you.

Following Directions

Because you did not trust Me to show My holiness in the sight of the Israelites, you will not bring this assembly into the land I have given them. —Numbers 20:12

Recon

God gives us numerous stories in the Bible to help us see why following His Word faithfully, honestly, and obediently is serious business. One of them is found in Numbers 20, where Moses forfeited his chance of leading Israel into Canaan.

God had told Moses, when the people had started complaining of thirst in the wilderness, "to speak to the rock while they watch, and it will yield its water" (v. 8). But when the time came to do it, Moses didn't *speak* to the rock; he *whacked* it twice—hard—with his staff.

Now maybe he was thinking back to the time in Exodus 17, when the sharp blow of his staff on another rock had produced water before—at the Lord's specific direction (v. 6). But God wants us listening carefully today and every day for how to specifically apply His Word to whatever situation we're facing now. He's ready to bring the water—ready to cause His power to be seen—but first He wants us to trust Him and do exactly what He says.

Actionable Intel

You'll find this account in Numbers 20:1–13. Looking at verses 3–5, and then at verse 10, what do you think perhaps caused Moses to overreact? What can we learn from this?

Hunger in the Heartland

*As you have received Christ Jesus the Lord,
walk in Him, rooted and built up in Him and
established in the faith. —Colossians 2:6–7*

Recon

Moldova, a small inland country near Russia, is among the poorest countries in all of Europe. But making this depressing fact even sadder is that much of the farmable land in Moldova is composed of what's known as "black soil"—dirt so naturally rich and fertile that it's capable of growing just about anything.

What a tragedy to see so much poverty in a land with so much potential.

Your enemy, I'll have you know, is well aware of the richness of your soil—the raw energy available to you because of the depth of God's righteousness within you. But unless you and I regularly yield to God's Spirit as He's growing our hearts and minds, making full use of what we've been given, Satan can deceive us into living shallow lives that bear little resemblance to the treasure we possess.

You should never know a day of hunger, child of God. And you must never let your enemy convince you otherwise.

Actionable Intel

Do a little research to find out the kind of nutrients that God has placed within the soil in your home area. To most people, it's just dirt. But like the power of God's righteousness within you, it's capable of producing all sorts of beautiful, nourishing things . . . if people will just plant something in it.

Of Mountains and Molehills

*If we have food and clothing, we will be
content with these.* —1 Timothy 6:8

Recon

There are people in the world today who honestly don't
know where their next meal is coming from. Or if they do,
they know it's most likely coming from the moldy, crusty,
bug-eaten leftovers inside a garbage dump.

Your enemy will try convincing you that your
problems are the biggest in the world—that nobody has
it worse off than you. But the truth is, you probably aren't
worried about what you'll eat later today, huh? Still, he'll
try causing you to focus on what *you're* lacking, what
you're enduring, what *you're* unhappy or uncomfortable
about. He'll try making you think there's no way you can
possibly deal with it or be thankful and content in the
midst of it.

God does care about what you're going through, just
as He cares for the suffering of others. But one of the
ways He cares best for you is by helping you walk through
difficult things with the shoes of peace tightly strapped on,
trampling on the enemy's attempts to blow everything out
of proportion.

Actionable Intel

How could you show kindness and care toward someone
who's struggling with some kind of problem today? Don't
just think about it. Do it. Go up and put your arm around
them. Say a prayer with them. Ask if you can help them.
It'll put your problems in a little better perspective.

Live It

*The life I now live in the body, I live by faith
in the Son of God.* —Galatians 2:20

Recon

You would never take your temperature with a tire gauge. You would never determine the final score of a ball game by comparing whose uniforms looked the cleanest. Neither of these is an accurate measuring stick. Well, the same is true when it comes to your faith. You can never get an accurate read on your faith merely by judging how you feel about it.

Faith is an action, not a feeling.

So if you *feel* a bit fearful and yet still *act* on the truth of God's Word and follow Him at His command, you are faith-FULL despite what you are feeling at the moment. But the opposite is also true. If you or I can't share any personal, firsthand stories of how we've trusted God and how He's shown Himself trustworthy—our faith isn't as strong as we think it is.

Don't let the enemy get in your head by making you think that your feelings are the appropriate barometer of your faith. Put him under your feet by marching out of the house today with a live-it-like-you-mean-it, shield-wielding faith.

Actionable Intel

Gather a couple of friends today who will pray with you about helping each others' faith to grow—by encouraging each other to live what you know.

I Quit

*Flee from youthful passions, and pursue righteousness,
faith, love, and peace. —2 Timothy 2:22*

Recon

Our strongholds are not all the enemy's fault. Every time
we nurse a grudge, every time we let a fear control us,
every time we choose to cheat instead of putting in the
effort we should, we may as well be working on the
Devil's construction crew. Yep, buying into his lies is like
putting on a hard hat, scooping up the mortar, grabbing
the next brick, and squishing it into the wall he's building
around us.

Why would we ever do that? Why would we willingly
partner up with him—working against ourselves on the
destruction plans he's been drawing up against us?

We do it because we don't always realize we've got
a choice. We do it because we confuse sin as giving us a
feeling of control. Most of all, we do it because we don't
remember what Jesus died to save us from so we don't
have to be tied down anymore.

Walk off the job today. Your work is done here.

Actionable Intel

Write your letter of resignation today from the enemy's
construction/destruction company. No two-weeks' notice—
you're quitting immediately. Tack it up with some of the
other prayers and Bible verses you've been putting on
your wall.

Speak Up

All the people listened attentively to the
book of the law. —Nehemiah 8:3

Recon

Soon after Nehemiah rebuilt the walls of Jerusalem and the people returned from years of exile, they held a celebration ceremony in the center of town. Ezra the scribe brought out the scroll bearing the Law of Moses—which is the first five books of the Old Testament. And he read from it—out loud, before all the people—from daybreak till noon.

There's something about hearing the Bible read. Aloud. Even reading it out loud to yourself. It makes the experience more like what the early Israelites discovered, hearing these old words—the Word of God—perhaps for the first time, or for the first time in a long time.

Hearing it aloud simply holds your attention better. It activates additional senses. It speaks differently somehow. You read more slowly. You don't skim over it as much.

One way to sharpen your sword is to do it out loud. Where you can hear it.

Actionable Intel

The next time you're reading the Bible, read it out loud. See how it changes the experience.

Threat Assessment

*Whoever thinks he stands must be careful
not to fall. —1 Corinthians 10:12*

Recon

Recent news reports about terrorist attacks in different parts of the world have made people everywhere more alert and vigilant about their safety.

But this is actually how spiritual warriors like you have always lived. They know to ask themselves questions like, "Where would the enemy most likely strike?"

One of the answers is this: Satan will try to hit you where you're the strongest—the area of your life where you pose the greatest threat to him and his plans.

So ask yourself: What are you the best at? What are some things you do really well? Expect him to strike there. Expect him to try to get you to admire yourself to the point of becoming proud, ego-tripping, obnoxious. Expect him to tempt you to tie your worth to your performance, tricking you into thinking you're a success or failure based on nothing other than your report card or your music recital or the number of points you scored. He'll look for any place—even the good places—to find an opening into your heart.

Actionable Intel

Write down some things that you'd consider some of your real strengths. How could the enemy try to twist them into spiritual trouble spots? Today, pray about these areas of your life, and ask the Lord to strengthen you against enemy attack.

Learn What's Important

The wise man must not boast in his wisdom. . . .
The one who boasts should boast in this, that he
understands and knows Me.—*Jeremiah 9:23–24*

Recon

I hope you're taking your schoolwork and education seriously. The opportunity to develop yourself as a student, as a learner, is a highly valuable thing to do. In fact, it doesn't stop when your formal school years end but continues on throughout life. I hope you'll always stay intellectually hungry, curious, and inquisitive. There's so much to discover.

But physical intelligence and educated opinion, although noble pursuits, are not the final word. *God's Word is the final word.* Whenever you're led to accept things as fact that contradict the truth of the Bible, understand you're veering off into areas that will always lead to needless rabbit trails and goose chases.

Logic and reason are God-given tools in your toolbox. Use them. Sharpen them. Be willing to ask the hard, brave questions. But realize that knowledge alone is never king; it is only a servant that ushers you more deeply into the eternal, unchanging strength and structure of God's truth.

Actionable Intel

What are some things you've been taught in school that are contrary to God's truth? Write them down and plan to talk about them with an adult you trust very soon.

Pre-Trial Hearings

*To someone who considers a thing to be unclean,
to that one it is unclean.* —Romans 14:14

Recon

If I were to mention the word *conviction* to you, you might think about police reports and court records. When someone is convicted of a crime, they're declared guilty by a judge or jury, then left to await sentencing for their unlawful deeds.

That's generally where your enemy is hoping to lead you as well. To act on his sinful temptations. To follow him into guilt and then suffer the consequences.

But God is one step ahead of him . . . because He's given you the Holy Spirit to "convict" you about sin (John 16:8). Not just *after* the fact, when the only thing left is to deal with the fallout. He convicts you of sin *beforehand*, when it's no more than the spark of an idea. He gives you both the time and courage to avoid a bad choice, reject it, and be spared from its aftermath.

Realize, by putting on the breastplate of righteousness today, you're wearing the protective coating of God's keep-away, keep-your-distance *conviction*.

Actionable Intel

Think of two or three times when you've felt convicted by God's Spirit about something you were saying or doing. How would you describe this to another person if they asked you?

Want to Feel Better?

Make every effort to keep the unity of the Spirit through the bond of peace. —Ephesians 4:3 NIV

Recon

Comparing yourselves to others is dangerous. For starters, it always gives us a false reading on ourselves. Either we think we're better than another person or we end up feeling like we're worse. Either way, comparison puts us in a bad place emotionally. And remember, the only thing that really matters is Christ's righteousness anyway. When you placed faith in Him, you received His perfect righteousness as your own.

There's nothing in the world that compares to the beauty of this gift you've been given.

So anytime you're tempted to be envious or jealous of someone else, here's a new strategy to try. Remember the redemption and power you've been given as a child of God. Then make the decision to *compliment* them instead of *compare* yourself to them. The enemy will hate the encouragement it brings to the other person almost as much as he hates the freedom it gives to you.

Comparison is the enemy of peace, just as unity is the goal of peace. Don't let anything drive a wedge between you and another child of God.

Actionable Intel

Go up to a person today who you're often tempted to compare yourself to, and give him or her a compliment instead.

Bigger and Stronger

*Grow in the grace and knowledge of our Lord
and Savior Jesus Christ. —2 Peter 3:18*

Recon

Knowledge is like a muscle. It gets stronger with use.

For instance, the reason you know you'll love that first cheesy bite of your favorite pizza is because you've experienced it so many times.

The life of faith is strangely similar. Every time you trust God, even if it comes with all kinds of struggle, you learn something new about Him—how He blesses you with joy and peace and the conviction to keep going. Every time you activate your spiritual senses, you get better at recognizing the subtle, gentle movements of His Spirit, how He speaks through His Word, leading you as you go, helping you recognize things and know what to do.

The first step or two may be baby steps—like all of ours were. But each step is leading you to a new learning experience. And the more of those steps you get under your belt, the more you'll know which one to take next.

Actionable Intel

Ask God to show you a way you could *experience* Him today—through faith—as you trust Him and follow Him.

Sure You Want to Trade?

What good is a birthright to me?—Genesis 25:32

Recon

Jacob and Esau were twin brothers. But because Esau was technically born first, the culture of their day said that Esau was the one who would receive the "birthright"—a doubled portion of their father's inheritance.

Esau's "younger" brother Jacob was a cunning deceiver. And one day when Esau returned home, hungry from a long day of hunting, Jacob offered him a bowl of homemade stew . . . in exchange for the birthright.

Esau was so hungry that it sounded like a good deal. But was it really? Think about it: a double portion of their father's estate as a gift he'd be able to enjoy throughout the rest of his lifetime and also pass on to later generations as well. Or . . . soup. He'd likely be hungry again before dinner.

So . . . what do you think? Good deal or bad deal?

Anytime we choose the deceiver's temptations over the rich inheritance of our salvation, those are the terms we're agreeing to. We're selling ourselves short.

Actionable Intel

Analyze one of your more common temptations. Break it down into what your enemy is really offering you, by the time you experience the guilt and shame of it. Ask yourself: How does he get away with this . . . when your salvation offers so much more?

No Such Thing as Secrets

"There is nothing covered that won't be uncovered, nothing hidden that won't be made known."—Luke 12:2

Recon

Satan loves secrets. He tries to get you to keep as many as you can. They give him room to maneuver. In the dark. Undetectable.

Show me someone who doesn't want anybody else to know what they're thinking, what they're doing, where they're going, or how they're occupying their time—and I'll show you someone who doesn't stand a chance against our enemy's way of fighting.

Although you might be sort of a private person—which is fine—I'm sure you know the difference between keeping something quiet because it's personal, because it's nobody's business, and keeping something quiet because you realize you're doing something you shouldn't.

The more others know about you, the more integrity you'll have. And that's the goal—to be the same person in public as you are in private. This leaves fewer areas exposed to surprise attack. The myth of a secret life is that secrets stay secret. Secrets almost always get revealed, and every secret contains its own consequence.

Actionable Intel

In today's verse, underline the word *covered*, and circle the word *uncovered*. Now ask the Lord to show you what things you may be covering up that you need to bring to the light so you can be free.

Conscience

I always do my best to have a clear conscience toward God and men. —Acts 24:16

Recon

Conscience is a powerful guide—a deep, internal instinct within every person, put there by God as a moral steering mechanism. You have a conscience and so do I. As Christians, our conscience gets even more effective, because the Holy Spirit awakens it by His power and His presence, making it even more reliable in helping us determine between right and wrong. And yet . . .

It's still not flawless. It's influenced by our past experiences and habit patterns. It's dulled by the layers of excuses and arguments we've papered across it. It's *good*, but it's not perfect. Our job is to stay humble and obedient, not compromising this gift we've been given, while God's Spirit continually transforms and realigns it toward His truth.

And we must always remember, even at its best, our conscience can only be a guide, not a final answer. Ultimately, God's Word, God's truth, God's opinion on any matter is the only thing that is *never* compromised. Totally reliable. Totally trustworthy.

Actionable Intel

Read Romans 12:1 to find out how you can cooperate with the Holy Spirit as He renews your conscience.

Power Sharing

You will receive power when the Holy Spirit has come on you, and you will be My witnesses. —Acts 1:8

Recon

Your armor can keep you safe in your spiritual battles. Not only that, but it will also make you confident enough to charge ahead with boldness and courage, knowing you're suited up for spiritual victory.

As you continue to recognize God's power in your life, as He equips you to walk in purity and righteousness, I'm praying that you will embrace the responsibility, as well, for telling others what He can do—not because you've *heard* about it, but because you've actually now *experienced* it.

That's what happened in Acts 1, soon after Jesus' return from the earth to the Father. He sent the Holy Spirit that He had promised His disciples. And perhaps the most noticeable result of the Spirit's arrival was how these once-timid, fearful men became eager to tell others about how they could experience God's power too.

You've received so much from Him. Take it. Use it. But don't forget to share it as well.

Actionable Intel

Ask the Lord for courage and opportunities to talk with others about some of what you've been learning from this devotional. You'd be surprised how many people, deep down, want to be strong and growing spiritually. Wouldn't you love to be part of helping them do that?

Out of This World

"I am not praying that You take them out of the world but that You protect them from the evil one."—John 17:15

Recon

My boys were doing a science experiment recently, looking at the difference between mixtures and solutions. A *mixture* consists of two or more substances that still maintain their own identity even after they're combined, like cereal in milk. A *solution,* on the other hand, is when one of those substances actually dissolves into the other, like salt that completely liquefies into boiling water. The solid is totally melted into its new environment.

Reread today's verse. Notice that Jesus never expected His disciples (or you) to completely pull out of the world and its culture. You can't help but be mixed up with it. But you also can't afford to be dissolved into it—to lose your identity, to start looking and acting and thinking just like the environment around you. Be distinct. Be different.

So, yes, while you live here on earth, love others and enjoy what God has given you here. Just don't *become* what's here . . . because you "are not of the world," Jesus said, "as I am not of the world" (John 17:16).

Actionable Intel

Look up how to make one of those easy "ocean in a bottle" mixtures of water and oil, where the colored water exists side-by-side with the other substance, yet also stays separate from it. Keep it on your dresser as a reminder to be "in the world, but not of it."

Next Steps

Your word is a lamp for my feet and a
light on my path. —Psalm 119:105

Recon

Look up "ancient oil lamps" in a search engine, and you'll see that these lamps were hardly the equivalent of a modern flashlight. What little light they gave out was pretty much encircled right around you. You might be able to see where to put your next step, but that was about *it*.

Exactly! That's it!

The only step that really matters in following God *is* the next step. Not ten steps ahead. Not the ten-year plan. Sure, you can try imagining some of that. As a guess. But the Word is designed for giving you next-step info, which is everything your faith needs to know for now. And as far as knowing which step to take after that? The Word will show you what to do when you get there.

Your enemy is impatient and impulsive, and he wants to make you feel pressured and hurried. But your God is patient, wise, and loving. And He will lead you where you ought to go. Hold on to the ancient life of His Word and . . . Keep. Moving. Forward.

Actionable Intel

Take what God's Word says to you today as your light. Let it guide you to the next step, even if just a little one. That's how steps of faith, over time, become leaps of faith into incredible things.

Steady Pressure

"By your endurance gain your lives."—Luke 21:19

Recon

Sometimes the most memorable victories are the slow victories.

Sure, we like the flashy ones—drop the bomb, deliver the knockout, slam the door shut, declare the winner. But most things aren't done that way. Most things require steady, consistent effort, played out over time. Like the person who faithfully saves a few dollars a week, then walks into the store a year from now with the cash to pay for something they really want.

Honestly, this is why so many people do more losing than winning, especially against their strongholds. They don't want to take the time and make the sacrifice. They don't want to keep doing what it takes. Because, yes, Satan is defeated. He knows it; you know it. But these strongholds of his aren't blown up in a day. They're chiseled off with one hammer blow after another. They're destroyed with daily doses of faith and trust. They *will* come down—don't doubt that for a second—but prepare to face a long battle. And win it with day-after-day obedience.

Actionable Intel

Mark a day on your calendar next month when you want to see a significant victory or progress in a particular area of your life. What's one thing you could commit to doing every day until then that will help you reach this goal?

Kryptonite

About midnight Paul and Silas were praying and singing hymns to God . . . and suddenly there was a great earthquake. —Acts 16:25–26 ESV

Recon

Kryptonite. It's part of the Superman legend. It's some kind of radioactive element that exists on his home planet of Krypton and is able to make even Superman weak and powerless.

Kryptonite is a comic-book creation. Although there is an actual gas called krypton that goes into fluorescent bulbs and photography lighting and stuff, Kryptonite doesn't actually exist.

But maybe something like it does. In spiritual form. *In prayer*.

Prayer is your enemy's Kryptonite. It's what weakens and unravels all his ploys against you. Prayer is the mechanism that brings down the power of heaven into your life. It activates your spiritual armor and makes it effective. It alerts the enemy that you're aware of his intentions and does the double duty of safeguarding you from his attacks.

So the next time you're praying, realize you're doing much more than just saying words. You're loading up with Kryptonite. And your enemy is too weak to stop it.

Actionable Intel

Try drawing a picture of what you think Kryptonite might look like. How cool is it to think you've been given a lifetime supply of it . . . in prayer?

Who Can You Trust?

"Watch out that no one deceives you."—Mark 13:5

Recon

We can trust our minds up to a point. We can trust our conscience up to a point. We can trust our feelings up to a . . . no, we can't really trust our feelings. But all of this stuff—logic, reasoning, conscience, emotion—is constantly feeding us information, and we need to think carefully about whether we can trust it to lead us in the right way.

Since none of these sources is ever foolproof, that's what makes them such delicious targets for the enemy. He knows that if he can make something sound logical . . . if he can make something seem right . . . if he can make something feel satisfying . . . we might just mistake it for truth.

This is why the Bible must be our constant, all-the-time, go-to guide. Because when we spend time every day in the Word, God's Spirit can use it to mold our thinking, to tenderize our conscience, even to capture our feelings in midstream, before they send us over the waterfall.

The Word stops deception in its tracks.

Actionable Intel

If you haven't already, I hope you'll make a commitment to spend at least a little time in the Bible *every day*. We're used to doing certain things every day—brushing our teeth, combing our hair, making our bed. Don't forget about *this* thing—the most important thing of all.

Who's Next?

Gideon and the 300 men came to the Jordan and crossed it. They were exhausted but still in pursuit. —Judges 8:4

Recon

Gideon and his extremely small band of soldiers had just witnessed a miracle. Despite their few numbers, God had enabled them to defeat an enemy of thousands, terrifying their foe in the dead of night with nothing other than torches, trumpets, and clay pots.

But often these are the exact moments your enemy is waiting for—when you are tired from a battle you've just won. You're celebrating and trying to catch your breath from exhaustion, and in satisfying triumph you unhitch your armor. Just for a little while. You stop reading the Word. Stop praying. Stop pursuing righteousness.

That's just the window your enemy is looking for.

Listen, I know you can get tired. I do too. Fighting an unseen enemy who never seems to relent, who's always looking for a way to deceive and take advantage of you, can be a wearying feeling. But learn the lesson of Gideon, who the Bible says was "weary yet pursuing" (NASB).

Keep your armor on, even when you're tired, even when you're resting. God will give you the strength to take on the next challenge—even if it's much sooner than you expected.

Actionable Intel

How do you typically feel after a big victory, whether on the basketball court or in some other kind of competitive arena? What temptations or unseen battles seem the strongest at those times?

War and Peace

Seek peace and pursue it. —Psalm 34:14

Recon

Do you see why "peace" is included in your battle armor? Because maintaining peace *is a battle*. Your enemy is always trying to take it away from you or to convince you that God can't really give it to you.

And, boy, does the enemy have the momentum on his side—because the most natural response to problems or pressure is to *lose* your peace. It doesn't require any effort to go there. It's like the black spots that grow on the bananas in your kitchen fruit bowl. Did you put them there? No. Bananas going from green to yellow to black to mushy is just what happens. Naturally. Without any help.

But when trying to restore peace with someone who's mad at you, or stay calm in a crisis, or restrain your hot temper—you will need to make a deliberate and almost unnatural decision to stay anchored in God. Trusting His Word. Trusting His heart. Believing He's there and will help you. And He *will* help you. To maintain and sustain your peace.

Actionable Intel

As you pray today, picture yourself aligning in battle formation, with God as your captain and commander. You're not just preparing for the day; you're preparing for war.

Limited Offer

"I assure you: They've got their reward!"—Matthew 6:2

Recon

Unlike all the religions of the world, Christianity is not a do-something-for-God religion. It's a look-what-God-has-done relationship. The amazing secret of living by faith is that we are "free" to follow Him (Galatians 5:1) instead of trying to impress Him. We don't follow rules; we follow God.

One of the nice things about this freedom is that it leaves room for you to enjoy things that you are uniquely interested in—a hobby or personal interest. As long as you're not entertaining yourself with something that offends God, you are free to participate in all sorts of activities and still enjoy God's blessing.

But even as you enjoy them, always remember—there's only so much benefit these things can provide you. They give limited rewards. Limited fun. They hand out their little payout, and then they're done.

So while lots of things may be acceptable things, they're not the highest paying things. They don't have any eternal benefits. The best things—the most rewarding things—are what you do by faith, not just for fun.

Actionable Intel

Write down a few examples of some "low-paying" activities that you participate in. How much time do you devote in a typical week to the things on that list? Ask yourself: Is this the kind of limited return you really want on most of your investments?

Know Peace

"There is no peace for the wicked," says
the LORD. —*Isaiah 48:22*

Recon

I'm not saying *you're* "wicked." But let's be honest, you and I both do some things sometimes that are not exactly, uh . . . nice, right?

Why do we do these not-nice things? Why do we get mad and shoot back smart-aleck answers? Why do we watch things on TV we might not want our parents or our pastor to know about? Why do we not care nearly as much about others as we care about ourselves?

Because we've let the Devil convince us there's a great ending to these actions, that somehow they'll give us peace and make us feel better. They'll satisfy us and give us all the things we think we deserve for all we've had to put up with in our lives.

But the truth is, "there is no peace" in the end for anyone who chooses to act in a way that dishonors God. So choose well. And then experience what it's like to have a life brimming with divine blessings.

Actionable Intel

Read the two verses leading up to the Lord's "no peace" declaration—Isaiah 48:20–21. What was God's command to His people who'd been exiled to wicked Babylon? What did He say they would experience by trusting that His ways are the ways of peace?

Memory Makers

I have treasured Your word in my heart. —Psalm 119:11

Recon

One day I was out shopping in a store, and an old song piped through the sound system. I heard the familiar lines and chorus of this song that I hadn't heard since I was a teenager. For just a quick moment, I suddenly felt like I was fifteen at summer camp, all over again. I could still see the shirt and sandals I was wearing. I could see the young faces of my childhood friends. And as I walked out to my car a few minutes later, I wasn't just humming the tune under my breath . . .

I remembered every word.

Every single word came back to me.

How interesting that I could remember words from a song I hadn't heard in decades, and hearing it could create such a transformative effect on me. Why wouldn't the Bible have even more of a lasting effect in our mind and memories?

It will . . . if we put it in our hearts the way we put *other* things in our hearts.

Actionable Intel

Consider taking one verse this week—you pick the one—and try committing it to memory. It's not really as hard as it sounds. I guarantee you, it's a memory you'll be making for life.

You Have It All

Didn't God choose the poor in this world to be rich in faith and heirs of the kingdom?—James 2:5

Recon

For much of its history, the ancient Roman army didn't have an established uniform for its fighting men. Soldiers who could afford better gear could wear what they bought, but those who were poor often did without and just hoped for the best. Despite being in the army, they simply couldn't afford every piece of equipment they really needed.

But not you.

No one on God's side ever needs to go out underdressed.

You may sometimes feel like you don't belong with the important group, that your faith in God is not the same caliber as people who seem to make a better spiritual impression. But the price of your breastplate and everything else you need for victory has been covered in full—just like theirs. You are covered in full. In Christ.

So put it on today. Every single piece you have. It's been purchased on the cross and provided at great cost. Even the weakest and poorest among us can now fight like the strong, well-supplied warriors He's made us to be.

Actionable Intel

Imagine being one of those penniless soldiers who was scarcely protected from the dangers of open warfare. Imagine your heart being exposed to any stray missile or arrow that came flying past. The only thing worse would be not realizing your armor was all there . . . all the time.

Save It for the Sanctuary

*If I had decided to say these things aloud, I would
have betrayed your people. —Psalm 73:15*

Recon

Psalm 73 was written by a man named Asaph, who was
struggling to stay at peace. Everywhere he looked, he saw
arrogant, ungodly people getting ahead. Getting what they
wanted. Yet here *he* was, trying to live for God, and having
nothing but trouble and problems to show for it.

And it was bugging him. Bad. To the point where he
wondered—like maybe *you* wonder sometimes—"Am I
doing this all for nothing?"

But Asaph chose to do something very important.
(Watch and learn.) Instead of blabbing his thoughts and
questions to others, whose faith he might have damaged,
he took his concerns into the "sanctuary," into worship
(vv. 16–17). And God met him there . . . with help, with
truth, with perspective.

With peace.

When the enemy riles you with lies and distortions,
take it up with God in prayer and praise. And see if His
good counsel doesn't calm you back down.

Actionable Intel

Read a few words from the last part of Psalm 73—verses
21–26. Notice what the writer is feeling at the beginning.
Notice what he's feeling at the end. Notice how God can
take us from peeved to peaceful.

The Faith to Forgive

"If you forgive people their wrongdoing, your heavenly Father will forgive you as well." —Matthew 6:14

Recon

One of the most daring acts of faith is forgiveness . . . because you don't know what will happen when you do it. For instance, the other person may do something bad to you again. They may tell you they don't *need* your forgiveness and that they don't think they've done anything wrong. They may even say *you're* the one at fault, that you ought to be apologizing to them.

Forgiveness. It's a sensitive area. You just never know.

But here's something you *do* know. *If you forgive, you'll be forgiven.* You'll be modeling Christ's heart of mercy to someone else. You'll be gaining a new appreciation for what your own sins have cost. And even if it doesn't lead to peace in a personal relationship, you'll be doing something that leads to peace, freedom, and a closer relationship with Him.

You'll be living by faith. By forgiving.

And that's the only way to live.

Actionable Intel

Take the faith dare today. If you haven't forgiven someone for something they've done or said, forgive them. Don't let the enemy keep you from walking in complete openness and freedom with Jesus.

Things to Remember

Do not kill them; otherwise, my people will forget. —Psalm 59:11

Recon

David was a man who attracted his share of enemies. Bad ones. A few even wanted to kill him, like King Saul—the enemy ringleader behind David's complaint in Psalm 59. But David was wise enough to know what God is *obviously* wise enough to know. If everybody loved us, if we faced no resistance, our natural tendency would be to "forget" some things that a battle helps us remember.

We'd forget to put God first. We'd forget that we are totally dependent on Him for everything. We'd forget that serving Him is better than serving our selfish desires. We'd forget what He's saved us from. We'd forget how easily we wander away from Him.

So yes, God *could* do away with our enemy so we could live without all the trouble he causes. But sometimes doing battle is the only thing that helps us remember. Let's use this enemy to our advantage where we can. Let's stay in battle mode so we never forget.

Actionable Intel

Write down five reasons today why you need God so much. Had you forgotten some of them?

Own the Words

*These words that I am giving you today are
to be in your heart. —Deuteronomy 6:6*

Recon

I'm sure you've watched enough movies and TV shows to be able to spot the difference between someone who's *saying* their lines and someone who *owns* their lines. The *owner* doesn't just look like a person playing a role. You almost believe they're actually the character they're portraying because they are so authentic. They're not just repeating words off a script. Those words are from the heart.

Good actors can accomplish this because they've said their lines a zillion times. They've read and repeated them, not only in rehearsals, but in the bathroom mirror, in the driver's seat of their car, while pacing around their living room, while falling off to sleep at night. The reason those words are *there* when the camera snaps on is that those words became *theirs* long before.

If you want to be someone who sounds like a believable Christian, then really be one—not simply by *reading* the Word, but by *knowing* the Word, rehearsing it, thinking about it. Being changed by it. Living it.

Own the Word.

Actionable Intel

Read Deuteronomy 6:6–9. Using these instructions as a starter, what are some practical ways that you can do what Moses told the Israelites to do?

Fearless

*I will say to the LORD, "My refuge and my fortress,
my God, in whom I trust."—Psalm 91:2*

Recon

One of my sons has always been prone to worrying. He's
not a scaredy-cat. He can just get something stuck in his
mind, and it's hard for him to get it out. To stop thinking
about it. To stop worrying about it. Are you like that?

So when I pray for this particular son of mine, one
of the things I very often—very *intentionally*—pray for
him is that God will instill courage within him. I ask the
Lord to keep a wall of protection around him that will
deflect the enemy's attempts to torment him with fear and
anxiety. Whenever I come across a Bible verse that speaks
about our confidence in God's care and how completely
He defends us, I turn it into a prayer for my son (and
sometimes for myself too).

This is how we turn God's Word into prayer. Since
Scripture is so specific, your prayers can be targeted and
precise. It can help keep your praying strong and sharp.

Actionable Intel

Read Psalm 91 today. It's pretty short. But it's tall on
promises for how God protects His people. Choose at least
one verse that you can reword into a prayer for yourself.

Journey to Freedom

"If you continue in My word, you really are My disciples."—John 8:31

Recon

One of the key verses we've seen that helps us understand why the belt of truth is so important is John 8:32: "You will know the truth, and the truth will set you free."

But equally important, though lesser known, is the verse from today—John 8:31—Jesus' lead-in statement to John 8:32. Other Bible translations say it this way: "If you abide in My word" (NKJV); "if you hold to my teaching" (NIV); if you remain faithful to my teachings (NLT); "if you hold fast to My teachings and live in accordance to them" (AMPC)—*then* the truth will set you free.

Your best life, I promise you—the one where you experience the most joy, victory, and freedom—will come from walking in God's Word and continually ordering your steps and decisions according to it. That's what makes the difference. That's what disarms the enemy's influence over you.

Actionable Intel

John 8:31 or 8:32 would be good verses to memorize. The best way to do it is just to break it into little chunks, little pieces. Memorize those. Then start mashing them all together, a bit at a time. Pretty soon, you've got a part of the Bible in your head where nobody can take it from you.

Let's Do This Quickly

If my people would only listen to me, if Israel would only follow my ways, how quickly would I subdue their enemies. —Psalm 81:13–14 NIV

Recon

When we haven't been living in a way that honors the Lord, the enemy's ploy is to make you think: *Boy, God is mad at me, and He is going to get me this time*. But let me tell you something important: He's a lot less into your punishment, and a lot more into your repentance.

Repentance is the idea of turning around. When you're going down the wrong path, repentance means stopping dead in your tracks, spinning yourself around, and taking off again in the other direction. The *right* direction.

Sure, that can be hard sometimes. But the quicker you "listen" to the truth of His Word and set yourself on the path to "follow" His ways, the more "quickly," He says, He will yank the chain on your enemy's leash and keep him at bay.

I promise you, the distance between your current state of discouragement and your future state of shame-free forgiveness is not as far away as you think. It's as close as your true repentance. That's what God really wants from you—not just this time, but every time.

Actionable Intel

Quick now—what are you going to do about that sin you've been clinging onto, the one you've been refusing to admit and get settled? You're going to repent. And you're going to do it . . . when? *Quickly*.

Pray for Me

All the assembled worshipers were praying outside. Then an angel of the Lord appeared to him. —Luke 1:10–11 NIV

Recon

Zechariah the priest was about to get the surprise of a lifetime. An angel, who unexpectedly appeared while he was performing his duties in the temple, was going to give him some incredible news. Zechariah and his wife—a childless couple who were pretty old—would soon be having their first baby, a baby boy.

But note this: the Bible says this angelic meeting occurred while "all the assembled worshipers" were outside praying. I love that.

Prayer is not only a good thing to be doing *for yourself*. Prayer is something powerful that you can enlist others to do *for you*. Their prayers will be like an incubator—those warm, protective environments where eggs are kept warm to hatch. They help put you in a safe place where God has easy access to you . . . and where the enemy must work even harder to reach you.

Have you ever thought about asking the Lord to place people around you who will incubate you in prayer? Their prayers will make a world of difference in your life.

Actionable Intel

List three people you can ask to be prayer warriors for you. Make a point of asking them about it today or the next time you see them.

Good News/Bad News

The Devil has come down to you with great fury, because he knows he has a short time. —Revelation 12:12

Recon

I've got some good news and some bad news. I'll give you the bad news first.

The bad news is: the Devil "knows he has a short time"—a reality that causes him to act with "great fury" toward you. Perhaps if he didn't know this, he wouldn't be so desperate to cause as much mischief as possible. But as I'm sure you've learned—like when the school bus is waiting outside or your big paper is due tomorrow—short time frames can lead to frantic activity.

The good news is actually the same: the Devil "knows he has a short time"—*but* he doesn't know exactly how short it is. Because even though a tight deadline is stressful, there *is* something worse—not knowing exactly when the end will come. It's like that feeling you get when playing musical chairs, not knowing when the music will stop. Intense, right? Well, when the music runs out on the Devil (and this is the good part), there will definitely not be a seat left for him.

Unless, of course, you're counting the hot seat.

Actionable Intel

Write down the main idea of today's theme alongside any other facts you've journaled about the enemy's motivations for attacking you. What kind of changes in strategy or mind-set could you implement, based on this information?

True Identity

We are in Him who is true, in His Son
Jesus Christ. —1 John 5:20 NASB

Recon

In the 1930s, law enforcement everywhere was on the lookout for a notorious bank robber named John Dillinger, America's most wanted fugitive. They could never seem to find him.

And yet they kept finding Ralph Alsman. Seventeen times he was arrested, locked up, and held for questioning. In places like Toledo, Detroit, Minneapolis, and Milwaukee. Even near Dillinger's hometown.

Alsman was the same height as Dillinger. Same weight. Same general appearance. Even had a mole next to one eye. (Like Dillinger.) A scar on his left wrist. (Like Dillinger.) Not until Dillinger was gunned down by federal agents in 1934 did everyone finally believe . . . Ralph Alsman wasn't Dillinger.

Mistaken identity. It's what your enemy keeps trying to pull on you as well. Saying you're not who you say you are—and definitely not who *God* says you are. But *you* know the truth. And that's what you need to keep tucked away inside your helmet of salvation. Always.

Actionable Intel

Someone has said, "If you were charged with being a Christian, would there be enough evidence to convict you?" Make some of those charges stand up by what you do and by how you think—today.

New Flight Plan

The path of the righteous is like the light of dawn, shining brighter and brighter until midday. —Proverbs 4:18

Recon

Like everyone, you're a day older today. You'll be another day older tomorrow. Stack those days up, and they eventually lead us all toward the same place—typically to old age, old bodies, and all the other things you associate with old people.

But you're a child of God, a warrior in God's army. You've been fitted with His armor, equipped with His weapons, sealed with His Spirit, and infused with the righteousness of Christ. You are part of a family who is destined for eternal life with Him.

And according to today's verse, this means your life on earth is different. Instead of sailing over the hill toward sundown, your trajectory is pointed straight up. Your destination is not the stroke of midnight but a steady climb toward high noon. You're heading into the light, not dying off in the darkness. Every day for you—from now until the day you die—is drawing you closer to the Son.

Actionable Intel

Draw a picture or try to design a personal logo that illustrates this truth—how the journey of life for a Christian is one that never has to leave the morning.

Constantly Communicating

Pray constantly. —*1 Thessalonians 5:17*

Recon

On average, people check their phones for calls, texts, e-mails, tweets, posts, news, and messages nearly 140 times a day! Not ten or fifteen or twenty or forty. More than a *hundred*!

In other words: constantly.

Yet when most people read today's verse, they get worried. "Pray constantly? Are you kidding me? I can't be praying all the time." But if prayer became as important to us as checking our cell phones, it wouldn't be a problem, now would it?

In the same way we might check to see what's new on what's-her-name's Facebook, and then go look up her profile and view her newly posted pictures, we should be eager to reach out to our God and see what wisdom He has for us. Prayer should be as quick and automatic as the way some people reach for their smartphones. Constantly checking. Constantly connected. In constant communication.

Actionable Intel

If you have an iPod or an iPhone—or anything similar—set a reminder or a screen saver that prompts you to say a prayer every time you check your device. Try doing it every day until constant prayer becomes a habit.

Armor Off

They cut off Saul's head, stripped off his armor, and
sent messengers throughout the land. —1 Samuel 31:9

Recon

It wasn't enough for the Philistines just to kill him, this tall king of Israel. No, they needed to strip him of his armor as well. Make him look even smaller and weaker. Defeated.

It's a historical fact that when Roman soldiers were being punished by their superior officers, they would be stripped of their belts and made to stand where everybody else could see them . . . just stand there in their long tunics, undone, looking nothing like the rock-hard fighters they were supposed to be. Because without their belt, they just seemed . . .

Ordinary. Weak. Not put together well. Even *embarrassed*, since the belt was what marked them as soldiers.

The belt of truth should be what marks us too. And we should be embarrassed and uncomfortable to ever be caught without it. Because even in this unseen war, people can see the difference when someone like you is wearing the belt of truth and when you're not. When you live by the truth, you'll stand out in a crowd.

Not wearing the belt is not a good look on you.

Actionable Intel

Have you ever arrived at school or church and realized you're missing a button, or you've got a big stain on your shirt, or your zipper is undone and broken? It's embarrassing. You end up spending all day trying to cover it up so others won't see. When you think of life without wearing the belt of truth, think of it the same way.

For the Record

I remember the days of old; I meditate on all You have done; I reflect on the work of Your hands. —Psalm 143:5

Recon

One of the great things about keeping a journal is that it helps you remember. When something is in the process of happening, you think you could never forget the specific events, feelings, and experiences that seem so important and memorable right then.

But you will. Forget, that is, because memories fade. But journals don't. When you keep a record of your life in a journal, you can read back over what you've written and see yourself changing. You can see God working. You can see growth happening.

You can see your enemy failing.

In fact, I guarantee you that if you make a point of pursuing a righteous lifestyle on an ongoing basis, the difference you'll notice in your strength and maturity— within the space of just one month or one year—will absolutely blow you away. But you can't trust yourself to remember it all off the top of your head—what you were thinking, the choices you made, who was in your life at the time. You'll need to be able to go back and read it from the journal history you created to capture it and prove it. And to worship Him for it.

Actionable Intel

You don't need anything expensive to do this. Even a spiral notebook will do. And don't feel pressure to write an entry every day. You can choose to jot things down once or twice a month if you'd like . . . so long as you are keeping a record of what you see and sense God doing in your life.

Prints of Peace

*To guide our feet into
the way of peace. —Luke 1:79*

Recon

The enemy works hard to convince you that God is like a grouchy neighbor, hollering at kids to get off His lawn—a rolled-up newspaper in hand, shaking His fist, ready to swat you because He's so easily irritated. An image like this would make you want to stay away from God.

But the gospel changes the whole direction of your life and the direction of your feet. Now you can walk "in the way of peace." You can move toward God instead of being afraid to draw near.

He loves your company. You can walk in His grass, right up to His door, and right in the house, right by His side. He *wants* you at peace with Him. He *wants* you eager to be near Him, familiar with His Fatherly company.

Peace with God is the welcome mat that invites your footprints inside. In fact, He's got some shoes in your exact size, all ready for you to help make that happen.

Actionable Intel

Remember as you pray today just how close you're sitting with God . . . and just how peaceful it feels to be there. Because *He's* there. And loves having you there.

My Goodness

"Disregarding the command of God, you keep the tradition of men."—Mark 7:8

Recon

If your enemy can't get you to do bad things, he can always try another approach: like getting you to do *good* things. For the wrong reasons.

That's what a religious group called Pharisees were always doing in Jesus' day. "Why," they asked Him, "don't Your disciples live according to the tradition of the elders?" Those traditions included things like never eating without washing their hands first. Which is a good thing, right? (Yes, it is.) But does it make you a better person than someone who doesn't? Did clean hands, clean plates, clean forks, clean cups—all those things that made the Pharisees feel so good about themselves—did they really make them any closer to God?

The Devil doesn't mind if you do good "religiousy" things, if the reason you're doing them is wrong—like to impress people or try to be better than them. The traditions of our culture and even of our churches can be good, but keeping *them* is not always the same thing as honoring *God*. Know the difference.

Actionable Intel

Ask the Lord to help you recognize anything you might do today for the purpose of impressing others or even to impress Him.

Mood Swings

They came and woke Him up, saying, "Master, Master, we're going to die!"—Luke 8:24

Recon

I know it feels that way sometimes. Like you're "going to die." Like it's the end of the world. When Jesus' disciples were out sailing with Him and saw the storm clouds rolling in, they certainly *thought* it was the end. By the time the rain finally hit—so hard and fast that the boat began filling with water—they'd worked themselves up into a panic. Even the professional fishermen among them were losing it.

Let Jesus be your picture of calm. For just as He quieted the storm that day, He is able to quiet the challenges that are scaring you as well. And even if He leaves some of them in place, you can still trust Him to care for you and be enough for you all the way through, all the way to the other side.

So take it easy. Take it to Jesus. And ride it out. You'll be okay.

Actionable Intel

Read the full account of this sea story in Luke 8:22–25. Watch the disciples go from calm to terrified to amazed, all in the space of four verses. What did they (and what do we) miss out on by being so up and down?

Truly, Truly

"Truly, truly, I say to you, we speak of what we know and testify of what we have seen."—John 3:11 NASB

Recon

Dozens of times in Scripture, Jesus introduced a statement He was about to make with these defining words: "Truly, truly, I say to you." Other versions translate it as "Very truly I tell you" (NIV); or "I assure you" (HCSB); or my all-time favorite, the old King James-sounding "Verily, verily, I say unto thee."

Every time Jesus spoke, He always spoke the truth.

If you and I have set as our goal a desire to grow more and more like Christ each day, then we need to be people who always, always, always tell the truth. Just like Jesus did. Even when it's hard. Even when it hurts. Even when we're standing alone. Truth is just how we should live, how we should think, how we should operate. It should come out of us whenever we speak.

Don't just *live* the truth. *Say* it, *speak* it, every day of your life.

Actionable Intel

Turn to Proverbs 8:7 and see how the wise writer of this Bible book described the difference between telling the truth and telling lies. Did you ever think of it with words like these?

Return on Investment

Honor your father and mother, which is the first
commandment with a promise. —Ephesians 6:2

Recon

You might recognize this verse from Ephesians 6 as being one of the Ten Commandments from Exodus 20: "Honor your father and mother" (v. 12). Show them respect. Submit to their authority. Be thankful to God for giving you someone to love you and lead you and take care of you.

But this statement is a bit unique among the Ten Commandments because, like Paul said, it comes "with a promise." Know what the promise is? "So that it may go well with you and that you may have a long life in the land" (Ephesians 6:3).

Boy, with a promise like that, you might want to keep it in mind the next time your enemy tempts you to disobey your mom or dad, or to smart off when they're correcting you, or to treat them without respect or like they're not as much fun as other friends' parents you know.

After all, the Devil has *his* agenda, and God has *His*. Which one's promise sounds like the best long-term plan?

Actionable Intel

Make a point of "honoring" your parents every single day. In fact, why not start today? What is one way that you can honor them before the day is over?

Push and Pull

You pushed me hard to make me fall, but the
LORD helped me. —Psalm 118:13

Recon

Pushing and shoving.

That's the enemy's way. Being the bully. Trying to intimidate. Forcing the issue. Hurrying you up. He wants you acting rashly, before you're ready, before your faith and common sense can come into play.

And if you're feeling pushed like that today, then you're feeling the enemy's pressure.

God's Spirit, however, doesn't push. *He pulls*. When the gospel came to you, it was God drawing you toward Christ, calling to you, inviting you to come His direction (John 6:44). He reached out to you with "ropes of love" (Hosea 11:4) so He could pull you to Himself, take you up in His arms, and care for you. And give you peace.

Sure, Satan's pushing can knock you down sometimes or distract you into overreacting. But no matter how hard he pushes, God will be there to pull your feet out of the net (Psalm 25:15), pull you out of deep waters (Psalm 18:16), and bring you back to a place of peace.

Actionable Intel

What about you? Do you *push* on others more than you *pull* them? As you go through the next day, through the next week, see if you can spot the difference.

On Second Thought

All things work together for the good of those
who love God: those who are called according
to His purpose. —*Romans 8:28*

Recon

Live long enough (if you haven't already), and part of your testimony will include any number of unpleasant events and goof-ups. Yet some of them, when seen through the eyeglasses of hindsight, you'll start to view as *good* things.

Perhaps these events stopped you from making an even worse mistake than the first. Perhaps they put you in connection with someone who proved important to you later in life. For one reason or another—a God reason—a negative became an overall positive.

This is one of the ways God thwarts your enemy for you. If the Devil had his way, you'd never triumph against all his temptations and deceptions. But as you take up your shield to fight, not only does God help you claim new victories in battle but He also overturns some old attacks that once fell into the loss column and puts them in the win column instead.

You're not only covered in advance but you're also covered in reverse.

Actionable Intel

Ask one of your parents to give you examples of how God has proved this verse true in their life.

No Snatching Zone

*"I give them eternal life, and they will never
perish—ever! No one will snatch them
out of My hand."—John 10:28*

Recon

I just want to be sure you know that when God saved you,
He saved you for keeps. You are a joint heir with Christ,
sharing in the Father's inheritance. You have been tucked
away, hidden inside the hand of God, where the evil one
may be able to snip and snipe at you around the edges,
but he can never pry you loose from your Father's grip.

You belong. You are forever connected to God's love.
You are seated with Christ in the heavenly realm. You are
free to relate to Him with every prayer, with every cry and
question on your heart . . . or simply because you want to
just sit there close to Him today.

Your enemy will come up with a million reasons why
you can't be confident in your salvation. But all the answer
you need is this one. "No one"—and God means *no one*—
can "snatch" you out of His hand.

Actionable Intel

Read 1 John 5:12–13. Anytime you doubt your salvation,
go back and read it again.

The Stronger Man

I will contend with the one who contends
with you. —Isaiah 49:25

Recon

No one's denying that our enemy is strong and quite capable of causing extensive damage in people's lives. He has just one problem, though—and it's a biggie for him. He is nowhere near as strong as our God is. And our God is on our side.

When some of the people in Jesus' day were questioning His power to confront demonic opposition, He told them there's only one way to take something away from a "strong man"—you tie him up first; then you can "rob his house" (Matthew 12:29). And that's exactly what Jesus has done to your strong enemy. Tied him up. He did it on the earth, did it on the cross, did it at the empty tomb, and still does it every day in the lives of His people.

Our God is the ultimate Warrior. No doubt. Every day of the week. Every week of the year. Every year of your life. The enemy may be strong, but our God is *stronger.*

Actionable Intel

Bring your requests one by one before God today, and remember with each item on your prayer list: He is contending with the one who's contending with you.

Something Better

They did not receive what was promised, since God had provided something better for us. —Hebrews 11:39–40

Recon

Noah had enough faith and courage to build an ark when everyone around him thought he was crazy. Abraham had enough faith and courage to leave the comforts of home for an unknown destination. Moses had enough faith and courage to stare down Pharaoh, the most powerful man in the world.

Most of us would say we don't have that kind of faith and courage.

And yet in Hebrews 11, where Old Testament heroes like Noah, Abraham, Moses, and others are specifically celebrated for their amazing lives of faith, the last verse turns its attention toward you. And says God has something even "better" for you.

This "something better" is life with Jesus. The heroes of old could only *hope* for the thing that we have the privilege to experience—abundant life and an eternal inheritance. Because of this, you can have an even firmer faith and emblazoned courage to stand firm and live well.

So let the testimony of Noah, Abraham, and Moses encourage you. But always remember that you have "something better."

Actionable Intel

Read what Hebrews 12:1–2 says you should do, knowing that you're surrounded by "such a large crowd of witnesses."

Grounded in the Air

*Guide me in Your truth and teach me, for You
are the God of my salvation.* —Psalm 25:5

Recon

By the time an airplane pilot sits down in the cockpit as a captain for a major airline, that person has already logged a minimum of four thousand hours of flight experience. Break that down into eight-hour workdays, and it would equal being in the air roughly a year and a half of his life. Every day.

And yet every pilot, no matter how experienced or how well-earned his confidence in his own abilities, doesn't just kick back and watch the clouds sail by across the nose cone, trusting in his flying skill alone to land the plane.

Pilots are always scanning their instruments. They're staying in close contact with the control tower. They're not depending on knack and feel alone to guide them. They're depending on the *truth* they're being told by readings on their dials and by people on the ground.

Our lives work the same way. If we ever think we've figured it out and don't need to worry too much with the Word and the truth, we're in for startling collisions as we travel throughout life. We never outgrow the need for truth. We never stop needing it.

Actionable Intel

The next time you see an airplane flying overhead, let it remind you that your ability to soar into spiritual growth is always dependent on keeping your heart grounded in truth.

Footloose

You have not given me into the hands of the enemy but have set my feet in a spacious place. —Psalm 31:8 NIV

Recon

No matter how much freedom and elbow room your enemy's temptations appear to offer, they always lead to the same spot. *A tight spot.*

Up till then, you're thinking you can handle it. You'll think you're doing fine. But then—*wham!*—you're trapped. Hemmed in. Bottled up. He's cut off your supply lines. He's cloaked you in darkness. He's separated you from the people who really love you and can help you. He's left you alone to wonder if you can ever truly escape.

But those shoes you're wearing—those gospel shoes—they mean you're never really trapped in a boxed-in place. They are peace-seeking missiles. Programmed to take you home. They will lead you by repentance back to a "spacious place," a peaceful place, a place where you can be restored and never return to any those other places.

Come out of Satan's spider holes and into the open fields of God's promises and blessings.

Actionable Intel

Don't let the enemy trap you in the loneliness of sin today, in the shadows of fear and worry. Seek out the "spacious places" of forgiveness, of obedience, of trust, of good relationships. No child of God is forced to sit in the corner.

What's in Your Wallet?

We have not received the spirit of the world,
but the Spirit who comes from God, so that
we may understand what has been freely given
to us by God.—*1 Corinthians 2:12*

Recon

One of the first things you do when get back from a foreign country is to go to the currency exchange desk at the airport, where you can cash in your foreign bills and coins for the kind that people use in your home country. No restaurant in America, for example, is going to want your European euros as payment. That currency simply doesn't work here.

When we talk about the unseen, spiritual battle we're each fighting—a war that's been initiated by our beatable, yet powerful enemy—I hope you realize you can't fight and win by using the wrong weapons. The kind that work on earth won't work in heavenly places. You need to make an exchange—your weapons for God's. Then you'll have victory.

Actionable Intel

Here's another illustration. The same plugs that charge your gaming device or cell phone in one country might not fit the electrical outlets in another country. They require an adaptor that works in that foreign land. Can you think of another kind of tool that might work fine in one situation but doesn't work so well in another?

Isn't It Obvious?

But where is the fury of the oppressor?—Isaiah 51:13

Recon

A rhetorical question is one where everyone should supposedly know the answer. It doesn't really even justify an answer, because the answer should be so obvious. Ever heard this one: "If everybody else jumped off a cliff, would you jump off one too?" That's one of the most famous rhetorical questions.

Today's verse from Isaiah 51 should be too. The Lord set it up by saying how the people of Israel were in "constant dread all day long," how they felt completely overwhelmed by an enemy who was intent on destroying them. "But where," He said, "is the fury of the oppressor?" How could you ever think he's bigger than your problems and more powerful than your God?

And if God intends this to be a rhetorical question—end of discussion—why should we ever treat it as though it's not?

Actionable Intel

Even though Isaiah 51:13 is meant to be a rhetorical question, God went ahead and answered it anyway in verses 14–15. Read those verses for yourself. How could you apply them to what you're going through today?

Up Close and Personal

*So that you may be able to resist in the
evil day. —Ephesians 6:13*

Recon

One of the newest advances in modern warfare is the use of drone attacks. Pilots sitting at computer screens inside a military base—miles away, perhaps even nations away—steer an unmanned aircraft into position, spotting their target. It's all very real, but hardly like being up in your enemy's face, tangling against one another in hand-to-hand combat.

Spiritual warfare, no matter how modern and clinical our smart weapons become, will always be the up-close variety. It will come against you at home, against your family, against things you take very personally and mean the most to you. You will feel sometimes as though the enemy is right up in your face—taunting you, spitting out lies, wrestling you with temptations, trying to strip you of the armor you've positioned around yourself.

That's why the sword that God gives you must be a dagger. Perfectly designed for the kind of close fighting He knows is coming—and the kind of winning His Word can accomplish.

Actionable Intel

Where's the enemy action been happening lately? Don't let it frighten you. Just let it take you deeper into the Word today.

Take That

But He answered, "It is written . . ."—Matthew 4:4

Recon

The Bible says Jesus was "tempted in every way, just as we are" (Hebrews 4:15 NIV). This means that the one passage in Scripture where Satan specifically tempted Jesus was hardly the only time.

But *one time* is enough to learn how to defeat temptation *every time*—with the stabbing, jabbing, Satan-stopping needlepoint of the Word of God. No matter what the tempter brought out of his bag, Jesus popped it with a direct response strike of Scripture.

These were *rhema* words. Remember those from page 91? Jesus was using specific statements for specific moments. He didn't need to start at the beginning each time, feverishly hunting the right word for the situation. He'd spent so much time reading and pondering it, the right verse was just there—hand-delivered by the Spirit—right on time.

That's the sword of the Spirit in action. And you can put it into action the very same way. Just like Jesus did.

Actionable Intel

Read about this whole event in Matthew 4:1–11. Detect the pattern. Different temptations, but always the same sort of response. You can become just as predictable yourself.

Words for Now, from the Past

*"My God, My God, why have You
forsaken Me?"—Matthew 27:46*

Recon

I can't think of any more powerful, emotional, heartbreaking words than this cry of Jesus from the cross. I mean, imagine never experiencing the drag of sin on your heart, never once feeling any strain or distance in your relationship with the Father. Then imagine suddenly feeling all the guilt, all the weight of *all* His people's sins, all who would ever live—all at once—dumped full force into His heart with one shock.

No words describe that pain.

And yet Jesus found them—in the words of a psalm written centuries beforehand. The Word of God remained His word list, even when experiencing the most intense anguish anyone could ever go through.

The answers you need, the comfort you're seeking, the words that say exactly what your current situation is demanding—they're in there, young warrior. They're in the Word of God. And He will give them to you as you need them.

Actionable Intel

Psalm 22 is fairly long—thirty-one verses. But what makes it so fascinating is how vividly it depicts Jesus' suffering on the cross, ages before crucifixion was even used as a means of torture. Just another proof of how amazing the Word of God is.

Centered in Scripture

How happy are those whose way is blameless, who live according to the LORD's instruction!—Psalm 119:1

Recon

Hold your closed Bible in front of you—the spine facing away from you, the page edges facing toward you. Slide your two thumbs till they meet at a point roughly halfway across, then peel your Bible back until it's opened almost at its center point. Equal weight on both sides.

You won't be far from Psalm 119.

It's the longest chapter in the Bible. Nearly two hundred verses. More than you'd probably want to read at any one time, especially since it's not a consistently running thought, but rather many individual statements, pieced one after another.

There *is* one consistency, however. Each verse in Psalm 119 contains at least one word that's synonymous for God's Word—instruction, law, statutes, decrees, precepts, commands—all the way through.

So if you ever don't know where to go when reading the Bible, just go to the center. There's always a verse there waiting for you—a word from God on the Word of God.

Actionable Intel

Try doing this with your Bible today. Maybe find a verse in there that you'd like to memorize.

Sword Drill

Mighty warrior, strap your sword at
your side. —Psalm 45:3

Recon

Along the way, as we've been traveling together, you've developed a specific prayer for each of the pieces of spiritual armor. Today is when you can do the same thing for the sword of the Spirit.

I've told you at other times to use Scripture verses to form these prayers. You never go wrong when you're asking for things that God has already specifically told you He will do for you. So ask Him, in the words of Psalm 19, to use His Word to renew your life (v. 7), to fill you with deep gladness (v. 8), and to prove His trustworthiness and reliability (v. 9). Ask Him to make His Word more desirable than gold to you (v. 10), and to give you the great rewards He promises to those who keep it (v. 11).

"May the words of my mouth and the meditation of my heart be acceptable to You, LORD, my rock and my Redeemer" (v. 14).

Actionable Intel

Pray—and keep praying—that the Spirit will keep that sword strapped firmly and ever-ready at your side.

True Worship

"God is spirit, and those who worship Him must worship in spirit and truth."—John 4:24

Recon

When Jesus spoke these words, He was talking with a Samaritan woman who wasn't really interested in having a personal discussion at that moment. She tried to change the subject, asking a theological question to this Man who appeared to be a prophet.

His answer, though, got right to the heart of the real issue. And His answer is for all of us who sometimes don't really bring our true selves to the experience of worship. And therefore, we don't really get to experience the truth of who He is and what He's done for us.

Worship—genuine, honest, heartfelt worship—is a key strategy that keeps us face-to-face with our deep need for God's forgiveness, as well as His compassion and ability to provide it. In worship we honor the truth of His greatness, His power, and His majesty, as well as His right to be our Lord.

Worship is for imperfect people who realize He knows we're imperfect people . . . and yet He still loves us.

Actionable Intel

What could you worship God for today?

Do Your Part

If possible, on your part, live at peace
with everyone. —Romans 12:18

Recon

This world is hardly a peaceful place. Bombs blowing up, civil wars raging, people arguing, blue lights flashing. Not to mention your own *personal* current events—disagreements at home, difficulties with friends, and other distressing areas of social discomfort. People you try to avoid, mostly because they're obviously trying to avoid you.

Since you're not the only one who contributes to these challenges, you can't control how others choose to behave or react. You can't force them to listen to your side or forgive you when you've acted badly. You can't convince them you didn't mean it the way they took it or that you're not the person they're making you out to be.

But where others refuse you the option of living at peace with them, you must remain dedicated to seeking peace as much as you can. So even if they've made it difficult for you, they should find you still standing there waiting whenever they return. Ready to forgive or ask for forgiveness. Wanting peace.

Actionable Intel

Is there a person in your life that you are having a disagreement with right now? Today, do something to pursue peace with them, even if it's something as simple as giving them a big smile. By doing this, you'll be thwarting the enemy's attempt to divide you.

Combat Training

Leave inexperience behind, and you will live; pursue the way of understanding. —Proverbs 9:6

Recon

I know you're young. I know you've got your friends. I know you enjoy hanging out with them and doing what you do. And while that's good and that's normal—and you should do it every chance you get—you can add an incredible layer of depth to your life by deliberately seeking out a few close relationships with older people as well.

Mentors help mature you in your faith. They ask questions you don't hear anywhere else. You'll learn in a hurry just how much their wisdom and experience and their journey with the Lord can teach you.

Do you really want to grow stronger as a warrior in this fight? Then let a seasoned warrior help you truly understand the value of your armor and the ways to wear it well. Pursue the way of understanding every chance you get.

Actionable Intel

Start making plans today to ask one or two key people— within your family, at your church—if they would consider meeting regularly with you to help you grow in your faith.

Always in Uniform

Stand firm. Let nothing move you. Always give yourselves fully to the work of the Lord.—1 Corinthians 15:58 NIV

Recon

Our youngest son is playing T-ball. And like any kid playing his first team sport, one of the highlights (to him) is being able to wear that uniform—the shirt, the pants, the shoes, the socks. He and his teammates wear that same outfit throughout the whole game. It is, after all, the uniform. Doesn't change.

But when he goes up to the plate, he carries a bat, and also swaps out his baseball cap for a batting helmet. When he's in the outfield, he wears a glove on one hand.

Your spiritual armor is sort of like that. The belt, the breastplate, the shoes—truth, righteousness, and peace—those are your uniform. They aren't things to *put on* as much as *keep on.* But depending on the occasion, you take up your shield, your helmet, or your sword—when they are needed. You use them to strike and defend against a specific threat.

So keep your armored uniform on all the time. And keep your weapons nearby, ready to use any time they are needed.

Actionable Intel

You'd never think of running to the locker room to change clothes between every inning. Instead it's game on—all the time. So your uniform stays on—all the time. Is yours on right now?

Keep Plugging

"Not by might nor by power, but by My Spirit,"
says the LORD. *—Zechariah 4:6* NASB

Recon

My son's handheld gaming device stopped working the other night. Shut off right in the middle of a game. He tried everything to get it to restart. Closed the lid. Opened it back up. Shook it. Finally plugged it in. Still, nothing.

But the charger he was using didn't belong to his game. It was a charger for something else. Although the plug fit, the power wouldn't transfer. Being plugged into the right source is critical.

Young warrior, you've completed 365 days of devotions. I am so proud of you. And if in the future your life doesn't seem to be working right—and you can't seem to figure out why—be sure you're being "charged up" by the right thing. Not your strength. Not your smarts. Not your money. Not your friends. You were made for God's Spirit. Plug into Him and you will excel.

Remember, this is not the end. It's your beginning as a spiritual giant who can defeat the enemy. Stay connected to the right source every "365 days" for the rest of your life.

Actionable Intel

My prayer for you: "Lord, give this warrior *Your* strength and *Your* power. Grant them favor and wisdom to live victoriously all their days. Amen."

The Winning Side

Do you want to live with power and enjoy all the benefits of overcoming the enemy? If you do, then your journey to victorious living begins by joining the winning side.

There's only one way to do this. You must have a relationship with the one true God who is already seated on the throne.

Although none of us deserves it, God has made a way for us to be part of His family and experience the victory that He has already achieved. He sent His only Son, Jesus, to pay the price for our sins so that nothing—nothing, never—could keep us separated from Him any longer. Jesus not only paid the horrific price of death for us, but He also claimed victory once and for all when He was resurrected back to life.

This salvation is a gift—a gift that you can receive right now.

Romans 10:9 tells you how. It's simple but critical and life-changing: "If you confess with your mouth, 'Jesus is Lord,' and believe in your heart that God raised Him from the dead, you will be saved."

That's it! By believing that Jesus is the son of God, and by placing your faith in His gift of salvation, you will be saved and enabled to live victoriously every day for the rest of your life. As you yield to His leadership and learn how to walk with Him, His armor will be available and activated, and you'll be able to stand firm against the enemy who already knows that his time is very quickly running out!

If that is a decision you'd like to make today, pray these words out loud:

Lord Jesus, I know I am a sinner, and I believe
You are my Savior. Today I place my faith in You

to remove the debt I owe for my sins. I believe You died for my sins and were resurrected from the dead. And because You were raised in victory, I can live in victory too. Thank You for saving me. Now please empower me to live for You . . . every day for the rest of my life. In Your name, amen.

Congratulations, Warrior!

Welcome to the winning side!

Now, as quick as you can, find another person—a parent, friend, relative, teacher—to celebrate with you, to help you fully understand what your decision means, and to learn how to walk with the Lord as you grow!

With Extreme Gratitude

. . . to one of the most skilled wordsmiths, humble servants, and patient ministry partners I've ever known. **Lawrence Kimbrough**, your heart is good through and through. The life lessons I've gleaned by watching the way you deflect glory to God and devote your craft to His kingdom have enhanced my perspective on what it means to serve the Lord well. I'm grateful for your example. Thank you for sharing your wisdom and your words with the world . . . and with me. Our mission to equip the next generation of Prince Warriors is more impactful because of you.

About the Author

Priscilla Shirer is a homemade cinnamon-roll baker, Bible teacher, and best-selling author who didn't know her books (*The Resolution for Women* and *Fervent*) were on *The New York Times* Best Seller list until somebody else told her. Because who has time to check such things while raising three rapidly growing sons? When she and Jerry, her husband of sixteen years, are not busy leading *Going Beyond Ministries*, they spend most of their time cleaning up after and trying to satisfy the appetites of these guys. And that is what first drove Priscilla to dream up the Prince Warriors series and her fictional story about the very un-fictional topic of spiritual warfare—to help raise up a new generation of Prince Warriors under her roof. And under yours.

Don't miss the rest of The Prince Warriors series!

The Prince Warriors

The Prince Warriors
and the Unseen Invasion

COMING SOON
The Prince Warriors
and the Swords of Rhema

Unseen:
The Prince Warriors
365 Devotional

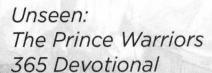

Unseen:
The Prince Warriors App

Thoughts and Action Plans